The Psychosis of Whiteness

*For Assata, Kadiri, Omaje, Ajani and all those who appreciate
that you can't spell slaughter without spelling laughter*

KEHINDE ANDREWS

The Psychosis of Whiteness
Surviving the Insanity of a Racist World

ALLEN LANE
an imprint of
PENGUIN BOOKS

ALLEN LANE

UK | USA | Canada | Ireland | Australia
India | New Zealand | South Africa

Penguin Books is part of the Penguin Random House group of companies
whose addresses can be found at global.penguinrandomhouse.com.

First published in Great Britain by Allen Lane 2023
001

Set in 10.5/14.5pt Sabon LT Std
Typeset by Jouve (UK), Milton Keynes
Printed and bound in Great Britain by Clays Ltd, Elcograf S.p.A.

The authorized representative in the EEA is Penguin Random House Ireland,
Morrison Chambers, 32 Nassau Street, Dublin D02 YH68

A CIP catalogue record for this book is available from the British Library

ISBN: 978–0–241–43747–6

Contents

Preface: Through the Looking-Glass   vii

1   Why Psychosis?   1

2   The Anti-Racism Industrial Complex   31

3   West Indian Slavery   53

4   Self-Segregation   73

5   We're Losing the Country   101

6   Cultural Misappropriation   133

7   The Post-Racial Princess   153

8   Black Skin, White Psychosis   175

    Epilogue: Out of the Rabbit Hole   199

    Notes   207

    Index   231

Preface: Through the Looking-Glass

I grew up in a generation where the TV was a focal point of the living room, but it was tightly controlled by my father and limited by the fact we only had four channels. We probably could have afforded Sky but my dad was too old and Jamaican for those kinds of luxuries. We rented our video player, even though we ended up paying three times what it would have cost to buy. As a child, the main way I interacted with the TV was to turn the dial to whichever station my dad wanted to watch. For those of you under thirty it will be difficult to imagine the TV of my youth, which had a remote we could never find and was housed in a gigantic wooden backing. Like in most houses the TV had an outsize impact on lives, framing the evening and sparking family conversations.

I was lucky enough to have been born too late to have to endure *The Black and White Minstrel Show* on the BBC, which, from 1958, ran for *twenty years*. Yes, White performers would black up and coon on mainstream TV. This was what publicly funded television had to offer, and there were only three channels to choose from. In 1964 it achieved its peak viewing figure of 16.5 million people. It was so popular that the album *On Stage with the George Mitchell Minstrels* hit number one in the charts in 1962 and Mitchell (who orchestrated the minstrels) remains the only person to hold first, second and fourth place in the charts at the same time.[1] The space for Black representation was so limited during this period that Sir Lenny Henry, now one of Britain's most cherished TV personalities, joined the cast in the 1970s to get his first break in the industry. Reflecting on his regrets in being in the show he remembers that 'people used to say Lenny was the only one who didn't need make-up' and talks about how it tipped him into a 'profound wormhole of depression'.[2]

I may have swerved the era of *The Black and White Minstrel Show* but when I was growing up Lenny Henry was one of the very few Black people on the shimmering box. ITV's *News at Ten* was appointment viewing when Sir Trevor McDonald, from Trinidad, became the sole presenter in 1992. On the rare occasions Black-led shows came on it felt like every Black person tuned in. I feel like I personally know all the characters in the Channel 4 show *Desmond's*, set in a barber shop in Peckham, which aired from 1989. I was probably too young to watch the comedy-sketch show *The Real McCoy* when it was first shown in 1991, but my parents never kicked me out when it came on. But these shows were oases in a desert of Whiteness. Blackface continued in hit shows like *Little Britain* until the early 2000s. This was before social media, so widespread condemnation from Black communities was completely ignored. It appears as though British comedians have an addiction to blackface: *The League of Gentlemen*, *Come Fly with Me*, *The Mighty Boosh* and *Bo' Selecta!*, all of which debuted in the twenty-first century, have now been removed from some streaming platforms. The removal of *Little Britain* from BBC iPlayer and Netflix caused the biggest stir; commentators decried their removal as 'censorship' and an example of so-called 'cancel culture'.[3] I have had far too much experience with this debate. I have gone from a child watching TV to becoming a talking head today, who gets invited onto news and discussion programmes to discuss the burning issues of the day. It is at once a gift and a curse to break the fourth wall for yourself. Once you have, it becomes clear that the normal rules of reason no longer apply, and that if you do not stay tethered to outside reality you may be consumed by chaos. It is a privilege to be able to act as a guide for others through this upside-down world that frames all of our lives.

The *Little Britain* debates I took part in on Sky News and for *Good Morning Britain* were full of the kind of deluded thinking that are the motivation for writing this book. The BBC had proclaimed that

'Times have changed',[4] and this seemed to be the baseline for the discussion. I patiently explained that blackface was offensive even in the eighteenth century, let alone at the turn of the twenty-first. On *Good Morning Britain* I found myself verbally sparring with Tom Harwood, who was apparently in his twenties but looked and argued like he was still in high school. Not for the first time in my television career, I wondered why I accepted the invitation. On Sky News I was pitted against Dominque Samuels, whom I later spent ten days with filming a BBC TV show called *We Are Black and British*. The only difference between Samuels and Harwood is that Samuels is Black, but they share the same right-wing certainty, which appears to the only necessary credential for appearing on these kinds of discussion programmes. The moment Samuels blurted out 'That's *communism* . . . and mind control!' when I explained that media companies have a responsibility to remove racist content might forever be my favourite of my entire television career.

The *Little Britain* debate took place during lockdown, so I was at least in the sanctity of my own home, witnessing the chaos over Zoom. When I have to visit sets in person it often feels like I have stumbled through Alice's looking-glass. The door to the studio acts as a portal to another world where the laws of reality have been fundamentally distorted. I can't count the number of times I have been involved in debates about whether racism still exists, as though the evidence isn't all around us. Walking into most TV studios, it should be impossible to ignore the number of Black security and cleaning staff compared to the minuscule representation of those working on the set, perfectly illustrating the economic effects of racism. But the first lesson you learn is: suspend any expectation of rationality if you want to make it through your segment. Prior to the murder of George Floyd there was very little discussion of racism in the liberal media, and the only consistent debates that took place were manufactured spectacles of the so-called culture war. For the viewer, too, the TV screen serves as Alice's looking-glass, a gateway to a world without reason. But swimming in the delusions of hyperventilating right-wingers, as I do on these programmes, has been a tremendously educational experience.

Arguing with someone like Piers Morgan about racism unveils the hidden face of Whiteness. The liberal conversations found on the BBC contain all the same irrationality that Morgan displays, but masked in pseudo-intellectual charm. When Morgan told me on morning television that if I hate Britain so much I should leave the country, the brazen racist logic was clear. He didn't quite tell me I should 'go home', but he did suggest Antigua in the Caribbean as my destination, which is not far from my dad's retirement home in Jamaica.[5] What provoked his national (af)front was my having explained that Winston Churchill was a White supremacist. Morgan couldn't accept that the Man Who Stopped the Nazis™ was a racist, despite his having beaten back the fascist threat of Hitler's Germany. Sometimes it takes a lot of ignorance to hold certain views. Churchill was an avowed White supremacist, so rabidly racist that his ghost probably haunted Morgan's dreams for a week after Morgan questioned his racist credentials. He supported the eugenics movement, which argued that racial hygiene by eliminating the inferior races was necessary for social progress, an intellectual movement that was instrumental in defining Jews as subhuman in the lead-up to the Holocaust.[6] During the Second World War, in 1943, he left three million Bengalis, subjects of the British empire, to starve to death; he refused to send food because he felt it was more important to keep it in reserve for the British army.[7] His own viceroy for India compared his views on Indian people to Hitler's,[8] and young members of his own party distanced themselves from him because of his racist views. He lost the very next general election after the war to Clement Attlee's Labour Party. Churchill might have been an important figure in the war effort, but the delusions of the great White men of history are offensive to many millions of soldiers who lost their lives in battle. The Second World War was a global effort: the British empire and her colonial subjects were vital for victory. Not to mention the Russians and Americans, without whom the Nazis would probably have won the war. We haven't even mentioned the women who were drafted into war industries, who were essential to victory. But no, it was Churchill alone who rallied the nation in its darkest hour. Through the distortions of history he has become a saintly figure, one you can only criticize if you hate Britain with a burning passion (believe me, I felt the wrath of the right-wing press when I talked about Churchill's real opinions).[9]

In my various tours of duty of the culture wars there have been times when I was internally dumbstruck by the nonsense being peddled by the other side. I thought there was a consensus that the murder of George Floyd was racially motivated, but when I was on the right-wing channel TalkRadio, a host (I can't remember which one, they all look alike to me) insisted that there was absolutely no evidence to support that claim. According to this host, there were no KKK hoods and the N-word wasn't used, which meant it couldn't possibly have been a racially motivated incident. It was just a coincidence that Derek Chauvin choked the life out of a Black man in full view of the public. How can someone know so little about the history of Black people and policing in the USA? But it's not only the unfettered right wing who are guilty of these wilful misunderstandings. In 2019 the Hollywood actor Liam Neeson admitted to wanting to kill 'some black bastard' after he found out that his White female friend had been raped. When I appeared on *BBC Breakfast* to discuss Neeson's admission, describing his desire as a lynching fantasy, I found myself 'corrected' for using inflammatory language. But when a White man in the US wants to kill a random Black man to defend the chastity of a White woman, what other word could one use but 'lynch'? I stopped being frustrated a long time ago and now look on bemused. When we discuss racism in the media, it's minimized or framed in ways that marginalize the issue. The media is incredibly influential and the delusional way it presents these debates is deeply concerning. For a brief few weeks after the death of George Floyd the tone of the conversation changed, and issues like structural racism and defunding the police were discussed. But it didn't take long for the backlash to kick in and then we were straight back into the culture wars – this time with feeling. Just a few short months after George Floyd's death, when light was still firmly shining on the Black Lives Matter summer of August 2020, a media panic about whether the song *Rule Britannia* was racist broke out.[10] (Spoiler: it is.) After that summer, we do talk a

lot more about race, but the conversations are so drenched in delusions that the increased attention does more harm than good.

I ask myself constantly: why do I keep going down the rabbit hole
when the result is a made-for-TV culture war? But I'm never trying to
convince people like Morgan or the audience of TalkRadio. Their
position is not a rational one. They are so deluded that the only metaphor I can find to liken it to is a psychosis, hence the title of this book.
But there is a secondary audience who does tune in to these debates,
whether live, online or in the aftermath of the social media chatter
these encounters generate. It's refreshing for them to see delusional
arguments they encounter everyday unpicked. When you hear the
fantasies of Whiteness on daily basis it doesn't take long before you
begin to feel that maybe it is *you* who is out of your mind. Seeing
someone bring some truth to these discussions can empower people
to keep a grip on reality. It's useful to demonstrate the irrationality
of Whiteness, to expose the faulty logic behind the verbal diahorrea
we deal with. Once we see that Whiteness is a societal psychosis we
can then understand that it is inoculated from all logic and evidence.
These platforms are spaces where we can reach an audience beyond
the one the producers imagined. I won't lie: it's also fun to wind up the
hosts. Watching Morgan's face turn red really brought home the
meaning of the term 'gammon'.

MEDIOCRE WHITE MEN

The media Wonderland's main character is the mediocre White man,
the typical debate host. There are other speaking parts, too: often a
female sidekick and a cameo from a Black or Brown person (who we
will discuss at length later in the book). But we are firmly in the court
of the White man, who comes armed with an indignant ignorance. It's
fascinating to see people blow hot air for hours, utterly convinced
that it is *they* who are correct. Delusions of grandeur are a sign of
psychosis, and disconnection from reality causes people in delirium to
believe they have an elevated status. I always chuckle at the irony of

being invited on to a show as a professor, a supposedly esteemed expert on the given subject, and then having my position treated as though it was of no esteem whatsoever. Some of the people I have 'debated' with are comical (see Tom Harwood, above). I appreciate that it is all a piece of theatre, but Malcolm X was right, as usual, when he warned that 'a clown can't play the part of a wise man'.

Symbolic violence in the media is replicated in the real world, which is dominated by mediocre White men. Amazon founder Jeff Bezos is worth over 200 billion dollars. His personal wealth is higher than the GDP of all but three African countries. In a single second he earns more than his average employee does in six weeks.[11] He is this rich *after* getting divorced and making a record-breaking settlement of more than 35 billion dollars to his former wife. Thankfully he recognizes the obscenity of his wealth and has pledged to give back, spending a billion of his own money on his pet humanitarian project. But worldly concerns like poverty, disease or famine are beneath this visionary. In Bezos's words: 'The only way I can see to deploy this much financial resource is by converting my Amazon winnings into space travel.'[12] He imagines himself a pioneer, facilitating the creation of an 'incredible civilization' of 'trillions of people across the solar system'. Whiteness is central to his fantasy: he imagines recreating cities like Florence in space, nurturing a thousand Mozarts and Einsteins. He is filled with imperial delusions: he's excited by the thought of a 'recreational colony', ideally with zero gravity, so you can fly without wings.[13] He seems to believe he will save the world through mining the solar system for raw materials. If he's successful we can look forward to a future filled with abundant resources, enabling us to buy cheap goods we have no real use for, that Amazon are so good at selling to us. The spoken-word artists the Last Poets summed up this kind of hubris best with the title of their track 'The White Man's Got a God Complex'.[14] But the uncomfortable truth is: we enable them to do it. Bezos's maiden flight with his private Blue Origins company was televized and celebrated like a NASA mission. If we weren't in the collective delirium of Whiteness, one that imagines that those with White skin should have complete dominion over the universe, we would have made it a one-way trip and redistributed his Amazon empire to the people. But delusions of grandeur are not just reserved for talk-show hosts and billionaires. Mediocre White men with egos the size of the universe (and much smaller intellects) are shaping the political moment.

At one point during the Covid-19 pandemic the most powerful country in the world was led by Donald Trump, the second largest economy in Europe was headed by Boris Johnson and the most populous country in Latin America, Brazil, had Jair Bolsonaro for president. It is no coincidence that these three countries were among the hardest hit by the pandemic or that all three leaders caught coronavirus. They are also all White, male and utterly incompetent. The wave of populism that brought them to power stumped commentators: why were bumbling charlatans and closet fascists being elected all over the world? But the answer is simple: delusions of grandeur aren't just reserved for the men themselves but are shared by much of the voting public. There is no other way to account for the majority of White women voting for misogynist-in-chief Donald Trump, or Boris Johnson, one of the most privileged men in the country, the epitome of the London elite, raised on the teat of the despised Margaret Thatcher, resonating with working-class voters in the north of England. Through the distortions of the looking-glass many voters see statesmen, while those with their senses see buffoons. Mediocre White men are popular because they are the living embodiment of White privilege. If Donald Trump was qualified to be president, then everyone who is White has a chance. As Chris Rock put it, referring to George W. Bush, 'a Black C student can't be a manager at Burger King. Meanwhile, a White C student just happens to be the president of the United States.'[15] The right to rule extends to even those without the basic competency to do so, and these delusions of grandeur were on full display during the pandemic.

Boris Johnson was hospitalized with Covid after bragging about shaking hands with the public. Trump downplayed the virus and refused to wear a mask; it wasn't long before he was in hospital too. The general reaction to coronavirus of many in the West was one of imperviousness, a feeling of being above the need to be protected from a deadly illness. There are good reasons for vaccine hesitancy, particularly in Black communities, given the history of racism and healthcare. But it is no coincidence that right-wing extremists and their conspiracy theories aligned when it came to rejecting vaccination efforts. Katie Hopkins, proving that there is some gender equality when it comes to mediocre White celebs, declared she was proud of being 'pure blood' to a cheering crowd of tens of thousands in the US in October 2022.[16] This delusion of imperiousness was an affliction also embraced by the small and insignificant country of Britain, when it decided it had the right to colonize a quarter of the globe. It also explains the colonial arrogance that exists long after the end of empire. Johnson, Trump and Bolsonaro were elected because they exuded the grandeur their White populations needed to see, promising to return their nations to former glory, to be the strongmen who could re-impose the dictates of White supremacy. The left has tried to counter the populist right-wing threat with reason and evidence, which simply does not work against delusion.

If people were looking for rational reasons to elect their leaders, this unholy trinity would not have made it to office. British Conservative politician Michael Gove gave the game away when he argued that 'Britain has had enough of experts' during the campaign for Brexit.[17] Vote Leave knew they would lose any debate based on facts, so their solution was simply to avoid facts altogether. Brexit, along with the elections of Trump and Bolsonaro, were victories for Whiteness as a symbol. The popular appeal of these politicians was immune to reason, as many voters were trapped in the delusions of the psychosis. They didn't need evidence to see that these great White men would lead them back to days of glory, and rejecting the evidence as being nothing more than part of 'Project Fear' was seen as pushing back against the machine that was trying to derail the project. Paranoia is the recurrent symptom of Whiteness: there is a fear of the threat of immigrants, a fear of losing their traditions and a fear of Black people in general.

The aim of this book is to demonstrate that Whiteness is deluded, irrational, and based on a set of collective hallucinations. The only metaphor we can use to understand it is a collective psychosis, one that shapes how we understand and move through the world. We have been trying to apply reason to the issue of racism, but that has failed.Whiteness is a set of ideas produced by the racist political and economic system, and as long as that system remains intact it will continue to reproduce delusions that prevent all of us from seeing the brutal reality of the social order we inhabit. There is no reasoning with Whiteness; instead we must destroy the system that creates it. I am hoping to save us all a lot of time and effort by lifting the veil. Once we realize that some battles cannot be won, we can truly win the war. I invite you to join me on a journey through Wonderland as we unpick the delusions of the psychosis of Whiteness.

I

Why Psychosis?

Black people do not have a happy history with the word psychosis. The term has historically been used as a stick to beat us with. I have family members who have received a diagnosis of psychosis, and I'm all too aware of its horrible history, the way that labels like psychosis have been used to stigmatize our community. I don't know much about my grandad, but I do know that one day he hit his breaking point and ended up in what was then called a 'madhouse'. Using a term like psychosis is something I have decided to do only after a great deal of thought. My aim is certainly not to further stigmatize those living with the diagnosis. While there are people who lose touch with reality, the truth is that psychosis is a political construct rather than an objective medical diagnosis. People do suffer very real symptoms that appear under the umbrella of psychosis: hallucinations, deluded thinking, and the inability to tell what is real and what is not. But the definition of psychosis has shifted in heavily racialized ways that specifically target Black communities.

'Psychotic' may be a term widely used to instil a fear of the dangerous (often meaning *Black*) mentally ill deviant, one we should all fear, but psychosis is not in itself a clear medical term. In medical literature, psychosis and schizophrenia are often conflated, and these terms used interchangeably. In *The Diagnostic and Statistical Manual of Mental Disorders* psychosis appears under 'Schizophrenia Spectrum and Other Psychotic Disorders'. I know how serious these conditions can be: I have a family member who has been schizophrenic since their early twenties. Brain scans of schizophrenics show observable changes to the structure of the brain over time. By any measure, schizophrenia is as 'real' a condition as there is.[1] Psychosis, however, includes the experiences of those with schizophrenia, as well as those who don't have the condition but do display signs of it. A diagnosis of psychosis is entirely subjective and is given if the patient displays two or more of the following symptoms: 'delusions, hallucinations, disorganized thinking (speech), grossly disorganized or catatonic behaviour or negative symptoms (i.e., diminished emotional expression, alogia [not speaking], or avolition [total lack of motivation to get things done])'.[2] But delusional thinking is in the eye of the beholder. Over the decades minorities have often been deemed deviant due to the overwhelming Whiteness of the profession of psychiatry. Consider the case of Steven Thompson, examined by Britain's first Black consultant psychiatrist, Aggrey Burke, in 1980. Thompson was just one week away from release from his six-year prison sentence when prison officers forcibly cut off his dreadlocks. He was a Rastafarian and his locks, grown over many years, were a sacred part of his beliefs. When he resisted this assault he was labelled 'delusional' for being so upset about a haircut, deemed to have a psychotic disorder and was sent to Rampton Secure Hospital on an indeterminate sentence. Only after outrage in the community was the Black psychiatrist Aggrey Burke brought on board, who managed to secure his release after what he diplomatically called a process of 'negotiation'.[3] This is just one of countless stories that tell us that accepting psychosis uncritically as an objective medical condition is, in and of itself, stigmatizing. One of the reasons this book was so important for me to write was so that we can all begin to understand just how problematic the very idea of psychosis is and the terrible ways it has been applied historically. I want to be very clear that in using the term 'psychosis' I do not wish to diminish the trauma that so many people sadly experience, but, importantly, I do want to capture how troubling it is and to question how this concept continues to be used and abused today.

RACIST PSYCHIATRY

We must problematize the term psychosis, a condition that does not exist outside the imagination of the diagnoser. Whoever determines what is delusional interprets the meaning of disordered thinking. In his excellent book *The Protest Psychosis*, which examines how race has always shaped psychiatric diagnoses in America, Jonathan Metzl explains how schizophrenia became a Black disease due to political 'changes in diagnostic criteria rather than their clinical symptoms'.[4] Metzl explains that in early twentieth-century America schizophrenia was associated with artists and middle-class women and was not considered to be a violent or aggressive disease. It was only in the 1960s, after the rise of the civil rights movements and Black power, that schizophrenia came to be associated with Black bodies seen to be violent and out of control. The United States has had to deal with a large Black population for much longer than the UK; it tells us something about where we might be heading. The US dominates the academic field of psychiatry, and it's helpful to look across the pond, as America's racial framework was mapped onto growing Black populations in European countries during the post-war period of mass immigration from the colonies. When large numbers of Black people arrived in their former mother countries they settled into the same patterns of racial segregation and institutional racism that have afflicted African Americans since emancipation.[5]

Metzl took the title of his book from a diagnosis dreamt up by the psychiatrists Walter Bromberg and Franck Simon, who were fixated on the impact of civil rights and the 'Musslims [sic]' on Black communities.[6] Supposedly delusional behaviours included the 'refusal to accept the syntactical language of standard English'; drawing 'pictures or writing material of an Islamic nature, elaborating their ideas in the directions of African ideology with a decided "primitive" accent'; the 'denial of Caucasian cosmology and values' in favour of 'Afrocentric ideology'; and the adoption of Arabic names or taking steps to 'de-Anglicize' their names.[7] I don't think I would have fared very well if I was trapped under their so-called care. But Bromberg and Simon do go to lengths to assure us that 'in these patients these productions are not *political* but psychological in form'.[8] Racist propaganda posturing as scientific diagnosis was nothing new to the discipline of psychiatry in the 1960s, and Bromberg and Simon were simply following in a long and undistinguished tradition.

It is impossible to discuss medical racism without talking about Samuel Cartwright, a physician from the Southern United States who died in 1863 after doing lasting damage to the profession. He was an enslaver as well as doctor to other plantation owners, specializing in the diseases of the so-called 'Negro race'. His ideas were so bizarre that you could be forgiven for assuming them marginal, but he was a prominent physician and his theories were discussed in journals and newspapers across the nation. Cartwright believed that Africans were inferior because, it was said, we naturally have a lower lung capacity, although there was no evidence that this was the case. Our supposedly deficient lungs meant that our red blood cells did not 'vitalize the blood', in his words, making us backwards and lazy. Cartwright used this as evidence that slavery was good for us because,

> under the compulsive power of the White man, they are made to labor
> or exercise, which makes the lungs perform the duty of vitalizing the
> blood ... it is the red, vital blood sent to the brain that liberates their
> minds when under the White man's control; and it is the want of a suf-
> ficiency of red, vital blood that chains their mind to ignorance and
> barbarism, when in freedom.[9]

Cartwright believed that the '"deficiency in the Negro"'s lung cap-acity was twenty percent lower than Whites'. He was in esteemed company and followed on from the work of one Thomas Jefferson, the third president of the United States, also an enslaver who peddled the fiction of a 'difference of structure in the pulmonary apparatus' of Black people in his 1785 *Notes on the State of Virginia*.[10] This notion was etched into the medical imagination when Benjamin Gould con-ducted a large-scale survey on soldiers in the US Civil War in 1864. Failing to account for huge differences in social class and living conditions among White and Black soldiers – Black soldiers had just been emancipated from slavery – he attributed his differing measurements to supposedly 'racial' characteristics. This observation became part of medical common-sense practice, particularly in the 1920s, when research into eugenics created evidence that, of course, confirmed this racist hypothesis.[11] Chillingly, racist assumptions of racial deficiencies originating from slavery are still shaping medical practice in the twenty-first century. Spirometers, which measure lung output, apply a 'race correction' factor of up to 15 per cent, meaning that they expect the lung capacity of Black patients to be less than White people's. This means that respiratory problems might be missed in Black patients; abnormal readings are being used as indicators of health. This 'race correction' is used in spirometers all over the world.[12] Kidney performance is also assumed to be lower, meaning that Black people's kidneys need to be more damaged than White people's before we are put on dialysis. It is noteworthy that in 2021, no doubt after an awakening following the Black Lives Matter summer, the National Institute for Health and Care Excellence (NICE) removed the recommendation for race-correcting Black patients' kidney function in the UK.[13] But it is a testament to the racism seeping through the pores of medicine that it was ever recommended. There is no good evidence that African Americans have a lower level of kidney functioning and there has never been any proof whatsoever that the wide variety of Black ethnic groups in the UK show reduced kidney output.

Dr Samuel Cartwright's most memorable legacy is in the field of psychiatry. Like many at the time (and far too many still) he believed that slavery was the natural state of Black people. Reading his articles in scholarly journals, it is bizarre to see how nakedly ideological they are. They are full of protestations about the historical inferiority of the 'Negro' and propaganda that Africa has produced 'no letters or even hieroglyphics – no buildings, roads or improvements, or monuments of any kind are anywhere to be found'.[14] He even quotes the Bible to prove our inferiority, explaining that we are meant to be knee-benders. He then claims that our knees are more pliable, thanks to this natural order. I would recommend reading some Cartwright to see what tumbling down the rabbit hole of the psychosis of Whiteness looks like. While writing all this he was venerated as a wonderful physician. One of the delusions of Whiteness is that 'science' is an objective pursuit, free from the constraints of politics and emotion. But science is always produced by the politics of its time. Cartwright is a somewhat extreme example, but his ideas were widely circulated and held to be true. But Cartwright wasn't objectively pursuing truth. His real motivations are clear: the 'illnesses' he was most concerned about were those that cost the plantations money.

Drapetomania is a 'disease of the mind' Cartwright dreamed up to explain why the enslaved ran away. (Of course, due to our natural state of servitude, wanting to be free could only be a mental disorder.) In a forerunner to the paranoia that is often painted onto Black patients, Cartwright describes how 'Negroes are jealous and suspicious ... they believe that they are poisoned ... but it is their mind that is poisoned'.[15] The cure for drapetomania was 'whipping the devil out of' the runaway to strike the fear of God into them and the rest of the enslaved.[16] This was, of course, done for their own good, because without the benefit of slavery they would fall into uncivilized savagery.

Not all cases of mental disease led to the enslaved running away in psychotic delusion. Cartwright developed the diagnosis of *dysesthesia Aethiopis*, a state in which the enslaved were

> apt to do much mischief, which appears as if intentional, but is mostly owing to the stupidness of mind and insensibility of the nerves induced by the disease. Thus, they break, waste and destroy everything they handle, abuse horses and cattle, tear, burn or rend their own clothing, and paying no attention to the rights of property, they steal other's to replace what they have destroyed. They wander about at night, and keep in a half-nodding sleep during the day. They slight their work, cut up corn, cane, cotton or tobacco when hoeing it, as if for pure mischief. They raise disturbances with their overseers and fellow servants without cause or motive, and seem to be insensible to pain when subjected to punishment.[17]

Black people are never seen as having agency, so therefore the everyday acts of resistance that Cartwright outlines above could not be a rational feature of fighting back against the system, but instead are used as evidence of our innate inferiority. The name he gave this affliction was 'rascality', which is basically shorthand for *when good niggers go bad*. He argues that there is no intent on behalf of the enslaved because the 'mind is too torpid to mediate to mischief': this, in his telling, was a biological problem caused by a lack of oxygenation of the blood. Cartwright's cure for rascality was hard labour (enforced with a whip, of course) because it increased the breathing, in turn vitalizing the red blood cells and boosting the so-called negroes' brain to a higher level of functioning. Inevitably, Cartwright used this pseudo-science to strengthen arguments against abolition. He died during the US Civil War, so his political motivations should be clear. But the idea that liberty would lead to the mental and moral decline of the formerly enslaved did not die with Cartwright; it lasted into the twentieth century and beyond.

In a 1913 scholarly article the US psychiatrist A. B. Evarts was sure that 'bondage was a great aid to the colored man', because we apparently 'had no racial preparation for freedom'. The situation on the plantation was better for our mental health because 'a crazy negro was a rare sight before emancipation'.[18] The notion that emancipation led to a spike in insanity for the formerly enslaved was picked up in other supposedly scientific analyses of the time.[19] As a sociologist by training I am used to reading wild misuses of statistical data, but looking at tables that compared reports of mental illness on plantations to those of the formerly enslaved in free society in order to illustrate the supposed 'benefits' of slavery, even I was taken aback. It is blindingly obvious why mental illness in the enslaved would be grossly under-reported: there was no financial benefit to reporting mental illness in the enslaver's property. On the contrary, it would lower the value of any potential sale and reduce the lucrative prospect of the enslaved being hired out to work elsewhere. Perhaps more importantly, the plantation owners had no interest in the mental wellness of their property and it was unlikely they would have even noticed any problems. In the tradition of Samuel Cartwright, any changes in behaviour were deemed to be solved with a good whipping. It wasn't believed the enslaved even had the capacity for mental illness. We were too childlike in our reasoning to be troubled by real diseases of the mind, which is why Cartwright made some up. Unsurprisingly when we were free to complain about our mental health, we did so, and there was a lot to complain about, given the immense trauma endured on the plantations. When apparently educated people so brazenly misuse data the only explanation can be that they are either deeply foolish, lying or in a state of delirium, and it is clear which of those labels applies here.

Psychiatrists of the period dreamt up fantasies and presented them as truths. In the literature one stumbles upon made-up generalizations like 'all negroes have a pronounced fear of darkness',[20] or, like Cartwright, proclaiming that all Black people cover our faces when we sleep because we need humid air; a fabrication to give credence to his lung capacity nonsense. What is striking across this so-called literature, a trend easily seen across all racial theories, is that the scientific promise to trust empirical evidence is dashed out of the window to support racist ideas. Where no evidence exists to support a thesis it is simply fabricated and mental gymnastics are undertaken to contort the available data to suit racist hypotheses. It was taken for granted that we were inferior and would therefore present differently as psychiatric patients. The psychiatrist Mary O'Malley, writing in 1914, paints this picture the most vividly:

> [P]sychosis in an obviously lower race, such as the colored race really is, must necessarily offer some features from a mental standpoint which distinguish it in a general way from a psychosis in a higher race. This is so apparent that it requires no further discussion. The lower psychic development of the colored race, under pathological conditions, offers some phenomena which are observed to approach more nearly the general features and characteristics of children.[21]

Mental illness was, likewise, not initially seen to be Black disease, because it was assumed that we were incapable of the complex thought required to produce it. The fact that Black patients were less likely to soil themselves, commit acts of public masturbation, self-harm, attack the nurses and spread faeces on the walls were used to make the case that we were *less* civilized. That White patients did do these things meant they felt the diagnoses on a more cerebral level.[22] White privilege apparently even extends to how flinging shit around is perceived.

These notions about the lack of capacity for non-Europeans to experience mental health issues are not as outdated as we may like to think. It took until the 1990s for psychiatry professor Vickram Patel to convince his profession that depression was in fact a problem in the underdeveloped world. Before then, it was believed that depression was only experienced by people in rich countries because the poor around the globe could not be suffering psychological problems in the same way as those in the West.[23] Partly this was due to the prolifer-ation of racist ideas, like those of J. C. Carothers, who argued in 1953 that Africans were incapable of the psychological development neces-sary to suffer mental health issues. There was also a feeling that 'if your baby died and you had seven already, you didn't experience it in the same way'.[24] It was also assumed that even if there were genuine mental health issues, they were less important than the life-or-death inequality many in the underdeveloped world experienced. To this day there is a chronic shortage of mental health professionals in the Global South. Some may try to apply the class argument here, to say that it is poverty, not race, that caused this faulty assumption, but this is truly a racial issue. It is commonly understood that poor people in the West are more likely to suffer from mental health problems due to the trauma of poverty, but when it comes to applying the same ration-ale to those in the underdeveloped world, these factors magically become separate: poverty is used as the reason that psychological dis-orders do not exist – and therefore do not require treating – rather than as one of the causes of said disorders. It is also no coincidence that those living in grinding poverty in the former colonies are Black and Brown. Poor Black subjects have never been seen as fully human and this has been because of perceived deficits of the mind. So we

9

should not be surprised about the logic that expects the poor Black and Brown around the globe to be incapable of mental ill health. This quotation, from the psychiatrist E. M. Green talking about African Americans in 1914, could equally describe the attitudes of many today:

> even under depressing environment, poorly housed, poorly fed, relegated to the most unattractive quarters, imposed upon, humiliated and contemptuously treated, still depression is foreign to their natures and happiness breaks through.[25]

How many times have we heard people comment on how happy people are in the underdeveloped world, even though they live in conditions that we would never accept? This is a throwback to the idea that the smiling native lives in a state of nature, unconcerned with the complexities of the modern world, that they cannot understand, and may even be better off for not experiencing the modern luxuries we would not bear to be without. Even as recently as 2015 a paper that appeared in a respected academic journal of psychology cited Green's racist screed as a legitimate source.[26]

Given these deep-seated notions that Black people are incapable of complex thought, it may seem surprising that we are now over-diagnosed with mental health issues in the West. In both the US and the UK Black people are more likely to be labelled as schizophrenic and significantly more likely to be sectioned and detained under mental health legislation than their White counterparts.[27] Young Black men in the UK are ten times more likely to be diagnosed with psychotic illness and four times more likely to be hospitalized.[28] Just like Cartwright's ideas about 'rascality', the cause of these disorders is assumed to be located in the body, not the mind, of the Black population. Biological or genetic differences are imagined, in the minds of those doing the diagnosing, to lead to the supposedly more violent, disordered and aggressive presentations of our mental health problems. As we have already discussed, these perceptions are rooted in the need to contain Black uprisings and protest in the 1960s, and gave rise to the stereotypical view of Black people as aggressive, rapists, criminals, beasts to be feared and controlled. Although there is a long history to that image, the idea of the 'good Negro', the deferential servant who would willingly do their master's bidding, was a major form, perhaps the predominant form, of Black representation – even as late as the mid-twentieth century. Think of those disgusting golliwog toys far too many people are still quick to defend today. Cartwright, again, is instructive here, taken as he was by the 'undoubted fact of the love they [the enslaved] bear to their masters', and he marvelled at the relative tranquillity on plantations, even though the enslaved significantly outnumbered the enslavers.[29] In the Southern United States the fear of Black people was seared into the imagination of Whites, given the demographic inconvenience of having to live next to the formerly enslaved. But it was only with the Great Migration, the movement of six million Black people from the south to cities in the north which began in 1910, the ensuing civil rights movement and, especially, Black power, that dominant media representation of Black people became the spectre of the Black threat. By the 1930s, a moral panic engulfed society that then created the conditions to transform schizophrenia into a Black disease, thus explaining the behaviour of the troublesome negroes. By the 1950s this idea had really taken root and the received wisdom that Black people had a higher propensity for mental illness was becoming taken for granted.[30] Now the bestial negro could be tamed with psychiatric medication and hospitalization alongside the already well-worn tactics of incarceration and police harassment. In a chilling echo of the idea that freedom was too much for the childlike brain of Black people, the idea that civil rights gains had raised our expectations too much was advanced as the cause for the disturbed bodies rebelling against White supremacy.[31] It seems we just can't handle being free.

In the diagnostic room everything became evidence of our disorganized thoughts and detachment from reality. We were too aggressive, spoke too loudly, gesticulated too much. We rejected White authority, not because it was illegitimate, but because we were unreasonable. Our cultural norms were too primitive to be rational and were taken as evidence that we were disordered. British psychiatry took its lead from the US in regard to race. A mental health nurse in the UK once revealed to me that, in the 1980s, they would observe patients picking out the brown bits from uncooked rice and chalk it up to obsessive-compulsive disorder (for the uninitiated, this is a routine practice in Black households, as is washing meat before you cook it, cleaning your legs and applying moisturizer). Sadly, it has become a self-fulfilling prophecy that Black people are more likely to suffer serious mental illness because living with racism is in itself a source of trauma.[32] Psychosis is a label that has been put on us for wanting to be free; trying to resist; and existing in ways that go against an established White norm. As such, it must be vigorously challenged when applied to us in ways that limit our freedom.

INTERNALIZED RACISM

While we should be wary of the notion that Black people are more *likely* to be mentally ill, we do also need to understand the impact that racism has upon those who live through it. Internalized racism is a phrase which describes how an external racist society assaults an individual's identity, and the impact of living with daily experiences of racism on the Black psyche cannot be understated.

In his classic book *Black Skin, White Masks*, Frantz Fanon eloquently captures the damage White supremacy causes, exposing the effects of racism on the psyche. He describes a White French child seeing him on the street and exclaiming, 'Look, mama, a Negro!', and being hurt by the fear in the young boy's face. The impact this had on him was intense:

> my body was given back to me sprawled out, distorted, recoloured, clad in mourning in that white winter day. The Negro is an animal, the Negro is bad, the Negro is mean, the Negro is ugly, look, a nigger.[33]

Fanon explains that the impact of internalizing these ideas is that 'the [way the] black man [behaves] towards the white, or towards his own race, often duplicates almost completely a constellation of delirium, frequently bordering on the region of the pathological'.[34] He shows that living in a society that depends on keeping you in an inferior position will have a disastrous effect on a person: 'to the identical degree to which that society creates difficulties for him, he will find himself thrust into a neurotic situation'.[35] Any Black person reading this will be either acutely aware of what Fanon is talking about or will still be in the phase of denial, trying to pretend that colleagues touching your hair is normal. Fanon's work is foundational because it so clearly articulates the internal struggles of navigating the world as a racialized other.

Following on from Fanon, so-called microaggresions[36] are the paper-cuts of racism, cuts bound to affect a person's mental health. In an academic paper Robin DiAngelo, author of *White Fragility*, along with researcher Cheryl E. Matias, states that 'interactions with White people are at times so overwhelming, draining, and incomprehensible that it causes serious anguish' to a racialized group. We strain ourselves to 'placate White neurosis due to real fears of White supremacy' in an interplay of what they call 'racial cray-cray' ('cray-cray' is an African-American euphemism for utter craziness).[37] I have worked for many years in academia, one of the very Whitest professions, and I can attest to a daily assault of microaggressions. A White staff member has physically pushed me out of an area they deemed I had no right to be in; I have been constantly harassed by security for my ID card to prove I do work in the building; and I have even had a White woman run crying out of a meeting room while accusing me of being 'aggressive', much to the bemusement of me and my Black colleague. To add insult to injury, after complaining about that last act of racial cray-cray I was subjected to a disciplinary investigation, because of course the tears of a White woman count for more than the complaints of two Black members of staff. It is no exaggeration to say that going to work is like walking on a tightrope or even tiptoeing through a minefield; constant vigilance is required, lest you accidentally trigger a racially charged explosion that will permanently damage your career. When I started lecturing I was so uncomfortable in the environment that for the first several years I refused to step inside any university without wearing smart trousers and shoes; I hoped that dressing differently to the students might improve my experience of being on campus. When I was made professor I said, 'to hell with it', and started wearing hoodies into work. I could actually see the discomfort on some of my colleagues' faces.

The novelist Ralph Ellison captures it best in his masterpiece *Invisible Man* when he describes the feeling of being an 'invisible man . . . a matter of construction of their inner eyes, those eyes with which they look through their physical eyes upon reality'.[38] Through the distorted lens of the psychosis of Whiteness, all Black people are a threat, aliens to be feared. Although I am probably the best-known person on my campus I can walk around almost anonymously because other members of staff look down, away or through the Black man coming towards them in the corridor. On the rare times I stop to say hello a momentary panic flashes across their face, until they breathe an 'Oh, it's *you*' sigh of relief. This is something that we just have to get used to, but there is a cost. I am mentally scarred from the constant assault of passive aggression, patronizing, undermining Whiteness, and have battled stress and depression as a result. There is evidence that for racialized minorities living in a predominantly White area is associated with increased rates of mental health issues.[39] Being the only Black person in a room (or even a building) is an experience you have to get used to if you want to navigate life as a racialized minority, and particularly if you hope to make it working in a university or other corporate environment. Learning how to exist/dance in such environments is as necessary a qualification for 'success' as any university degree. One of the most basic aspects of White privilege is to be able to avoid the perils of the racial performance.

The fact that my wounds are not larger is a privilege. As my mom once told me, having to deal with racism 'is what being Black is' and we delude ourselves if we think that we are protected from racism because we have earned the privileges of working in the 'house' rather than the 'field'. The truth is, my position protects me from the starkest consequences. I can take sick leave and when I was Amy Coopered I was dealt with through HR proceedings rather than the police. I have the luxury of financial security and being able to retreat if necessary. The same cannot be said for those at the coalface of White supremacy, harassed by the police and living on the economic margins of society.

We must confront the reality of what racism does to our communities more directly, and we can start by destigmatizing how we talk about mental illness. In 2021 the actor David Harewood made a powerful documentary called *Psychosis and Me* discussing a breakdown he experienced in his twenties. He opens by saying we need to re-examine how we think of the term: 'When someone is psychotic we instantly think crazy, dangerous mad, sort of raving, looney . . . that's what we think when we talk about psychosis.'[40] He spoke to a number of young people suffering with the diagnosis who look very different to the way that they are represented in the media. Harewood's own psychosis clearly demonstrates the impact racism can have on mental health. During his time at the prestigious drama school RADA he had to change the way he spoke and took elocution lessons to that end. He vividly remembers the stress of living up to being a 'Black actor' and having to come to terms with how his Blackness meant his 'aspirations, dreams, hopes' were restricted. He received racist reviews during his performance of Romeo that said he 'looked more like Mike Tyson' with his 'thick neck' and 'threatening physical demeanour'. But it was his performance of Sloane in *Entertaining Mr Sloane* which tipped him into a psychotic break. He was the only Black actor in the play and the role could not have been more of a racist stereotype: Sloane is described as 'a scheming, murderous, sexual deviant who ends up in servitude'. At the start of the second act Harewood had to perform a particularly sordid monologue and watched as Black members of the audience stormed out in disgust every night. I can only imagine the out-of-body experience that must have been. He describes how he 'was struggling with my black identity in a white world and I was rejected by people who looked just like me . . . I started drinking, before and after shows, manically throwing myself into performances'.[41] When he was hospitalized he hallucinated the voice of Martin Luther King giving him a mission to bring peace to the world. When his friends took him to the psychiatric hospital he was heavily restrained by six police officers 'sitting on' him and was filled with enough sedatives to 'knock out a horse', as one of the nurses described it. If ever there was a story that illustrates how racism makes us lose our minds, it's this one. Once recovered, Harewood never suffered another episode. He is fortunate that he did not get trapped within his diagnosis, as so many Black people do.

THE PSYCHOSIS OF WHITENESS

Given the racist history of psychiatry and its inheritance of a deeply racialized idea of what mental health is, I use the term 'psychosis of Whiteness' as a provocation. I want to be abundantly clear I am not arguing that all White people are psychotic. I am not using the term in the individualized way psychiatry has, to describe so-called 'deviants'. We cannot see racism as an individual disease of the White mind; to do so would mean the solution would be to treat the sick people, rather than to address the societal issues that cause this psychosis. I use psychosis here as a metaphor to diagnose the delusional thinking that is necessary to maintain a racist society. If we were able to fully accept that the barbarity of White supremacy is the keystone of our prosperity, then we would be forced into action, creating an alternative economic system to the one we have, one that no longer reproduces the material conditions of White supremacy. To avoid facing up to its true nature society creates myths and distortions, resulting in what I am calling the psychosis of Whiteness.

There is a distinguished tradition of Black authors explaining racism as a psychological problem. Author Toni Morrison famously explained in an interview:

> the people who do this thing, who practice racism, are bereft. There is something distorted about the psyche. There is a huge waste, a corruption, a distortion. It's like it's a profound neurosis . . . it feels crazy, it is crazy.[42]

Fanon described the 'neurotic orientation'[43] of Whiteness that is visible whenever White privilege is challenged: defensiveness, anxiety, irrationality and discomfort are the result. Professor Beverly Daniel Tatum's classic book exploring racial identity formation in children, *Why Are All the Black Kids Sitting Together in the Cafeteria?*, provides a perfect illustration of this 'neurotic orientation', although she doesn't articulate it in this way. In that work, Professor Tatum describes visiting schools that were predominantly White but which had been going through the desegregation process (bussing in Black children), and where the titular question was often posed to her by teachers in these schools. It was routine for White people to cluster together, but when the Black kids did it it was suddenly a problem. Seeing a group of Black children put the White educators on edge, made them question what the Black kids were saying and whether their generous efforts at desegregation were failing. The urge to focus on and disperse the Black kids from their groups in the cafeteria is based on that neurotic itch, White racial anxiety.

Perhaps nothing evokes that anxiety like White people being plunged into a situation where they are the only White person or one of a few White people within a group of Black and/or Brown people. You'll see beads of sweat on their brow, they'll clutch their handbags and be overcome with general nervousness. Perhaps this is the historical anxiety of the colonial so-called 'pioneers', constantly fearing being overcome by the savages surrounding them. In 1926, observing the growing rates of neuroses among colonial masters, Dr Hugh Stannus diagnosed the condition as *tropical neurasthenia*, one brought on because 'the colonist could not understand the natives' language and this made him edgy. What were they saying behind his back? Was a violent revolt being plotted under his very nose?'[44] The colonists couldn't sleep and felt constantly anxious. Alone in the twenty-first-century British equivalent of a colony, the inner city, White people can still experience the same full-on neurosis. The ultimate White friend test is to see if they can get through a Black family barbecue alone, with no other White comrades to lay cover fire in a crisis. I wouldn't recommend that as a first hurdle unless you secretly dislike the person and don't mind risking them having a complete (psychotic?) breakdown. Get them to dip their toe in the water by watching some *Fresh Prince* re-runs first. Pre-slap Will Smith managed to be so disarming we should just go ahead and designate him Ambassador of Black men. After adding in some degrees of difficulty to the TV portion (maybe some *Desmond's*, accents can be triggering), try taking them to a shopping centre in a 'diverse' area and see if the *tropical neurasthenia* kicks in. If they make it through that without having a panic attack you can bring them around your family. If you are White and reading this then ¯_(ツ)_/¯.

The term 'neurosis' captures these relatively small examples of White discomfort as it articulates the impact on an individual level. (I say relatively small, but these anxieties can be devastating for the mental and physical health of Black and Brown people, whether expressed through microaggressions in the workplace or through police violence.) But the violence that underpins White supremacy goes far beyond a neurosis. George Zimmerman calling the police to report that the seventeen-year-old African-American Trayvon Martin was a 'bad dude' walking around the neighbourhood may have been neurotic. But Zimmerman's pursuit and then murder of the unarmed teenager requires a very different metaphoric diagnosis. Robert Williams, the legendary civil rights activist who advocated for armed self-defence, declared that racism was a 'mass mental illness'. He argued that in order to comprehend it we needed to see racism 'as a mass psychosis ... the racist man is crazed by hysteria at the idea of coming into contact with Negroes'.[45] Psychosis differs from neurosis because it represents a complete break from reality, marked by delusional thoughts and behaviour. How else to explain the mirage of the dangerous Black savage that Zimmerman thought he saw that night? Perhaps seeing Zimmerman's actions as a symptom of a societal psychosis might help us understand how they occurred.

In order to understand the psychosis of Whiteness we need to first accept that the West was only made possible due to unimaginable levels of brutal colonial slaughter. We have never seen, and will hopefully never see, a system as bloodthirsty as the one we still inhabit.

White supremacy necessitates delusional thinking in order to sustain itself. From the genocide in the Americas that cost tens of millions of lives to the savagery of slavery and the inhumanity of colonial barbarity, the West was built on the blood and bodies of the Black and Brown.[46] Historian Carol Anderson wrote an excellent and heartbreaking book called *White Rage*, recounting countless tales of savagery in the name of Whiteness; they are difficult to read. Perhaps the most gruesome is the story of Mary Turner, who was lynched in Valdosta, Georgia, in 1918. After an African-American man named Sidney Johnson killed a White man, in retribution for a savage whipping he'd received, the town erupted into a five-day 'lynching orgy', where eleven Black people were brutally killed. Mary Turner and her husband were not involved in the murder, but Mr Turner had already been lynched when the mob came for her:

> they dragged Mary to a tree, stripped her, tied her ankles together, and strung her upside down. The men then ran to their cars, brought back gasoline, and began to 'roast her alive'. Then they saw her naked, eight-month-old pregnant stomach convulsing, that only set the mob . . . into a deeper frenzy, as one man took out his knife and sliced away at her charred flesh until the baby, now ripped from the womb, fell to the ground and gave to cries. Someone in the lynch party then stepped forward and smashed the child's head into the red Georgia dirt with the heel of his boot.[47]

There was nothing unique about this gruesome spectacle. Lynchings were a common practice, used to terrify African Americans into submission and mass mob violence erupted frequently. There are numerous other examples: in 1863 thousands of angry Whites carried out an orgy of lynching in New York City to protest against the Civil War draft. They murdered over 1,000 people in the space of just a few days. In 1919 Tulsa, Oklahoma, saw three days of violence during which 35 blocks of a prosperous African-American neighbourhood were razed to the ground and up to 300 people were killed.[48] In New Orleans in 1866 fifty African Americans were lynched solely for having the audacity to meet to discuss voting. Grotesquely, lynchings were a family affair:

everyone, including children, would take a day off to go out and watch the entertainment. To this day photographs of the 'strange fruit' hanging from Southern trees remain with us because they were used on postcards; a macabre holiday snap. Moreover, 'severed body parts became souvenirs and decorations hung proudly in homes'.[49]

This barbarity was not a case of American exceptionalism; scenes of brutality have been perpetrated by the West across the globe. Christopher Columbus, the great-grandfather of White supremacy, unleashed a reign of terror on the Americas that included man-eating dogs and a practice of mutilating the natives if they didn't meet their quotas for mining gold. Belgian King Leopold II instituted the same system upon the Congolese when he was given the 'free state' in the nineteenth century. His system of exacting tribute included maiming children for not meeting their rubber-gathering quotas. His regime was so brutal – he killed half of the entire population of the Congo – that the Belgian government intervened and removed the Congo Free State from his personal possession. Nor were scenes of pregnant Black women hanging upside down from a tree and being beaten alien to British plantation owners. Alternatively, they would dig a hole in the ground for a pregnant woman's belly, make her lie down, and whip her severely. Not to mention the vicious and industrial sexual violence that enslaved Black women were subjected to in order to make them breed subsequent generations of the enslaved. Across the globe White people have enforced their will with a barbarity that is so X-rated we simply cannot bear to acknowledge the unspeakable truth.

The only explanation for such exorbitant levels of savagery is that they were produced by a psychosis, not a psychosis of individual perpetrators but of the collective consciousness of an entire society. This societal psychosis reduced Black people to the status of non-human, only slightly above animals. We were bought, sold and slaughtered without troubling the White psyche. Sometimes it seems as if the US is 'worse' than Europe, because we can see American violence and barbarity so clearly, but this is just a result of their greater proximity to the subjects of their violence. Europe managed its colonies at arm's length, and it is only recently that large numbers of Black and Brown people have come to live in the mother countries of the colonialists. European societies were not required to be as violent and, in any case, settler colonies like the USA and Brazil, where we witness the extremes of racial violence, are just the homes of ex-pat Europeans enacting colonial barbarity without limitations. Due to their colonial settler demographics, they cannot hide from their histories of violent White supremacy. President Andrew Johnson's declaration in 1886 that 'this is . . . a country for white men, and by God, as long as I'm president, it shall be a government for White men',[50] just one year after the 13th Amendment was passed outlawing slavery (except as punishment for a crime), shows us how racism was baked into the very formation of the US nation state. The fact that Mississippi didn't officially ratify the 13th Amendment until 2013 is an indicator of how little has changed.

In Britain it is easy to point the finger at America as a uniquely racist society; the distance between violence in the colonies and their respective mother countries has given European nations a deluded sense of moral superiority. It is essential that we do not fall into the delusion that racism exists uniquely in one country. There is no such thing as American, British or any other nation-state racism. Racism is a global system that developed from European nations devastating the Americas, plundering Africa and conquering the globe. We cannot simply focus on the obvious violence of settler colonies like the USA while former seats of empire like Britain, France, Spain and the gang have built on colonial violence just as much. It is sometimes imagined that these great nations were forged long before racism emerged and, though they may have benefitted from plundering the colonies, racism and violence were not the making of them. I have been told on multiple occasions that because the British monarchy predated colonialism it must surely be independent of it; a perfect example of delusional thinking, as the British monarchy did not predate the British empire. Prior to the Act of Union in 1707, Britain simply did not exist, but only the *English* crown. It was the wealth derived from empire that gave England the might to expand across the island and which gave Scotland and Wales the incentive to join in the colonial feast. It should be impossible to consider Britain as separate from the empire that produced it. The monarchy may predate empire, but its wealth, role and even its symbolism are rooted in colonial exploitation. The king is the head of state of fifteen nations and leader of the Common-wealth, which is just a polite way of saying 'empire'. It is no coincidence that Queen Elizabeth II was in Kenya, staying in a 'treetop' hotel, when she heard the news that she would be taking the throne. The jewel-encrusted crowns that she paraded at public events are perhaps the biggest symbolic link to the looting her position is based upon. The imagery, pomp and costumes of royal pageantry are built firmly on colonial expansion. Though the violence was done at a distance, ideas of empire and White supremacy were just as important to the national identity in places like Britain as they were in settler colonies; the psychosis of Whiteness is shared across all Western countries, banded together by colonial violence.

To return to Fanon, he underscores how racist ideas permeate the mother countries just as much as the colonies. He was born in Marti-nique under French rule, and although in the 1940s and 1950s there were very few Black people in France, racist ideas and stereotypes were just as prevalent there as they were in the Deep South of the United States. In Fanon's own words, 'France is a racist country. For the myth of the bad nigger is part of the collective subconscious.'[51] Black people remain disproportionately arrested and imprisoned in European nations; it should be easy to identify the source of this racism. I say *should*, but the opposite is true: because of the psychosis of Whiteness, it is impossible for society to understand how racism plays out. Delusions obscure an honest accounting of history.

The West conveniently forgets about its dark side, a phenomenon named the 'epistemology of ignorance' by philosopher Charles Mills.[52] We ignore that the Industrial Revolution could not have occurred without slavery and that the loot of colonialism fuelled the modern world. There is some truth to the idea of wilful forgetting, but the dominant understanding of the world is distorted beyond simple ignorance. Not only have we forgotten colonial brutality, we revel in it. It is utterly mind-bending that I went through *every* level of education in Britain and never once heard the word empire uttered in a classroom. The British empire is undoubtedly the most important feature of the nation's history, the foundation stone without which nothing makes sense . . . and we *never* spoke about it. It's no surprise then that the majority of the British public believe that the British empire was a force for good in the world: the same empire that enslaved millions of Africans and was responsible for the deaths of tens of millions of people around the world. But when supposedly intelligent people do sit down to examine the history and legacy of the British empire, the same disease, the psychosis of Whiteness, continues to plague their imagination.

Case in point is empire apologist-in-chief Niall Ferguson, whose prominence is a case study in the deification of mediocre White men. Ferguson is one of Britain's highest profile historians, regularly on television and author of several bestselling books. I listened to his screed *Empire: How Britain Shaped the Modern World* on a road trip to a speaking engagement. I expected that it might present at least some evidence I would need to respond to about the value of the British empire to the world. Instead, more than once I had to be careful not to drive off the road because I was laughing so hard. I have heard more sensible reasoning from my five-year-old. In fact, it is only a slight exaggeration to say you would learn more about the reality of the British empire listening to the crying of a new-born baby; after all, it is better to learn nothing than to risk being seduced by racist propaganda! There really is no other way to describe a book that would have us believe that the British empire 'unfailingly act[ed] in the name of liberty'.[53] That the British empire should be celebrated in part because they built railways is not the most ludicrous argument in its defence (although of course it appears in Ferguson's whatever-the-opposite-of-a-masterpiece is). Displaying an egregious example of a White saviour complex, he describes the explorer and missionary David Livingstone as a 'superman'. Livingstone was an nineteenth-century missionary who was determined to open Africa up to the British, to so-called free trade and of course to the mercy of Jesus Christ. His success in charting routes into Southern Africa is lauded by Ferguson, who goes as far as to call him the 'Médicine Sans Fron-tières' of his time, as he also happened to be a doctor. Ferguson recounts some of his childhood memories of his family's sojourn in Kenya, so growing up in Livingstone's colonial playground may explain his obsession with the man. Perhaps *tropical neurasthenia* has decayed his ability for rational thought.

Ferguson also promulgates the 'it was Britain that won the war' narrative, saving the world from the Nazis, but takes it to stomach-churning lows. The millions of Black and Brown people in the colonies who were integral to the wars are usually forgotten. Ferguson does highlight the brutal racism with which Britain exploited the subjects of its colonies: almost half of the two million Africans who served in the Second World War lost their lives. But he somehow concludes that we should be proud of the British empire nevertheless, for defeating the most evil of empires. The racist means apparently justify the sup-posedly anti-racist ends. In fact, he goes as far as to opine that the British empire 'was dismantled, not because it had oppressed subject peoples for centuries but because it took up arms for just a few years against far more repressive empires'.[54] Britain's problem was that it was *too* noble, and depleted itself by taking on the true enemies of history. Even though he quotes Hitler's admiration for the British empire and notes that the racial exploitation which Britain pioneered laid the blueprint for the horrors of national socialism, Ferguson remains firmly of the belief that Britain is a (and maybe *the greatest*) source for good in the world.

Ferguson argues that free trade and so-called democracy are Brit-ain's gift to the world, and that after the British empire collapsed, the blueprint and language they put in place now underpin the modern world. This is certainly the case, but it is nothing to be proud of. We live in a world defined by White supremacy, today as much as in the day of the British empire. A child dies every ten seconds in the under-developed world; nine million almost exclusively Black and Brown people die from hunger each year; and in the West people are still having to make pleas for Black Lives to Matter because of the brutal impact of racism.[55] The so-called 'free trade', American-empire-led framework that Ferguson is so proud of is the very same one that expresses the logic of colonial brutality today. I too argued that the emergence of the American world order underpins the world today in my previous book *The New Age of Empire: How Racism and Colonialism Still Rule the World*, but with exactly the opposite conclusion. Ferguson accepts Malcolm X's thesis that the United States took over leadership of the world from Europe. But while Malcolm X describes the system ruled over from Washington as 'benevolent colonialism' ironically,[56] Ferguson believes that it is a beacon of light in the world. In a conclusion stunning for its transparent White supremacy he opines that the real problem with the United States is that the new seat of empire 'lacks the drive to export its capital, its people and its culture to those backward regions which need them most urgently'.[57] He effectively calls on the United States to take up the White man's burden, to bring light to all the dark, savage parts of the world, a particularly pertinent example of the delusional thinking that is the hallmark of the psychosis of Whiteness.

Neither empire nor the colonial barbarity it depended upon are in the rear-view mirror. The current world order is shaped in the same image and relies on creating cannon fodder out of Black and Brown bodies to this day. Ferguson's work only highlights the deep-seated nature of the psychosis. Possessing, as he does, a lucrative professorial role at a university in the USA, he cannot simply claim ignorance. His book is full of misinterpretations, so much so that the stupidity of his reasoning must be intentional. The philosopher Lewis Gordon argues that there is a 'bad faith' element to White ignorance[58] and with Ferguson it is on full display. His work is high profile and legitimated by academia and the mainstream media. The nature of his work enables scholars of his persuasion to allow the public to feel comfortable in their inherited ignorance. Intentionality has been a major part of the debate on Whiteness; whether scholars in the West are purposefully distorting historical evidence to nefarious ends[59] The metaphor of 'psychosis' shifts the discussion away from individual intentions and instead allows us to focus on how these ideas function on a societal level. Society is based on White supremacy, and a key mechanism for maintaining our political and economic system is to convince the population that this is not in fact the case. Think of the fact that we never discuss global inequality in terms of White supremacy, even though it is clearly the most obvious feature of economic injustice. It cannot be a coincidence that Black people live in the poorest parts of the world (so-called sub-Saharan Africa) and White people reside in the richest (the West). That is the purpose of the psychosis of Whiteness, to delude us into thinking there is nothing wrong, despite mountains of evidence to the contrary. Once the problem is located at the societal level we can understand that these distortions are both intentional and comfort-seeking. We deliberately look away because the truth is too hard to bear and convince ourselves that everything is OK by embracing the delirium. Trawling through old racist psychiatry articles, I stumbled upon the perfect definition of the psychosis of Whiteness. Psychiatrist John Lind was, ironically, discussing what he saw as the 'colour complex in the Negro', arguing that we had to construct an alternate reality in order to resolve the deviancy of being Black. But nonetheless he manages to perfectly capture how the psychosis of Whiteness operates on a societal level:

> Entrenched behind rows of defences which shut out the world of reality effectively and within which he finds life bearable ... he has constructed a maze of unintelligibility in which we who attempt to penetrate his psychic secrets find ourselves wandering around dazed in a labyrinth of neologisms, irrelevances and digressions ... He developed his psychosis which solves [for] him his problem.[60]

The problem we face is the question of how to exist in a world that is dependent on the exploitation and deaths of millions of Black and Brown people for its prosperity. It took a distorted worldview for families to take their children to picnics where they watched Black people being lynched, the same dysfunctional worldview we inhabit when we make a donation to a charity helping some wretched African children, via a phone built from stolen materials from their very country. Looking away is not enough, we must look through deluded eyes, which mistake the blood soaking our hands for the sweat of good, honest, hard labour. In our blindness we see that blood as the evidence of our earned privilege in the world instead.

The mind develops psychosis to deny a problem, to distort a person's connection to reality so thoroughly that the utterly irrational becomes logical. Whiteness, the controlling set of ideas that order the world, is not a rational beast that can be reasoned with. In order to sleep at night White society has created a psychotic way of understanding the world and when racialized people struggle to navigate it this is used as evidence of our deficiencies. This psychosis is found when deflecting the realities of violence, an obfuscation that the modern world depends upon, and is also located in so many more places besides. We are embarking upon a journey to explore the hallmarks of the psychosis of Whiteness, drawing out the delusions, collective hallucinations and often violently irrational defences that masquerade as reasonable thought in our society.

Further on in this book we will continue our journey onto slave plantations, and nowhere could be more appropriate. The so-called Atlantic system that laid waste to generations of indigenous peoples and enslaved tens of millions of Africans is White supremacy's original sin, the engine that powered five centuries of colonial brutality. Delusional representations of transatlantic slavery are an essential building block of this psychosis. The wealth generated means that legacies of slavery continue to shape the present and an honest accounting of those legacies is impossible if the status quo is maintained. Acknowledging the debt owed to the descendants of the enslaved would collapse the Western economic framework, which is why most governments refuse to utter even an apology. They must maintain the delirium, reinforced by historical hallucinations which allow us to imagine that that period of history was not really that bad after all, an important mechanism for the psychosis of Whiteness.

Most White people do not live near nor socialize with racialized minorities, and this segregation is both a cause and effect of the psychosis of Whiteness. This distance from the so-called 'other' allows hallucinations about the 'ghetto' to feed delusional thinking about issues of race. One of the most powerful of these hallucinations is that a bloodthirsty dark horde will overrun majority White nations to seek control and revenge. This is pure paranoia, a delirium that posits White people as latter-day victims, and a delusion that racism is an unfortunate element of the past.

Delusions of grandeur are central to any psychosis. This is most evident in the way that museums defend their holding onto stolen goods plundered from the colonies. Of course, in their telling, the artefacts belong in the Western museums, in the hands of White people, the only ones esteemed enough to value them. Hoarding objects that belong to other cultures speaks to the narcissism of Whiteness: the value of this loot bolsters collective esteem and reinforces ideas of White supremacy. There will be more discussion of Western museums and arts, and the delirium contained within them later in this book, but for now it is sufficient to know of the terrible delusions of grandeur that underpin them.

Another idea indispensable to the psychosis of Whiteness is the presumption that we have moved into a post-racial society, which will be explored in Chapter 7. Our final stop will consider the role that Black and Brown people can have in feeding into these delusions. It cannot be reiterated strongly enough that the psychosis of Whiteness is not reserved just for those with White skin. There are countless historic and present-day examples of racialized shucking and jiving to the tune of White supremacy to pocket some pieces of silver. This is perhaps the most dangerous element of the psychosis, because putting a Black face on White racism provides a veneer of legitimacy to these ideas.

A parade of right-wing commentators have been frothing at the mouth recently, convinced that White privilege and critical race theory are being rammed down the throats of the unsuspecting youth. Before we delve into our journey, we must first understand the controversy they have created. Their claims alone should alert us to how completely detached from reality the mainstream understanding of the world is. Issues of race are barely taught at all in schools, let alone complex academic theories. But the more disturbing truth is that despite their howls of protest, Trump and his disciples have nothing to fear. So complete is the grip of the psychosis of Whiteness that even the study of Whiteness and anti-racism initiatives are now engulfed in the delirium. Once we accept that even genuine efforts to overcome racism are clouded by the psychosis of Whiteness too, we must acknowledge that we should train our focus on creating a new society, rather than trying to convince those poisoned by the old one to lend us a hand in allyship.

2

The Anti-Racism Industrial Complex

It was the first Black History Month debate in the British Houses of Parliament following the Black Lives Matter summer of 2020, and the Equalities Minister took to the dispatch box. Kemi Badenoch, the proud daughter of Nigerian immigrants, was riding on a wave of anti-racist feeling sparked by the killing of George Floyd and was in no mood to mince her words. As minister, Badenoch clearly had a lot to get off her chest. Wasting no time, she got straight to the point, stating proudly that 'our curriculum does not need to be decolonised, for the simple reason that it is not colonised', in opposition to those protesting for a non-Eurocentric school experience. Badenoch championed the existing curriculum, one that potentially offers some children the opportunity to choose a few very limited options of non-White history, as a beacon of anti-racist schooling. Appeals to learn about Britain's leading role in the enslavement of millions of Badenoch's ancestors were dismissed out of hand, because according to her that is an American issue. All those who came from the Caribbean, including those who were deported back in the *Windrush* scandal by her own government, were voluntary migrants who came because of their lovely 'connections to the UK'. As justification, the minister told the house that in Africa they didn't fool around talking about White people's responsibility for racism because they were too busy learning about the 'Black slave traders who existed before and after the transatlantic slave trade'. We heard of her horror that all this propaganda had convinced her own daughter of the need for Black History Month 'because every other month is about White history'. Not only did she reassure us that there was nothing wrong with the curriculum, but Badenoch was keen to make clear where the real problem lay: those teachers who 'teach their White pupils about White privilege and inherited racial guilt'. But, never fear, Badenoch was here to bring all that woolly-headed liberal nonsense to an end, declaring 'any school that teaches those elements of critical race theory as fact . . . is breaking the law'.[1] It was truly a command performance, providing the most complete, shining, ebony example that the psychosis of Whiteness is not just reserved for those with white skin. For now we will avoid falling into the various delusional fantasies that appear to be the basis of Badenoch's worldview. Ironically, Badenoch accused sensible people in Britain of importing our politics from the US when the truth is that her ~~minstrel~~ ministerial show was taken directly from Broadway.

Trump made a presidency out of his embrace of White nationalists, a racist immigration policy and a pledge to 'never allow an angry mob to tear down our statues, erase our history, indoctrinate our children or trample on our freedoms'.[2] As part of his commitment to White supremacy he launched a crackdown on the 'un-American' ideas of critical race theory (CRT), specifically against calling out the problem of Whiteness. Trump banned the spending of federal funds on any education or training that taught that 'any individual should feel discomfort, guilt, anguish, or any other form of psychological distress on account of his or her race or sex'.[3] To ban talking about White fragility is peak White fragility. There is perhaps no more 'American' set of ideas than CRT, which through examining the history of the US concludes that racism is a permanent feature of that society. In a strange way, this assault on the discussion of Whiteness shows just how mainstream it has become.

In a perverse (or perhaps entirely logical) way the backlash against critical Whiteness studies is the crowning achievement of an academic field of study that has developed over the last several decades. Its aim is to shed light on the concept of Whiteness so that it can be addressed, dismantled and/or overcome, and often attempts to be 'essential to the liberation of people of colour around the globe'.[4] Central to this project is the idea that, if the processes of Whiteness can be uncovered, they can then be overcome through rational dialogue. In the extensive literature Whiteness is categorized as a Eurocentric worldview, one that produces the privilege of white skin as a property that is owned and therefore needs to be defended.[5] There is a heavy focus on the unseen nature of Whiteness and exploring how, when it is produced, it becomes normalized and invisible to the White population.[6] This concept shifts over place and time, in terms of who is and who is not included in the exclusive club.[7] Whiteness is also seen to be key to a global system of oppression; the West over the rest, mobilizing the so-called civilized over the uncivilized world.[8] Importantly, Whiteness has been retained in the post-racial imaginary idea that racism is a thing of the past and shapes how we see and understand the idea of Whiteness beyond biological understandings of race.[9] Finally, the first rule of Whiteness is: you do not talk about Whiteness. To acknowledge that it exists is to admit that racism is real.

Critical Whiteness studies is seen to be a development of our understanding of racism as it identifies that it is White people's responsibility to change, instead of putting the responsibility on the shoulders of racialized minorities, and is meant as a decolonizing call to action.[10] By forcing White people to confront their complicity in the system, it aims to rebirth them as allies to the dark oppressed peoples of the world by taking a 'comprehensive theoretical approach' to expose and dismantle Whiteness.[11] Participating in critical engagement with Whiteness is seen as a cathartic and cleansing experience for those with white skin, so that they can no longer avoid race and racism.[12] The reason that Trump and Badenoch railed against Whiteness studies is because it has used education as the primary tool for social change. The fear is that if critical Whiteness studies is taught in the school system it will open society's eyes to the reality of White supremacy. Unfortunately, their fear of critical Whiteness studies is entirely misplaced, as it is no bastion of subversive ideas.

THE PROBLEM OF PEDAGOGY

The practical application of Whiteness studies has been to engage White people in what is called critical pedagogy. The aim of this process is teaching (pedagogy) to uncover the silences and irrationalities that underpin the Whiteness that permeates society. The philosopher Charles Mills argues that the system of White supremacy is maintained by an 'epistemology of ignorance',[13] a purposeful forgetting of the racial violence necessary for Western progress. As most people never confront their Whiteness, the idea is that this process will be transformative, opening White people's eyes to the uncomfortable truth.[14] This is nothing new. Black activists have been trying to explain White people to themselves for centuries. As Mills explains, 'we know where the bodies are buried because so many of them are our own'.[15] Radical writings about white privilege are so embedded in Black intellectual traditions that, as US scholar Zeus Leonardo quips, they only seem new to 'white audiences who read mainly white authors'.[16] One of the earliest examples is found in David Walker's *Appeal*, an anti-slavery document published in the USA in September of 1829, which called for enslaved Africans to revolt against their masters. The African-American abolitionist also brought attention to the fact that 'whites have always been an unjust, jealous, unmerciful, avaricious and blood-thirsty set of beings, always seeking after power and authority'.[17] Perhaps the most influential framing of the issue came from the sociologist and activist W. E. B. DuBois over a century later, who was one of the most prominent intellectuals of the twentieth century. He described Whiteness as a 'psychological wage' that all White people benefit from, regardless of whether they were rich or poor, that knowing there was a group forever below you was a valuable currency in itself. For another prescient example we can look to Malcolm X, who spent a large amount of his time touring the United States addressing White audiences. These talks contained a very different message to the ones he gave to Black folk. Angela Davis recalls a speech he gave at Brandeis, a majority White-university:

I was shocked to hear him say, speaking directly to his audience, 'I'm talking to you! You!! You and your ancestors, for centuries, have raped and murdered my people!' He was addressing himself to an all-white crowd and I wondered whether ... other Black people in the audience felt as uncomfortable and outrageously misplaced as I did ... For White people, listening to Malcolm had been disorienting and disturbing.[18]

Angela Davis's experience of Malcolm X's talk highlights one of the main problems with the idea of critical Whiteness studies. Her White colleagues found the talk 'disorienting and disturbing', but they were not cleansed and reborn as allies for Black liberation. In fact, there is no evidence that engaging White people in discussions of Whiteness makes any difference to how they see the world, not even to the practitioners who advocate these discussions.

Evidence from a range of studies shows that the process of critical Whiteness studies draws out feelings of anger and aversiveness[19] and that once confronted with the guilt of Whiteness, White people try to avoid these feelings and simply reinterpret whatever they have learned in ways that maintain their 'sense of entitlement and comfort'.[20] Obviously not all White people who encounter such pedagogy ultimately reject it, but it does appear that those who are hostile to accepting the reality of White supremacy remain so. The critical Whiteness studies literature is full of such nauseating notions that the brave White souls confronting their privilege are engaging in 'heroic acts of confession' where they realize their unjust place in the world.[21] To suggest this process is in any way redemptive reduces racism to the realm of personal moral failing, rather than a systemic issue.

Probably the best example of the psychosis of Whiteness in the anti-racist industrial complex is the so-called 'new abolitionists', who do not want to reason with Whiteness; they want to destroy it. The historian Noel Ignatiev, author of *How the Irish Became White*,[22] has been at the forefront of the new abolitionism. It is not too far a stretch to say that Ignatiev is to critical Whiteness studies in academia as Kant is to moral philosophy. In 1997 he argued that,

So-called Whites must cease to exist as Whites in order to realize themselves as something else; to put it another way: White people must
commit suicide as Whites in order to come alive as workers, or youth,
or women, or whatever other identity can induce them to change from
the miserable, petulant, subordinated creatures they now are into freely
associated, fully developed human subjects.[23]

The basic argument of new abolitionism is that White people need to
give up their Whiteness, in order to, as Leonardo puts it, 'acknowledge their unearned privileges and disinvest in them'.[24] On the surface
new abolitionism sees the rootedness of Whiteness in the system of
oppression, but, if you dig deeper, they actually downplay the structural role of racism. If Whites can simply disinvest in their privileges
by 'defying white rules',[25] then Whiteness itself cannot be systemic. It's
not comparable to owning a few shares in the stock market; Whiteness *is* the political-economic system itself. In Ignatiev's analysis the
reason that the police treat Black people as enemies is because they
assume they are criminal due to their black skin. By contrast, White
people are assumed to be loyal to society and therefore not always in
need of attention. Ignatiev wonders what would happen if Whites
started to commit treacherous acts against Whiteness and the police
could no longer dole out beatings based on these perceptions. It is
entirely unclear what these supposedly 'treacherous acts' might
include. One of the examples he gives of defying White rules was to
be 'reverse Oreos [the cookie that is black on the outside, white on the
inside] flagrantly, publicly. When someone makes a racial slur in your
presence, say, "You probably think I'm white because I look white."'
Perhaps he imagined White youth walking around the ghetto with
oversize boom boxes in hoodies excitedly waiting to tell police they
have abolished their Whiteness. He concludes that if Whites disobey
the rules, then,

[W]hites who are poor would find themselves on the receiving end
of police justice as Black people now do ... With color no longer serving as a handy guide for the distribution of penalties and rewards,
European-Americans of the downtrodden class would at last be

compelled to face with sober senses their real condition of life and their relations with humankind. It would be the end of race.[26]

The problem with Ignatiev's logic is that he reduces the problem of police brutality to the level of individual police officers' perceptions and behaviour. Police treatment of Black people is based on a system of oppression that produces over-policing of Black communities and disproportionate use of force and arrests. Police do not beat Black people because they are seen as disloyal; they beat them because they exist as quasi-citizens at best, and quasi-human at worst. There is no mechanism for White people to 'become Black' in this way. But Ignatiev's argument contains a deeper psychosis of Whiteness, too: that, without the benefits of their Whiteness, poor Whites would be able to see the 'real conditions' that they live under. Ignatiev seems oblivious to the reality that the conditions facing poor Whites are not the same as those facing poor Blacks, due in no small part to police abuse. Mass incarceration is a feature of poor *Black* communities, who are being caged at truly unprecedented rates. In 2005, African-American males born in 1975, who didn't have a high-school diploma, faced a 70 per cent chance of going to prison by their mid-thirties, compared to a risk of less than 20 per cent of similarly positioned White males.[27] The difference between being poor and Black and poor and White is not a mirage that can be lifted by treason to Whiteness; these are real structural inequalities that exist for the Black population.

In a complete departure from reality, Ignatiev espouses the notion that Whiteness has 'held down more whites than blacks',[28] as it has tied them to a capitalist system that relies on their oppression. This bizarre reasoning is underpinned by the same psychosis as exists in orthodox Marxism, which denies the central and structural importance of racism in maintaining the capitalist world order. Marx managed to create a theory of the oppressed and ignore the most brutalized victims of the capitalist system. Poor Whites have been shielded from the worst forms of oppression essential to capitalism (genocide, slavery and colonialism), and continue to be so, in the form of neo-colonial trade policies and exploitation around the globe, as well as vicious institutional racism within the West.[29] Even poor White people have a lot to lose if they give up Whiteness, which is precisely why the psychosis is so pervasive. To argue that White people suffer the worst from Whiteness is an offensive retreat from reality.

The title 'new abolitionists' should immediately set alarms bells ringing. Ignatiev argues that nineteenth-century abolitionists succeeded against a system of slavery that was strongly rooted in society; therefore, he argues, Whiteness is equally moveable if concerted pressure is applied. He has dived so deep into the Kool-Aid that he is swimming in it. For a start, the abolition of slavery did not end racism, it just shifted its form. Black people were only freed from their shackles; they remained subject to brutal racial exploitation. More importantly, the narrative around abolition is rooted in the White saviour complex, which we will explore more fully in the next chapter. Celebrating the heroism of the abolitionists is an historical delusion that is key to the psychosis of Whiteness. Slavery ended because the enslaved themselves made the plantation system unworkable and because mechanization and urbanization meant a shift to new economic forms of exploitation. Slavery was halted as this benefitted Whiteness, not as some great concession to the moral power of the abolitionists. Once slavery was abolished different forms of racial oppression simply took its place: segregation and Jim Crow in the United States, and colonialism in the rest of the Americas. Not to mention that it took slavery's depletion of Africa's people to enable European powers to colonize that continent. After those systems were dismantled they were replaced by the economic and social discrimination that is still in place today. Abolition is no model to follow if you are interested in transformative change. But if you aim to maintain the delusions at the heart of the status quo and position White people as the saviours of the future, it's perfect. The new abolitionists are perhaps the most extreme of the critical Whiteness studies brigade, but they highlight the limits of this intellectual movement. Although much of the discussion of Whiteness has moved out of the ivory tower of the university and conversations about Whiteness have now become more mainstream, it retains all the worst features of the academic debate.

SELF-HELP FOR WHITENESS

I recently started listening to audiobooks and stumbled into a decidedly new genre of what I can only call self-help books – for readers to overcome their internal White supremacy. The narrator's soothing tones guide the listener through 'exercises to discover your own Whiteness'.[30] Through hours of listening and self-reflection it is promised that your inner ally will be awoken because 'to dismantle the system we need all of us . . . as someone who holds white privilege your contribution has the utmost of importance. No matter who you are you have the power to influence change in the world.'[31] I certainly had an emotional reaction to my journey through Whiteness self-help literature. I laughed. I (almost) cried. But mostly I was just utterly bemused at the idea that we can combat racism with a handy toolkit or by writing self-reflections in a journal. The genre is the strange fruit of critical Whiteness studies: a systemic analysis totally and completely reduced to the mindset of individuals.

Robin DiAngelo has become the figurehead for the Whiteness self-help racket, and her bestselling book *White Fragility* is now a sacred text. The popularity of *White Fragility* is the perfect example of the fact that talking about Whiteness can be the opposite of tackling White supremacy. Her central idea is a rehashed version of what Black intellectuals have been saying for years, that 'the mere suggestion that being white has meaning often triggers a range of defensive responses. These include emotions such as anger, fear, and guilt and behaviours such as argumentation, silence, and withdrawal from the stress-inducing situation.' This fragility makes it impossible for White people to address racism and therefore inequalities remain in place. As if sensing the critique that the book's focus on individual attitudes ignores the structural issues, we are reassured that through an individual recognition of Whiteness 'not only would our interpersonal relationships change, but so would our institutions . . . because we would see to it that they did'. Ironically, given the criticism from right-wing commentators, it is pretty clear that DiAngelo is not a critical race theorist, because if she were, her starting point would be that changing individual attitudes does not alter racist systems. DiAngelo herself admits the futility of trying to train Whiteness out. In what I can only compare to the rock-bottom moment of clarity alcoholics can experience, she confesses that,

> I have been engaged in this work in a range of forms for many years, and I continue to receive feedback on my stubborn patterns and unexamined assumptions. It is a messy, lifelong process, but one that is necessary to align my professed values with my real actions.[32]

Not wanting to sound too preachy but, to quote the Bible, 'Physician, heal thyself!' You wouldn't go to an AA meeting run by someone sipping from a wine bottle, but you can book DiAngelo to talk through her white fragility for a fee that can be upwards of $30,000 (but don't worry, that doesn't include expenses).[33] I suppose it's good to know that at least someone is benefitting from diversity training.

If you work in any sort of corporate environment (this unfortunately includes institutions like schools and hospitals), it's likely you will have come across the dreaded diversity training initiative. They have become so tokenistic nowadays that it's often little more than an online tick-box exercise. Personally, I am still refusing to click on the link to complete my mandatory online diversity cleansing. Strangely enough, even though completing the form is a condition of the job I have been working in for almost a decade, no one has said anything to me about it so far. I think by now it is lost on no one that diversity training routines are simply there to make companies feel better. I mean, the key to 'unconscious bias' is in the name: if it's unconscious, you can't teach it out. It's extraordinarily easy to book a speaker to do a performance that keeps up the spirits of equality and diversity (if you want to pay lots of money to a Black person with real credentials, I am available!). But the truth is that you can't train racism out of people, let alone institutions. The fact we think diversity training is any kind of solution is entirely the problem.

For a television show I appeared in on BBC2, *We Are Black and British*, I attended a diversity scheme at a very large company based

in the Shard. We shared our experiences and agreed that it was important to pronounce each other's names correctly, but there was nothing
of substance done to address the company's issues with racism. It was
a facilities company, making billions from the privatization of the
public sector, holding contracts in areas like cleaning and security.
Both are disproportionately staffed with Black and Brown people.
These jobs, which are undertaken for public-sector buildings like
schools and hospitals, have been outsourced to the private sector, and
predictably the workers receive less pay, smaller pensions and poorer
working conditions than if they were directly employed by the public
sector. In 2010, after the Conservative government implemented a
policy of austerity, more than a million jobs were moved into the private sector, disproportionately harming the living standards of Black
women in particular.[34] Worse still, one of my fellow trainees was head
of the 'Care and Custody' division, running immigration detention
centres and deportations. As I said to my colleague for the day, if
you're deporting my grandmother I don't really care if you do it in a
sensitive manner. The company's business model is based on exploit-
ing the market of institutional racism but their approach to equality
was to try to train their privileged staff to be nicer to each other. The
experience was the perfect metaphor for the limitations and failures
of the anti-racism industry: from books to diversity training, they are
nothing but window-dressing.

White people feasting on the gravy train of anti-racism are part of
a long and undistinguished tradition. The greatest beneficiaries of
affirmative action in the US, which was won through the blood and
sacrifices of Black people in the civil rights movement, are White
women. When institutions built in programmes and measures to
boost their diversity the gains for White women in education, employment and career progression far outstripped those of racialized
minorities. White female enrolment at university increased 26 per
cent in the US between 1978 and 1994, compared to only 1 per cent
for African Americans in general.[35] When Trump labelled Elizabeth
Warren 'Pocahontas', because she identified as a Native American
until she got hired by Harvard University, it was a rare moment of

THE PSYCHOSIS OF WHITENESS

rhetorical perfection from that flawed yet entertaining president. These revelations caused a crisis for her presidential campaign and she doubled down, publicly submitting to a DNA test. The results revealed she did indeed have a Native American ancestor, six to ten generations ago. Only by stretching the one-drop rule beyond breaking point could this be called vindication. In an act of ultimate karma her presidential run was submarined by this act of cultural appropriation. We could spend a few more pages ridiculing the pronouncements of White authors/practitioners/gurus, especially when they include such stomach-churning insights as 'the self-reflection I am advocating goes beyond cognitive understanding. It affects our hearts as well as our minds.'[36] But some of the most high-profile spiritual leaders of the self-help genre are, in fact, Black.

Layla F. Saad's international bestseller *Me and White Supremacy* promises to take the reader through the necessary steps to 'recognise your privilege, combat racism and change the world'.[37] I should disclose that I listened to the audiobook and so did not complete the reflections suggested at the end of each chapter, so I may well have missed out on its healing power. The book's daily topics explore cultural appropriation and anti-Blackness and the reader is constantly encouraged to reflect on their biases throughout their 'anti-racism journey'. We are assured that we will need just three things to succeed: our 'truth, love and commitment'. As you proceed on this perilous path, you add tools in 'your metaphorical antiracism backpack' that you can use to overcome obstacles in the future. Saad insists that this 'is not a personal growth book designed to make you feel better about yourself', but that statement is as accurate as her analysis of White supremacy. Throughout this quest the reader-hero is encouraged to attend to 'self-care whilst confronting your internalised racism'. Had I known that overcoming White supremacy was as simple as filling out a journal I wouldn't have wasted years studying, protesting and organizing. At the end of their Herculean effort of self-examination, after conquering their inner White devils, the overall effect of going through the process of this book is likely to make White readers feel that they have conquered all the 'levels' of anti-racism, that they are the masters of their own White supremacy and are fit to go forth in the world. There may be worse ways to address the issue of Whiteness, but they escape me. I would prefer people to fully embrace their demons, don KKK hoods and burn a cross on my lawn. At least then I would know where I stand. The genre is peddling deeply dangerous ideas that will ensure that we continue to die as a result of institutionalized racist practices. They are based on such shallow understandings of racism that there is only surface with nothing underneath. Once, I was doing the washing-up while listening to a different book that purported to explain racism in society written by an esteemed African-American academic I won't name because I have already made too many enemies. My late wife walked in and asked, 'Why are you listening to a pamphlet?', as she listened to a superficial description of different kinds of racism. We may have more books about racism than ever before but we somehow have less understanding of the issues. In a rush to placate White audiences and gently lead potential allies on the path to salvation it is as though we have abandoned serious, critical and challenging work. This problem has only worsened in the post-George Floyd era. As a rule of thumb, if someone had nothing meaningful to say about racism before watching Floyd's murder, they are the last people we should be turning to in the aftermath. If Floyd's death was your awakening to racism then there are years' worth of steps you need to go through before you have the credentials to talk publicly about White supremacy. No matter if you have been on TV or how well you play a professional sport.

Shallow understandings of racism have led to serious misdiagnoses and only paint-by-numbers solutions are being offered. Firstly, White people are suggested to be the key agents of change, a legacy of critical Whiteness studies, which confuses criticizing White people with needing them. Black intellectuals focused on Whiteness in order to understand the problem, but when the academy took over, creating allies of White people became a solution through critical pedagogy. As problematic as much of the rhetoric that White people are actual devils sent to bring terror to the world is, at least when Black activists like

Malcolm X invoked this metaphor they were not relying on evil to reform itself.[38] We understood Whiteness to avoid being killed by it. Whiteness is the problem, not the solution. The purpose of activists studying Whiteness was a call for us to embrace our power as Black people to strive for independence. But the anti-racism industrial complex has reversed the equation, disempowering Black people and focusing on White allies as the ultimate goal. The African-American author and journalist Kenrya Rankin's statement of resignation – 'Black people aren't going be the ones who fix racism . . . a racist dude ain't listening to my black ass, they will listen to someone that looks like them' is a good example.[39] Bestselling anti-racist author Ijeoma Oluo argues that if 'we are going to continue to make progress' then 'liberal white men need to address their personal issues with race and gender'. She cited a discussion with the queen of the Whiteness hustle, Robin DiAngelo, to make the case that 'we absolutely need' White men if we want to make progress.[40] The genre moves from irritating to nauseating. If we are waiting for White men to deliver our freedom, then all hope is lost. Not only do these wrong-headed ideas locate the solution in fixing White people but they also place responsibility firmly at the level of the individual.

The genre concentrates on mobilizing against the immediate, day-to-day experiences of racism to lead to wider social change. In *So You Want to Talk About Race* Ijeoma Oluo argues that 'these daily interactions are how systems of oppression are maintained but with awareness they can be how we tear those systems down'.[41] To do so, the author recommends campaigning for more diverse hiring practices, ensuring cultural diversity amongst company staff and thinking differently about where we shop and how we vote. We are assured that if

> we all pull levers of this white supremacist system every day the way we vote, where we spend our money, what we do and do not call out . . . we cannot talk our way out of a racially oppressive system. We can talk our way into understanding, and we can then use that understanding to act.[42]

It would be comforting to think that it is this straightforward, that we can change how White people think and build a better world. But this would be to be deluded by the psychosis, which reduces the discussion of racism to the small scale, the actionable problems that make us believe society is improving when it is not. Oluo highlights specific campaigns as signs of progress, like getting a racist district attorney removed from office and stopping funds being spent on a shiny new police station in Seattle. But in the words of Marlon Peterson, a formerly incarcerated activist, 'a newish America is still America'.[43] A new district attorney does not mean the end of mass incarnation and the police will be able to fulfil their role enforcing racism well enough without a fancy new station. We might be able to win some of these battles, but we will never win the war if we engage on these terms.

Ironically, in trying to avoid the mistake of individualizing the problem it is possible to fall further down the rabbit hole of the psychosis. In his book *How to Be an Anti-Racist* Ibram X. Kendi tries to locate the problem within the structure of society rather than at the level of the individual, arguing that we need to focus on uprooting racist policy. It would be easy to see his work as the antithesis to the self-help for Whiteness literature. In his account, we should create 'anti-racist policies geared towards reducing racial inequities and creating equal opportunities'.[44] It would be difficult to be against such an idea, and indeed it formed the basis of the post-civil-rights settlement until it was overturned by the recent whitelash against so-called multiculturalism (more on that later). But Kendi goes further, arguing that 'only an exclusive few have the power to make policy. Focusing on "racial discrimination" takes our eyes off the central agents of racism: racist policy and racist policy makers or what I call racist power.'[45] He rejects terms like structural and institutional racism as too vague and gives the impression that these are essentially distractions from the real work at hand. No doubt the way that these terms are often used, or more appropriately, misused, today strips them of their usefulness. But the idea that we should abandon theorizing racism to focus on anti-racism is the same misstep that landed us in the predicament we are currently in. Perhaps unintentionally, Kendi has hyper-individualized the problem to those who control the levers of policy. If we can just change their minds or get new (anti-racist) people at the head of the table, then we can deliver anti-racist policy and outcomes. The book masquerades as a structural argument when it is the classic liberal account of changing the individuals, which is exactly how the psychosis of Whiteness distorts the anti-racist agenda.

This is most clearly seen when Kendi reflects on his own politics. He, helpfully, recognizes that Black people can be racist, not in the nonsensical reverse-racism way, but in the sense that Black people can themselves replicate racist ideas, such as the myth of Black inferiority. He cites a powerful example: when he was in high school he entered an oratory competition, and in his speech chastized the community for their low morals and lack of work ethic. In a passage that captures the essence of one of the manifestations of the psychosis of Whiteness in Black right-wing circles (that we will cover in depth later) he explains that 'I thought I was serving my people when in fact I was serving up racist ideas about my people to my people'.[46] Reflecting on his position now, he describes how 'I used to be racist most of the time. I am changing.'[47] This process of becoming an anti-racist is in truth no different to the self-help journeys of discovery, where we arrive at the other side of the rainbow ready to enact anti-racist policy. The truth is far more uncomfortable: the very structures we are seeking to remake are built on a foundation of racism, even if they are filled with well-meaning 'anti-racists'. The purpose of the psychosis of Whiteness is to delude us into believing we are on the train to racial justice even when all the signs are telling us the opposite. We find solace in taking action that will lead us nowhere.

The cul-de-sac of the anti-racist framework has most clearly been stated by critical race theory founder Derrick Bell. CRT is based on the acknowledgement of the permanence of racism in society and many theorists have been leading the field of critical Whiteness studies, which is why people like Trump and Badenoch are so afraid of it. But CRT should not present an existential crisis to either the right or left wing. On the face of it the movement continues Black radical analysis, but being immersed in the academy means that theorists like Bell are unwilling to embrace revolutionary solutions. If the system isn't broken but produces racist outcomes by design, the solution must be a new system. But by rejecting this radical solution Bell has resigned us to 'both a recognition of the futility of action ... and the unalterable conviction that something must be done, that action must be taken'.[48] Apparently we are meant to keep busy in an unending and useless struggle against a problem we can never solve. This is how the struggle gets reduced to a 'social justice puzzle', according to Crystal Fleming, that you can ask your friends for advice on how best to use your talents to solve.[49] We seek refuge in the individual account because we have given up on transforming the system. In this individualized narrative we can think, dream or even love our way out of White supremacy.

On my torturous journey through the field of anti-racism I found some priceless examples of what happens when we individualize the problem of racism. According to the US civil rights attorney and anti-racist organizer Rickell Howard Smith, 'parenting my children is the most revolutionary thing I can do in this world'.[50] Malcolm X warned us in 1963 that 'this word *revolution* is being misused'. They might as well have buried Malcolm on a spit because by now he must be spinning in his grave. Seeking a revolution vicariously through your children is just the latest way to individualize our role to our immediate circle of influence. I have four children and see it as my role to educate them about the world and the Black liberation struggle. But teaching your children is not revolutionary, it's just a basic responsibility. I have seen this kind of retreat for years across the community. People are convinced that their role is just to educate their kids (which really means ensure they are successful). If it takes a village to raise a child, the people must come together to make a village in the first place.

When it comes to freedom it seems many of us have given up on actual liberation. Absent any substantive change, author Kenrya Rankin reassures us that she has found 'a place where we can be our whole free black ass selves right now: group text'.[51] I hope this was tongue-in-cheek, but when we seek refuge in an encrypted WhatsApp

THE PSYCHOSIS OF WHITENESS

group we know we have a serious problem. The revolution will not be a voice note. One of the most egregious example of the delusions of anti-racist dreaming, thanks to its hyper-individualism, comes from author and women's rights activist Adrienne Marie Brown, who apparently has 'white friends [who] are non-believers in White supremacy' and can therefore be trusted for intimacy. She takes this argument further, declaring her parents' interracial love 'radical' because 'to truly love someone of another race, particularly when the other person is white or has white skin privilege can be a direct act against white supremacy'. I can hear Malcolm's voice chiding her that she 'left [her] mind in Africa' on that one.[52] Apparently, Brown's credentials on this issue are rock-solid because her parents, through their interracial union, 'built a foundation where it was very difficult to leap into a framework of white supremacy'.[53] Who knew that interracial unions were the route to radical progress? Maybe we should put Thomas Jefferson's head up on Mount Rushmore due to his commitment to his so-called relationship with Sally Hemmings. The argument somehow manages to get even more bizarre in Brown's book *Pleasure Activism*.

Brown genuinely offers to be a guide on your 'pleasure journey' as she explains that finding 'pleasure is a source of freedom'. We are encouraged to make time for pleasure, to let our happiness guide our lives and decision making, because when you are happy you are good to the world. When we are overwhelmed we should remember that 'there is another path that isn't filled with stress, doubt, pain, victimisation and suffering'. Imagine how much better the world would be if Nanny of the Maroons, who resisted slavery in Jamaica, and Harriet Tubman had avoided stress and instead lost themselves in sex and magic mushrooms, as Brown appears to be advocating. It's called 'the struggle' for a reason – it's supposed to be hard, uncomfortable and difficult. Transforming the world is not about an individual pursuit of happiness but sacrificing individual privileges for the good of everyone. I don't want to make it sound like there is no room for joy in revolution, of course there is. Listen to a Malcolm X speech or to Elaine Brown reminiscing about the good times in the Panthers and it is obvious there was plenty of fun amidst the struggle. But that is an entirely different proposition to advocating that individual pleasure should be at the heart of activism. The indulgence involved in being able to follow your own pleasure seems lost on Brown. The vast majority of the world live in conditions under which following their heart simply isn't a choice. Too often we forget the privileges that living in the West confers on us and that they are built on the exploitation of those in the rest. The sordid concept of pleasure activism is the result of individualism seeping into our politics, and little could be more dangerous than that, because it causes us to lose sight of those who are at the real coalface of oppression in the underdeveloped world. The mechanism of social change in pleasure activism is that 'by tapping into the goodness of all of us we can create liberation'.[54] This is hyper-individualism that goes beyond even the delusions of critical Whiteness studies. It says that we don't even have to educate people; if everyone finds their inner happiness, we can build the new world out of rainbows. Hopefully it's obvious how obscene this reasoning is, but like many of the other texts that have bemused me *Pleasure Activism* is a bestseller. The genre is so popular because it feeds the psychosis of Whiteness and allows people to remain comfortable in their delirium.

I realize Brown might be an extreme example, but the logical end point of reducing racism to the individual level is an analysis so ridiculous that I still am not sure I didn't dream it. In this sense it perfectly illustrates the nature of the psychosis of Whiteness. Brown is in keeping with the rest of the anti-racist industrial complex, where we are told to focus on trying to be our whole selves, to be freed of the racist expectations of society by ignoring the racism around us. We are invited to 'move differently without our chains, pretend yours are gone and they will be someday'.[55] If wishful thinking were enough to end racism then Wakanda would be a real place instead of belonging to the Marvel fantasy universe, a corporate cash cow designed to get reverse reparations from representation-starved Black audiences.

*

Talking about racism, or deconstructing Whiteness, is not necessarily a progressive step on a long march to social justice. The psychosis of Whiteness infects every interaction, distorting even our anti-racist efforts. It is no coincidence that the study of Whiteness falls into delusions once it reaches the halls of the academy. The university is defined by Whiteness, built to reinforce the status quo, and continues to be the primary site through which the knowledge necessary to ensure Black lives do not matter is produced. Understanding Whiteness was an essential tool of survival for Black communities suffering racial terrorism. The same is true of anti-racist mobilizations like the civil rights and Black power movements, which were born out of the struggle to exist. But when this work was co-opted into the university the stakes changed; they were no longer life and death, the study of Whiteness became an academic arena, an intellectual game removed from the struggle of everyday life. University debates did not have a meaningful impact on the lives of the oppressed. Instead these ideas were picked up by people in the halls of privilege who had good intentions and they were distorted through a prism which allowed the status quo to remain intact, and soothed those benefitting from racial oppression with the platitude that they were at least doing something. The mainstreaming of anti-racist critical Whiteness studies thought is, ironically, a logical outgrowth of the gains made in struggles for racial justice. The door was opened just enough for some of us to prosper and for an industry based on soothing the conscience of White society to flourish. Right-wing reactionaries like Trump and Badenoch railing against CRT and diversity training only make so-called liberals feel even more righteous in their convictions, strengthening the delusion that we are making progress. I have seen the way Black Power gets watered down to an 'equality and diversity' strategy that does more harm than good. To see the reality of, and our complicity in this system, we must strip away the comfort blanket of well-meaning anti-racist initiatives.

Our knowledge of the past is filtered through the lens of the psychosis of Whiteness, meaning that our understanding of the present is no less a delusion. Transatlantic slavery is probably the most misrepresented period in human history. Three hundred years of murdering and treating Black people as animals provided the fuel for the industrial revolution that has shaped the world we live in today, and the efforts we go to in order to avoid that reality and the necessity for reparative justice are startling. Seeing this period of history distorted has made the psychosis of Whiteness clear to me; the misrepresentations are so utterly *irrational*. If we are serious about education as anti-racist practice then beginning an honest accounting of the horrors of transatlantic slavery would be a good start. But, as we will see in the next chapter, our narrative around slavery is already so diseased that it is beyond repair.

3

West Indian Slavery

In 2019 my family and I took a much-needed break to Jamaica to visit my dad, who had retired to his place of birth a couple of years before. I was also attending an academic retreat discussing intersectionality near a tourist beach in Negril. The north shore of the island is an entirely different place to most of the country. There, a series of hotels owned by foreign companies section off parts of the beach for their visitors' exclusive access. We arrived on a plane full of tourists and caught one of the countless coaches ferrying people from the airport to their hotels. We saw racial profiling in action at the airport: White tourists waltzed happily into the country, while those who looked like the locals were subjected to searches. Negril is a tiny place but there were thousands of tourists scattered across its various resorts. Going through the gates of your hotel, you are granted access to a mirage of an island paradise, one that you never need leave. Your food is provided, you are showered with more drinks than you could ever need and the hotels even import the local 'culture'. Each night there is some activity, always involving music, to get you into the Jamaican vibe. I only learned that the limbo had anything to do with Jamaica at one of these resorts, where the drunken guests were challenged to try to contort themselves under the stick. If the beach or the bar aren't enough to fill your vacation, the hotels will arrange excursions, taking you to see parts of the island but maintaining the bubble of the tourist illusion. After all, you are there to enjoy yourself – this is not the time to witness the reality of Jamaica and how your visit participates in the racist logic that keeps the population in poverty.

If you do stray out of your hotel room alone, you will notice the façade peeling away. Take a walk down the main street of Negril and it feels like a ghost town. Most of the locals live in the hills and the thousands of tourists in the area stay locked in the virtual reality created by the resort. If you stray inland, you will notice that the roads become treacherous and full of potholes, in stark contrast to the well-preserved road taking you from the airport to your hotel hideaway. Development extends only insofar as it maintains the tourist fantasy. It is reminiscent of when Queen Elizabeth visited Antigua in 1977 – they only paved the roads her car would travel on. She could wave to her adoring fans on a nicely tarmacked road while believing she had brought development to the region.[1] As the majority of the resorts are foreign-owned, most of the money you spend in Jamaica is offshored immediately.[2] Tourism provides employment for many, but it is low-paid, seasonal and insecure. The fact that we have the money to sit on a beach in the Caribbean drowning in alcohol while residents in this former British colony struggle should tell you enough about global power and wealth imbalances. Your dream holiday is only possible because of the economic devastation wrought on the island and on the wider Caribbean, which is far from a paradise for most of the people who live there.

In the aftermath of the 2010 earthquake in Haiti the cruise line Royal Caribbean came under mild criticism for continuing to make stops to its private beach on the island. One of the tourists who had booked a ticket spoke about the dilemma her family was facing: 'How can you sit there and say, "Waiter, bring me a drink" while on a private beach ... knowing that 100 miles away, people are dying?'[3] Apparently there were many punters who had absolutely no problem with the situation and the cruises continued, with the blessing of advocates like Brian Mullis, chair of Sustainable Travel International (which supposedly advocates tourism that protects the environment and vulnerable people), who argued that the money from such tourism would 'trickle down' to the rest of the island. The formula we saw for Jamaica also applies to Haiti, where it is estimated 70 per cent of tourism money leaks directly out of the country.[4] The only trickle-down analogy for partying on a beach in the aftermath of such devastation is to compare it to metaphorically pissing on the 250,000 dead bodies. The Caribbean as it exists today is a creation of White supremacy. So-called tourists' paradises exist so that privileged Westerners can visit and be served by people who are only in the region because they are descendants of the enslaved, whose labour built the supposedly modern world.

When visiting Montego Bay I made sure to take my family to see Rose Hall, a place that terrified me when I was younger. It is supposedly haunted by the ghost of Annie Palmer, who murdered her three husbands. The site of Rose Hall is spectacular, a Georgian mansion sitting on 290 acres of land. To get to the house one drives up a long and winding road, taking in the beauty of the manicured lawns and palm trees. The Great House is advertised as an 'architectural masterpiece' and there is even a golf course. The grounds are so breathtaking that it has become a premier wedding destination for couples with the means to take their vows in luxury.[5] The website provides only a couple of clues to the place's dark history. Describing the golf course, they let slip that it is built on what once was the Rose Hall Plantation. The Great House is in fact the Big House, where the slave master lived and ruled over more than 2,000 enslaved Africans. It should be blindingly obvious that a mansion house built in the eighteenth century, set on acres of land, was the site of a brutal plantation, given the country it sits in. My dad's generation refer to Jamaica as home, but really it is nothing of the sort. Black people only populate the island today because our ancestors were stolen in chains to work on plantations like Rose Hall. My family and I experienced what felt like the Black version of the tour; the Jamaican guide didn't hold back when she explained the brutality of what took place in the house. From the top floor there is a beautiful view of the sea and a courtyard where some couples choose to have their nuptials. This is also where enslaved Africans were publicly flogged and sometimes murdered, as the slave master watched on from the balcony. Surely there is no better representation of the psychosis of Whiteness than feeling comfortable enough to get married on a site where thousands were enslaved, beaten, raped and murdered. The place is most defin-itely haunted, not by the ghost of the master but by the tortured souls whose blood seeped into the ground.

Unfortunately, Rose Hall is not an aberration. So-called 'plantation weddings' are common across the Americas. People revel in the splen-dour of sites where crimes against humanity were committed.[6] At least the Hollywood couple Ryan Reynolds and Blake Lively showed public remorse for choosing the Boone Hall Plantation in South Caro-lina for their special day.[7] They might have sounded more sincere if this apology had appeared before their eighth wedding anniversary and not amidst the meaningless declarations of allyship following the brutal killing of George Floyd. This kind of vulture tourism isn't just reserved for former plantations. In Bali, Westerners party on beaches where bones and skulls are still being unearthed following the slaugh-ter of communists by US-backed regimes in the 1960s.[8]

Visiting former slave plantations has become a tourist industry and there are many critiques of how the history of these sites is remem-bered. The modern-day sites downplay the violence, freeze the brutality in the past and present the plantation as an idyll that has moved beyond its dark history.[9] While Whitewashing history to that extent is distasteful, there is something frankly macabre about revel-ling in beauty built on bloodshed. The Magnolia Hill Plantation Hotel in Natchez, Mississippi, advertised its converted slave quarters as 'our poolside suite'. The Caledonia Farm in Virginia offered its former slave quarters (although of course they referred to them as servants' quar-ters) as the 'honeymoon suite' with 'the best-sleeping bed you've ever been [in]'. I can't imagine how delusional a mindset you have to have to lay your head and rest in a place that was once home to enslaved people. I couldn't sit there, let alone sleep. It's a tortured logic that makes such actions possible, like the rationalizations of one of the guests at the Tezcuco Plantation in Louisiana. Amanda Schwegler, a twenty-six-year-old student at the time, defended her vacation choice by reasoning (sic) that 'perhaps they were, as the slaves' residences, generally happy places where rest and family interactions took place ... perhaps they were the happiest place on the plantation for

56

the slaves'.[10] In 2022, Airbnb caved to social media pressure and removed an ad for a luxury stay in a '1830s former slave cabin' in Mississippi. The cabin had a 4.97 star rating, with one reviewer saying how they had enjoyed splitting their time between sleeping in the 'sharecropper cabin' and eating in the 'main house'. Apparently the breakfast was outstanding. In another eerie comment, a different reviewer explained how the whole experience 'felt like you were stepping back in history'. I shudder to imagine the content of the rosy reflections on this particular period of history.[11] There is no rational basis to this logic; it exists only to make oneself feel better about the indefensible.

In Britain slavery took place offshore. But Rose Hall is distinctly British, as until 1962 Jamaica was part of the British empire. When I take my family to the island it is always part vacation, part family reunion, because when my dad was a child he moved from one part of Britain (Jamaica) to join his mother working in another part (England). Part of the psychosis of Whiteness is to imagine that Britain is not haunted by the very same violent past and deluded present as settler colonies like the United States. We remember the horrors of the system as 'West Indian slavery' and claim that Britain's only active role was to abolish that awful trade. On the island of Britain we continue to feed the psychosis by downplaying the history of slavery by Whitewashing the term 'plantation'. Slave plantations should not be the site of destination weddings, slave quarters should not be converted into cosy vacation homes with Wi-Fi, and 'plantation' should not be a word we are happy to slap on a restaurant. These are sites that should be treated with the same dignity with which we treat former Nazi concentration camps, not remodelled to make even more money from the delusions of colonial nostalgia.

A person who is experiencing psychosis suffers delusions, which are reinforced by hallucinations that convince the person that their distorted reality is real.[12] Whiteness shapes mainstream culture, producing visual and auditory hallucinations on our big and small screens. Movies, therefore, exist as celluloid fantasies that reinforce a distorted version of the world. The irrational justifications that lead someone to sleep in former slave quarters are supported by how slavery is (and, even more so, by how it is not) represented in the media. It is a feedback loop that helps to maintain delusions. By analysing cultural texts we can expose media hallucinations that feed into the psychosis of Whiteness. There is no conspiracy behind media representations of Whiteness, no orchestration by a grand puppet master as the psychosis of Whiteness creates a distorted view of society that is replicated on film. Given the importance of slavery in building the modern world, the lack of movies covering the topic is astounding. What is absent is as important as what is present and the lack of films speaks to the general silence around, and society's avoidance of, the history of slavery. The system was so abhorrent and so brutally racist that it gets buried away to hide the realities that built the modern world. There have been calls for more attention to be paid to the parts of history that the White majority would like to forget. But we should be careful what we wish for. Anything addressed through the lens of the psychosis of Whiteness will be distorted by it. Film production is rooted in the same system of White supremacy as everything else and, rather than working to challenge the Whitewashing of history, films about slavery have served as digital hallucinations that only feed the psychosis.

DIGITAL HALLUCINATIONS

Hollywood has been cashing in on slavery movies over the last decade or so. Prior to Quentin Tarantino's *Django Unchained* in 2012, Spielberg's 1997 *Amistad* was the only big budget film to dive into the topic of slavery since *Mandigo* in 1975. A bit like buses, once one turned up, they just kept coming. *Twelve Years a Slave* (2013), *Birth of a Nation* (2016) and *Harriet* (2019) are entirely about the enslavement of Africans, and *Lincoln* (2016), of course, featured the plantation system heavily. If we include *Abraham Lincoln: Vampire Hunter* (2012) (it isn't much less realistic than the fantasy of Lincoln we are usually sold) that makes six movies that have the enslavement of Africans at the centre of their narrative. Given how important slavery was to the founding of the United States, it was perhaps inevitable that there would be contemporary movies made about it. Of course *Gone with the Wind*, one of Hollywood's highest-grossing films of all time, is built around the plantation, but you would be hard pressed to find a better example of digital hallucination than that romanticization of the noble slaveholding South. The topic of slavery was deemed worthy to explore in more depth and with more care, especially once Black directors became less of a rare sight in Hollywood. There is much I could say about the hallucinations of Whiteness present in US films (and in fact my colleague Dr Eugene Nulman outlines these clearly in regard to *Amistad* in our 2017 documentary *The Psychosis of Whiteness*). But here I am going to focus on the only two big budget British films centred on enslavement: *Amazing Grace* (2006)[13] and *Belle* (2013).[14] For a start, because there are only two – demonstrating that we either must have missed the Hollywood memo or that the nation is far behind the US in trying to address the history of slavery – but mainly because they beautifully demonstrate the hallucinatory effects of the media when it comes to understanding the nation's involvement in slavery. These two films bear forensic analysis precisely because they contain perfect examples of the historical hallucinations that are an essential ingredient of the psychosis of Whiteness.

Spoiler alert: if you have seen either film, I hope this analysis will make you unsee, to appreciate the delusions you were invited to engage in. If you haven't, I have tried to detail enough so that you can follow the story and spare yourself a couple of hours. The last thing I would encourage you to do is to spend money supporting either of these projects, so if you are really interested in seeing them, then either try and record them off the television or in absolute desperation pick up a bootleg DVD. But do remember that video piracy is a crime! I appreciate I am showing my age here and that many of you will have no idea what a DVD is.

Belle and *Amazing Grace* were made by different studios, with different writers and directors. Yet the two films reproduce remarkably similar historical distortions, even though both the writer (Misan Sagay) and director (Amma Asante) of *Belle* are Black women. The psychosis of Whiteness is not reserved for White people; it is a delusional worldview rooted in Western society and can be reproduced by those of any hue. Both films make attempts to shed light on some of the horrors of transatlantic slavery and give nods to the economic impact of the trade on Britain. But if you scratch the surface it is easy to see the underlying psychosis which has infected the narrative and movie-making of both projects.

THE WILBER-FARCE OF THE WHITE SAVIOUR

Both movies suffer from a chronic lack of Black characters. Even when taken together, there are only three Black characters with speaking roles; in *Belle*, there is the title role, plus one maid, who has a few lines. In *Amazing Grace*, Olaudah Equiano, a formerly enslaved African whose real-life counterpart wrote one of the first accounts of an enslaved African in the British empire,[15] is the only Black speaking character and his role is little more than a cameo appearance. Both films credit abolition to White agents who emancipate passive and tortured slaves.

Amazing Grace is based on the exploits of William Wilberforce, the former Member of Parliament who campaigned for the abolition of slavery in the nineteenth century. The narrative of the film is built on the premise that Wilberforce alone is the driving force behind abolition. In what could be an allegory for the entire movie and the White saviour narrative in general, *Amazing Grace* opens to a scene of two men whipping a Black horse lying collapsed in the driving rain. A carriage approaches, gallantly pulled along by two White horses. Out of the carriage steps William Wilberforce, whose name is enough to stop the men from beating the poor black horse. The movie describes abolition as his God-given mission and, at one point, he is told that it is 'you against them', referring to the 300 Members of Parliament who are in the enslavers' pockets. The film's crescendo shows Wilberforce being honoured in Parliament, and we are told that 'The slave trade is no more' because of this great man.

Amazing Grace presents a number of distortions to support the Wilberforce-as-saviour narrative. The most glaring one is the misrepresentation of both his abolitionist project and what it achieved. Wilberforce was indeed instrumental in the passing of the Abolition of the Slave Trade Act in 1807. However, the film repeatedly gives the impression that the act, and by extension Wilberforce, brought about the end of slavery itself. At a key point in the film, when assuring the group involved in the fight for abolition that they must press on with the legislation, the abolitionist character James Stephen gives an emotive appeal, explaining that in Jamaica he had 'heard a woman saying that someone was coming across the sea to save them ... they said it was King Wilberforce'. The film elevates Wilberforce to a messianic figure, relying on a complete lie. The act that Wilberforce worked so hard to pass did nothing to end the system of slavery in the British empire, but merely prohibited the kidnapping of more people from Africa. The Abolition of Slavery Act was not passed until 1833 and did not become law until 1834. Even then, it included a four-year period of so-called apprenticeship when the supposedly emancipated had to spend three-quarters of their time working for free on the plantations. Slavery was not fully abolished until 1838, more than thirty years after the 1807 act, and five years after Wilberforce died. The enslaved Africans in Jamaica addressed by the character played by James Stephen would have derived no benefit from Wilberforce's mission. In fact, the evidence is clear that, after they stopped stealing Africans, conditions for those already enslaved got worse. There was more pressure to 'breed' the next generation and more was expected of those on the plantations.[16]

In the Wilber-farce which is *Amazing Grace*, Black people are reduced to mute ghosts, haunting the hero of the piece. The first Black character is only introduced ten minutes in, a young enslaved African in chains, pleading for help from Wilberforce as he looks at his reflection in a mirror. It's eerily reminiscent of the emaciated figures of pot-bellied African children who tug at your liberal heartstrings from the television screen. Such images appear dotted around the film and are used to show the horror that spurs Wilberforce on. The only speaking part afforded to a Black abolitionist is Olaudah Equiano, who is introduced as part of the delegation that goes to Wilberforce's house to convince him to get involved in the campaign. Even in this scene Equaino is marginalized and it is the White abolitionist Thomas Clarkson who speaks of the torture and brutality of slavery; the highest level of White-splaining. He has a very limited role in the film, but in reality figures like Equaino, Ottabah Cugoano and Mary Prince, all formerly enslaved on British plantations, were indispensable to the abolition movement through their writings, speeches and organizing. The same is true of African Americans like Frederick Douglas and Henry 'Box' Brown (so-called because he packed himself into a large box and put himself in the post to freedom), who toured the British abolitionist speaking circuit.[17] But they are entirely absent in the Wilberforce lovefest *Amazing Grace* presents us with.

Though the titular role in *Belle* is a Black woman, the film also produces a narrative that excludes Black agency from abolition. *Belle* is the story of Belle Elizabeth Dido, who was raised by her uncle, Lord Mansfield, the Chief Justice of England and Wales. The fact that the only British movie centred around an enslaved African (at least in theory) tells the story of perhaps the only one of the landed gentry who rescued his child from the horrors of the plantation system should be warning enough. Belle is truly an historical exception, and the exceptional is used here to overrule our common sense. The movie has Belle growing up as a Black woman in the English aristocracy, and the narrative is intertwined with the famous court case of the massacre on the slave ship *Zong*, in 1781, over which Lord Mansfield presided. However, as in *Amazing Grace*, there are very few Black characters. Belle is the central feature of the movie, of course, but she is a passenger on the vehicle of abolition. She is represented in the film as being almost completely unaware of the horrors of slavery, locked away on the wealthy estate of Lord Mansfield. She eventually tries to influence her grandfather's ruling over the case of the slave ship *Zong*, but she is convinced to do this by her fictional White love interest in the film, John Davinier, who works tirelessly to provide evidence. Agency is only afforded to Chief Justice Mansfield, and the film accords him the power to 'bring down the institution of slavery' with his ruling on the case, a disgraceful distortion of the reality of both Mansfield himself and the *Zong* trial.

The *Zong*, infamously, was a slave ship whose captain murdered 132 enslaved Africans by throwing them overboard. The case ended up in court because the insurers did not want to pay out for the captain's false insurance claim over his lost cargo of enslaved Africans. The captain's rationale was that the ship was running low on water and otherwise everyone on the ship would have perished, so he had no choice.[18] In the finale, Mansfield rules against the ship captain, much to the delight of Davinier and Belle. It is this ruling that paints Mansfield as a great abolitionist hero, beating blows upon the slave trade. 'Let justice be done, though the heavens fall', a legal maxim that Mansfield was fond of, repeats throughout the film, denoting his credentials as a campaigner for justice in the court system, consequences be damned.

As with *Amazing Grace*, however, this representation does not stand up to even the slightest scrutiny. The *Zong* ruling was made in 1783 and the institution of slavery managed to survive for another fifty-five years despite it. Rather than being a gigantic blow to transatlantic slavery, in fact the ruling supported the system, as it sided with the ship's insurers, who were an essential part of the trade. To rule in favour of the ship's captain would have been a stronger blow for abolition; if his actions were deemed reasonable, it would have become much harder to secure insurance for voyages. The case was actually an appeal by the insurers, for this very reason, after the courts had previously ruled in the favour of the captain.[19] If insurance companies had left the sordid marketplace then the framework facilitating the slave trade would have collapsed.

Contrary to the portrayal in the film, the case was not a major event at the time, going almost completely unreported in the press.[20] It was only when the abolitionist movement picked up the story as a vivid demonstration of the barbarity of enslavement that the *Zong* case became iconic.[21] *Belle* conflates the aftermath with the case itself. The grand finale in the film is completely fictitious: Mansfield never formally ruled in favour of the insurers and the case only ended when he ordered another hearing because he felt there was sufficient evidence to cast doubt on the insurance claim. In effect, this meant the insurers would not have to pay out, because the follow-up hearing never took place.[22] It is understandable that such an anti-climax would not satisfy a cinema audience, but that does not justify distorting the meaning or importance of the case.

Though at times Mansfield displayed a certain antipathy for slavery, his ruling in the *Zong* case had nothing to do with an abolitionist crusade. It was simply due to his desire to uphold his reading of maritime law. Mansfield refused to even acknowledge that the criminal act of murder had been committed because, in the British empire, enslaved Africans were not considered as human beings. In his actual ruling, airbrushed from the film, he focused solely on the issue of insurance and made it abundantly clear 'that the Case of Slaves was the same as if Horses had been thrown overboard. The Question was, whether there was not an Absolute Necessity for throwing them over board to save the rest.' He ruled in favour of the insurers because evidence showed that the ship had ample opportunity to stock up on water and therefore the captain was unable to claim for his own incompetence. This was not a moral crusade against slavery and, as the historian Jeremy Krikler has argued, Mansfield 'in effect . . . kills the victims of the *Zong* a second time. The slave-traders had physically destroyed them in the massacre; Mansfield refused them a posthumous human existence under the law.'[23]

The film 'kills the victims' a third time, as it endorses Mansfield's line of thinking, emphasizing the evidence that the captain was at fault as the eureka moment in the narrative. There is no suggestion that this should be a murder trial, it is limited by the logic of Mansfield's courtroom: that enslaved Africans are legally chattel and should be treated as such. Despite this, *Belle* paints both the case and

Mansfield as abolitionist heroes. In the scene where Mansfield gives his ruling, he states the following lines, giving the impression that at the heart of the judgement was an issue of principle and morality:

> The state of slavery is of such a nature, that it is incapable of being introduced on any reasons, moral or political; but only positive law, which preserves its force long after the reasons, occasion, and the time itself from whence it was created, is erased from memory: It's so odious, that nothing can be suffered to support it, but positive law.

These words were never uttered in the *Zong* case; they are taken from a ruling in an earlier trial that Mansfield presided over. In the case of the *Zong*, Mansfield provides a legal justification for the murder of the enslaved and sides with the insurers on a technicality. By quoting the lines above, the film presents an alternative reality, one which places Mansfield at the centre of abolition. The quotation is taken from Mansfield's ruling at the trial of James Somerset, in 1772, a case of an enslaved African in Britain whose master wanted to send him back to Jamaica to be sold.[24] Mansfield ruled that slavery was contrary to English common law, meaning that Somerset could not be sent to Jamaica, and he was set free. The result of the ruling was to effectively outlaw slavery in England, although of course, in practice, this did not happen. In keeping with the *Zong* ruling and his overall judicial career, Mansfield strictly applied the law of the land. There was no provision in English law legalizing the practice of slavery and therefore the courts could not uphold it. It is telling that in the quotation he twice mentions 'positive law', which means only a direct statute from Parliament could be enough to legalize slavery in England, and as none existed, it was illegal. But his ruling in the *Zong* case makes it clear that, had such a law existed, he would have enforced it like any other. There was a clear separation between English law and that of the empire, and courts insisted on certain laws in England that simply were not applied elsewhere. Mansfield's ruling had no bearing on the legal basis of slavery in the empire, or even on the maritime law which was so pivotal in the *Zong* case.

BRITAIN, THE 'COUNTRY THAT ABSOLISHED SLAVERY'

Deep in the psychosis of Whiteness, slavery is thought to have happened far away and is certainly not counted as part of Britain's legacy. Britain's only role in slavery is remembered as its abolition, and it's thought that mighty Britannia should be proud of our heroism. Prime Minister David Cameron, arguing against Scottish independence in 2015, claimed that Britain was a nation worth saving because breaking it up 'would be the end of a country that launched the Enlightenment, that abolished slavery, that drove the industrial revolution, that defeated fascism'.[25] I was part of a team that carried out an analysis of the press coverage of the bicentenary of abolition of the slave trade in 2007. It was startling to see how many newspapers conflated the slave trade (kidnapping Africans) with slavery itself (forcing them to work on plantations). From the coverage, you would have thought that the slave system had been laid to rest 200 years ago, but at the time of writing there are still more than fifteen years left for that particular anniversary to arrive. That Britain had 'abolished the West Indian trade' appeared over and over in the newspapers, as if to say that was the *only* active role Britain played and as though the West Indies were being run by some other evil entity! It was entirely lost on the press and obviously on David Cameron too that Britain was the premier slave-trading nation and that the Royal African Company, a monopoly set up by the English crown, trafficked more human flesh than any other company in the world. The delusions of the psychosis reinforce the illusion that there is something to be proud of within Britain's dark and sordid history of enslaving Africans, a view that spilled over into the 'celebrations' of the bicentennial.

The historian Anita Rupprecht captured the spirit of these celebrations perfectly when she described a large-scale event in London which involved a contemporary warship sailing down the Thames accompanied by a replica of the *Zong*. The event was titled 'Free at Last: The Spirit of Wilberforce' and she explains how:

The combined might of the military, church and state had come together to commemorate their own historic roles in the abolition of the slave trade. It also seemed to be a straightforward exercise in reinforcing the image of the British Navy as the global humanitarian maritime police swathed in imperial nostalgia.[26]

This same discourse underlies both *Belle* and *Amazing Grace*, which are celebrations of abolition, not explorations of slavery. Imperial nostalgia is resplendent from the outset; both films are set in the grandeur of eighteenth-century London, made possible only with the loot from empire, and most of the action takes place in the grand estates and mansions of the nobility. The films pay the same attention to detail – the ornate costumes and majestic staging – as period dramas, and, like other examples of that genre, they both involve a love story. In fact, the director of *Belle*, Amma Asante, explained that she wanted to give 'little [Black] girls' a protagonist 'who wore those clothes, the fine silks and the lovely jewellery and who was the love interest' in the 'romance of the Austen-esque British drama'. She embraced the 'production design, the costumes, just the entire romance of it all'. No setting for films about slavery could be so far removed from the horrific reality of the system. Before its release *Belle* had been billed as the 'British version of *Twelve Years a Slave*' in the press.[27] But the contrast between these two films could not be any sharper. The American film *Twelve Years a Slave* focuses on the brutality of enslavement while the British film eschews any scenes of violence or, in fact, slavery at all. There is perhaps no better evidence of the pathological nature of Whiteness than a Black female director giggling over the thought of placing a formerly enslaved African woman in the romantic finery of the era. It is as if looking at history through a rational lens is too painful, so in order that we may look past it, we fabricate fairy tales.

Both films promote the narrative that Britain is progressive. *Amazing Grace* takes place in the crucible of the House of Commons, where Wilberforce battles to make the abolitionist case. By the end of the film he has won over the house, who applaud his endeavours and life's work. The closing scene is the epitome of imperial pomp: words on the screen tell the viewer that Wilberforce's fight for a better world was successful, while a British army regiment of bagpipers, in full dress, plays the titular song outside Westminster Abbey. This heraldic ending of the film reinforces the idea that Wilberforce's victory was one for Britain, the country that 'ended the slave trade'.

In *Belle* the key setting is the ornate British court system and, in considering the *Zong* case, Mansfield deliberates and rules in historic settings. As in *Amazing Grace*, the message is that the case is a victory for the British legal system, which *Belle* puts forward as being central to the abolition of slavery. It is no coincidence that these settings are used in the films. They work to distance the period-drama Britain presented onscreen from the brutal system of slavery, rewriting the narrative of Britain's involvement. The system becomes something that happens elsewhere, in the colonies, not in the nation. Across both films we only see one enslaved African on British soil. He is owned by one of Wilberforce's enemies, the Duke of Clarence, who calls for an aide to 'fetch his nigger' and offers him up in a bet with Wilberforce. The moment is memorable because it is so exceptional to see an enslaved African in either film and the scene tacitly admits that slavery did happen in the British Isles. But the entire sequence of the Duke of Clarence calling for his 'nigger' and using him in a bet is presented as being so controversial and outrageous that the film gives the impression that enslaved Africans in Britain were not commonplace. If a viewer took all their knowledge from these two films they could be forgiven for assuming that slavery only took place in the colonies, but when Mansfield gave his ruling in 1783, there were an estimated 15,000 Africans in Britain, the majority through the slave trade via the Caribbean. This wilful forgetting is a necessary feature of the psychosis of Whiteness, airbrushing away the nation's uncomfortable truths.[28]

POST-RACIAL SLAVERY

The psychosis of Whiteness minimizes the importance of racism, embracing a post-racial way of understanding problems in society instead. The gains made in the civil-rights era are offered up as having solved the problem of racism, which has been relegated to the bad old days. One of the main ways to do this is to argue that racism is no longer important and that other factors are more significant when discussing inequality. In Britain invoking class is the main tool used to delegitimize the complaints of racism. The notion that poor Whites suffer equally to or more than Black communities is one of the hallmarks of the psychosis of Whiteness and *Belle* consistently reinforces this idea.

The film opens with a scene in which her father rescues Belle from a slum, telling her 'I am here to take you to a good life, a life that you were born to'. He then leaves her with his uncle, Lord Mansfield, while he undertakes a voyage. Belle is raised in the splendour of the Mansfield Estate. The film does not entirely ignore the racism that she faces; among other things, Belle is forced to eat dinner out of sight when guests dine with the family and it is made clear to her that she will never be able to marry because of her colour. However, through the relationship with her cousin Elizabeth Murray, brought up alongside her, the film creates a narrative that minimizes the impact of race in comparison with both class and gender.

Elizabeth Murray is portrayed as a lady in title, but absent of wealth. She is raised by Mansfield but her father has left her no estate to speak of. She searches fruitlessly for a husband, is consistently rejected as 'penniless' and, therefore, not thought to be a good match for prospective husbands. Belle was led to believe she would never marry, but when her father dies at sea he leaves her a substantial inheritance of £2,000 a year. One of the suitors who eventually rejects Elizabeth, Lord Ashford, courts Belle so he can secure the bag. Friction ensues between the two cousins and Elizabeth tells Belle that she is beneath the lord because of her colour. Belle's response is, 'It is not *me* who is beneath him.' Belle's wealth is portrayed as overriding the privileges of her cousin's Whiteness. In the end Belle chooses to reject the lord so that she can marry the clerk to Lord Mansfield, who stokes her abolitionist passions, and whom she loves, instead. But this story is entirely false, a filmmaker's hallucination, a classic symptom of the psychosis.

In reality Belle and Elizabeth did not enjoy equal status or wealth in the Mansfield household. Elizabeth's annual allowance from the Mansfields was five times that of Belle's, who received slightly more than a first coachman would have done at the time, an income that would have kept her far away from her lofty social position in the film.[29] Although Belle did receive an inheritance from Lord Mansfield (not her father, as the film portrays), her annual allowance was £100, nowhere near the £2,000 stated in the delusional world of the movie.[30]

The real Elizabeth Murray had no problem finding a husband and was married at the age of twenty, while Belle was still living at the Mansfield Estate. Although Belle did marry a John Davinier, the film's representation of him is completely fictitious. The crusading abolitionist lawyer who caught Belle's eye is a celluloid hallucination. Little is known about Davinier and her marriage took place after Lord Mansfield had died in 1793, ten years after her cousin had left. Elizabeth's jealousy of Belle was a narrative based on fabricated economic positions of the two cousins that create an entirely false, *delusional* impression of Belle and her Blackness. Using class to undermine ideas of racism is commonplace across society, as we will discuss in depth in Chapter 5, and is a key reinforcing myth of the psychosis of Whiteness.

Gender oppression also has a starring role in *Belle*. Lady Elizabeth's plight is largely tied to her gender, dependent as she is on a husband to secure her future. We are introduced to marriage as a transaction: Elizabeth tours country estates to find a match, with Belle tagging along for the ride. Succumbing to the idea that she must marry to secure her social position, Belle agrees to marry Lord Ashford, spurning her true desire. At one point in the film, Belle equates the bondage of gender to that of slavery, lamenting to her cousin that 'we are but their property'. It is this intersection of class and gender that makes Lady Elizabeth's character so downtrodden. She is unable to break the shackles of her gender because of the limitations of her class. She ends up becoming engaged to the brother of Lord Ashford, James, who is presented as a villainous character who scares Belle by grabbing her by the arm and racially abusing her. Even the brutish James

Ashford spurns Lady Elizabeth, who only learns of this rejection when she reads about his marriage to another woman in the newspaper. Belle, in contrast, is presented as extremely desirable and has her pick of suitors, like the heroine of an eighteenth-century version of *The Bachelorette*. By the end of the film Belle has managed to overcome both her race- and gender-based oppression and she pushes through the all-White male crowd at the courthouse to see Lord Mansfield's momentous ruling on the *Zong* case. Her class has cleansed her of racial oppression and she is free to take her place in the world. You would be forgiven for thinking that racism was not a problem in eighteenth-century England, that the wonderfully just British court system ensured the freedom of the enslaved: these celluloid hallucinations reinforce the distortions of the psychosis of Whiteness.

Coming to terms with the history of slavery would mean that we would have to address the impact it has had on the present, which is impossible without undoing the current world order. Violence and death built the modern world and created the wealth we see in the West and the poverty we see in the rest, particularly in the Black world. An honest accounting would only lead to the conclusion that the West owes trillions of dollars in reparations, a crippling amount of money. But the psychosis of Whiteness allows us to believe that slavery was confined only to the past and requires no atonement, so we get married on former slave plantations and comfort ourselves with movies that downplay the brutality of slavery. All the while, hallucinations of the psychosis allow us to refrain from addressing racism.

Amazing Grace and *Belle* are just two films but they demonstrate how the nature and mechanisms of the digital hallucinations reinforce the psychosis. Across the media and wider society the same messages present White saviours or pretend that we have moved beyond racism and should be focusing on class, gender or even discrimination against regional accents. The screens we are glued to are mirrors whereby we can see the distorted reality that helps us to ignore the racism that brings us our relative prosperity. Just like someone gripped in a psychosis, these hallucinations are the only confirmation we need to make us feel secure in our delirium. Making matters worse is that the vast majority of White people live completely separate lives to those suffering from racial oppression. The wretched of the earth are oceans away, in the sweat shops or coltan mines that allow society to function. In the West racialized minorities are almost exclusively clustered away from the rest of society in the deprived areas of a handful of major cities. The digital hallucinations may be the only exposure to Black and Brown people and issues of racism that many White people have at all.

4

Self-Segregation

In August 2019 the British government launched the latest phase of its war against knife crime. They had already wielded the hard power of the state: an increased police presence, ramping up stop and search, and issuing stronger prison sentences for carrying a weapon. Now, they decided to try the diplomacy of soft power, setting aside a million pounds for their #knifefree campaign, which aimed to send out positive messages to dissuade young people from carrying knives. Policing Minister Kit Malthouse hoped it would 'bring home to thousands of young people the tragic consequences of carrying a knife and challenge the idea that it makes you safer'. Ignore the cringeworthy, trying-to-be-hip old-people idea that a hashtag will somehow reach into the souls of young people for a moment. It was a patronizing campaign, one that essentially blamed young people rather than the conditions they were trying to survive, conditions that made it seem like they had no alternative but to carry a knife. This is classic conservative personal responsibility nonsense, and funnily enough this kind of thinking always manages to neglect the responsibility politicians have for improving people's lives. The campaign caused an outrage: more than £57,000 of taxpayers' money was spent on purchasing 321,000 boxes to replace the standard containers of fried chicken at Chicken Cottage, Dixy Chicken and Morley's, emblazoned with empowering #knifefree messages. No, I am not joking, the government really used fried-chicken shops for public service announcements about knife crime. If you have ever listened to Grime music you will likely be familiar with the name Morley's; it is immortalized in a number of verses. Rest assured: these are the ghetto-est of chicken shops (KFC was apparently too upmarket). Public health messaging about the dangers of 99p fried chicken might be warranted, but even I can barely imagine the thought processes that led to this racist waste of time and money. Picture the meeting when they hit on the idea of unfortunate little Leroy, who seeks refuge in the chicken shop, and whose attention is rapt by the #knifefree hashtag adorning his three-piece meal. It should terrify but not surprise us that the government relates to the Black community through the latest Stormzy album.

It shouldn't be necessary for me to explain why this campaign is racist, but both violent crime and fried chicken are long-held racist stereotypes associated with Black people. Combining these together is the Mighty Morphing Power Ranger of racism. No matter what the television and news media may have you believe, most knife crime in the UK is not committed by Black people (we are only 3 per cent of the population: no further explanation needed). But understandings of Black communities in Britain are dominated by what sociology professor Elijah Anderson calls the 'iconic ghetto':

> The 'ghetto' is where 'the black people live', symbolizing an impoverished, crime-prone, drug-infested, and violent area of the city. Aided by the mass media and popular culture, this image of the ghetto has achieved an iconic status, and serves as a powerful source of stereotype, prejudice, and discrimination.[1]

The ghetto follows us around, projecting an image of fear and distrust. When someone crosses the road when they see me, or clutches their handbag that much tighter, it is not me they are afraid of but of the iconic ghetto they assume I represent. One of the ironies of the pandemic for many Black people is that we were already well prepared for social distancing. Among the few perks of being Black and male is usually having two seats to yourself on the bus because people aren't eager to invade your personal space. Covid-19 meant we could wear face masks without the police being called. When I was younger you couldn't buy a ski-mask in Birmingham city centre because of the fear of the so-called mugger.

The late Professor Stuart Hall led a team at the Centre for Contemporary Cultural Studies in Birmingham who published *Policing the Crisis* in 1978. The book was a forensic examination of the moral panic that had emerged over the issue of 'mugging'. It is important to note that there is no such modern-day crime as 'mugging'; street robberies are nothing new. They have even been immortalized in legends of the great highwaymen, like Robin Hood. But fears about immigration and dark hordes disturbing the so-called British way of life transformed an old crime into a new sinister wave. By the 1970s the inner cities of major metropolitan areas, like Handsworth, Birmingham, where my father grew up, were transformed by the immigration of former colonial subjects. These were, not coincidentally, deprived neighbourhoods, and when Black and Brown immigrants committed street robberies in these areas the media panic ensured they became 'muggings'. These neighbourhoods became synonymous with the term and were depicted as dangerous ghettos where savage youth were on the prowl. *Policing the Crisis* examines how the media, police and courts fell into these delusions, conspiring to create a crisis that only policing and incarceration could fix. The media amplified the ghetto as a place of disorder, and publicity around this new crisis fed the collective psychosis of Whiteness with hallucinogenic imagery. It should come as no surprise that Rupert Murdoch's *The Sun* was a key architect of the panic. Stories sensationalizing street robberies and the ghetto began to appear, like this example from 1973:

> Handsworth, that sprawling Birmingham slum where the three muggers grew up, is a violent playground . . . Paul Storey, son of a mixed marriage, tried drugs, then theft – and finally violence, in a bid to find excitement in his squalid environment. Paul's mother, 40-year-old Mrs Ethel Saunders, said 'What chance do young people have in a lousy area like this?'[2]

Responding to the supposed crisis, police saturated the area using sus laws (that gave police powers to take a person into custody on the mere suspicion of a criminal offence) with abandon. In the year lead-ing up to the 1981 Handsworth urban rebellions, when predominantly Black young people took to the streets in desperation at the condi-tions they faced, 40 per cent of Black youths in the area had been stopped by the police.[3] The courts poured petrol on the fire; judges doled out harsher sentences to those convicted of so-called 'mugging', referring to the offence in their decisions, despite the fact that it has never existed as a legal term. This framework of understanding the iconic ghetto remains in place today: Black people are disproportion-ately stopped and searched, wildly over-represented in the prison population,[4] and over half of all young people incarcerated are from a racialized minority.[5] Such is the power of the psychosis of White-ness, which shapes how we are understood in society.

The problem of youth violence becomes a crisis of *Black* criminal gangs. While most murders involve White people killing other White people, when both the victim and the perpetrator are Black it is chalked up to the pathology of supposed Black-on-Black crime. Alarmingly, if you are Black in Britain, you are five times more likely to be murdered than a White person, a pattern we see repeated across the Black world.[6] Jamaica sees twice as many murders yearly than England even though its population is fewer than that of the Mid-lands. In South Africa it is cause for celebration if there are less than 20,000 murders a year. And yes, there are far more murders within Black communities than at the hands of the police, but this is not due to a pathology in Black people: it is simply another manifestation of institutional racism. The reason that we are more likely to be mur-dered is rooted in the same reason why we are more likely to be killed by the police: it is a result of the same problems that mean we have higher rates of unemployment and that even mean that Black women are more likely to die in childbirth. We experience second-class citi-zenship even in countries where we are the majority. Black life is marginalized across the globe, economically, politically and socially, with the result that we are subject to vicious inequalities. The result of surviving this oppression is a host of negative outcomes, and one of those is a higher murder rate. The fact the person doing the killing is also likely to be Black is more an indicator of racial segregation than it is of any cultural deficit. No genuine attempts to understand the issues are made; instead, delusions of Whiteness cloud the collective vision. #Knifefree chicken may be laughably ridiculous but it is also the perfect example of how the psychosis of Whiteness both distorts our understandings of the world and ensures that the racist status quo is maintained. By justifying the unjust social order and displacing responsibility on to the victims of racism, these delusions worsen the problem.

SEGREGATION NOW, SEGREGATION FOREVER

I want to stress that the psychosis of Whiteness is not based on ignorance. Nor is it caused by a lack of understanding, rooted in the fact that most White folks have little contact with us. The classic liberal lie says that if only we could all meet in multicultural harmony we would all hold hands on our march to freedom. But contact is not the solution. Psychoses are not rational. Meeting Black people who aren't 'ghetto' does not disprove stereotypes. Instead the civilized negro is seen as the exception to the rule, not like the rest of 'them'. If having a Black friend does not mean you are not racist, then it also is no inoculation from the psychosis of Whiteness. Elijah Anderson talks about the precarious nature of being the token Black, accepted because they can 'dance' to the correct cultural tune. But he warns that you are only one slip away from the 'nigger moment' when your status as not 'one of them' is removed and you are treated with the same contempt as any other nigger. I am sure most Black people in professional circles will relate; having to make sure to never show any anger, annoyance or frustration at work, in case the dreaded accusation of being 'aggressive' is thrown your way. So contact is not the solution, but segregation is a key source that helps to feed the psychosis.

Part of the reason that the 'iconic ghetto' is so powerful is due to racial segregation in housing. We are accustomed to seeing this as an

American problem, and it *is* blindingly obvious there. I've spent a lot of time in Boston and Philadelphia and quickly learned to be attentive to the racial make-up of whichever public transport I was riding on to make sure not to miss my stop. In the city centre the train or bus is fairly mixed, but once everyone on board is Black, you know you're getting closer to your destination. I was once on a bus in Boston, going from a predominantly Latino area to an overwhelmingly Black one. A commotion was caused when the most stereotypical White guy I have even seen embarked. He looked straight out of a movie: stone-washed jeans, a brown leather jacket with badges sewn on and a cap on top of untidy long hair. I'd only ever seen three White people on this bus in the six months I'd been catching it. Once someone brought their White girlfriend on board and the other passengers heckled them so badly they got off a couple of stops early. The other time, two White female missionaries, dressed in full garb (like they were trying to civilize the African savages) were visiting the ~~jungle~~ neighbour-hood. So, when this White dude got on, we were all convinced he was on the wrong bus and the passengers were vocal about it. So much so that the bus driver asked him to double check. After stepping off to look at the number one last time, he realized that of course he *had* got on the wrong bus. My entire time in Dorchester, a Black neighbour-hood in Boston, felt like living in a 'hood movie, like (showing my age) *Boyz n the Hood* or *Menace II Society*. The only White people I saw were maintenance people or the police. There was even a run-down convenience store, complete with rotting fruit, run by a Korean family. It felt every bit like a colony and the missionaries (bloody missionaries!!!) were just the icing on the cake.

The stats back up my experiences of the city. The situation is said to have marginally improved in the twenty years since I lived in Boston, but two-thirds of Black Bostonians still live in the neighbouring areas of Dorchester, Roxbury and Mattapan. In fact, 69 per cent of residents of the city would have to move to racially balance housing in the city.[7] Segregation is worse in other cities like Washington (a so-called chocolate city, because African Americans are the largest demographic), and Chicago is a model of racial segregation.[8] It only took one ride on the EL train to the famous Black neighbourhood the South Side to witness the stark racial divisions. The University of Chicago has a campus in the 'hood, serving as an oasis of Whiteness for those looking to escape the dark ghetto. Most American cities have followed a pattern: as Black people moved into inner-city neighbourhoods White residents fled to the suburbs, leaving the cities incredibly 'diverse'. For the iconic ghetto to hold sway, it is necessary for deprived Black neighbourhoods to exist, to haunt the White imagination. Importantly, these neighbourhoods were created by White flight and barriers created by town planners, public officials and banks to ensure that African Americans could only reside in particular (disadvantaged) locations.

Much is made of the history of segregation and of efforts to desegregate the South, but it was largely an empty victory. Stark housing segregation means that US public schools are now more racially segregated than they were after the landmark Brown vs the Board of Education ruling in 1954 that outlawed segregation in schools.[9] Millions of African Americans fled the Jim Crow racism of the South but found that conditions in the North were just as severe. Malcolm X is famous for comparing the vicious, snarling Southern Wolf, who 'will show their teeth in a snarl that keeps the Negro always aware of where he stands with them', to the cunning Northern Fox, who prefers to 'show their teeth but pretend that they are smiling'.[10] There is truth to this analogy, but even while liberal White Foxes pose as friends to African Americans we should never forget that the North is full of Wolves too.

The wolf is used to symbolize the violent repression of African Americans in the Jim Crow South. One of the most traumatic books I have ever read, Carol Anderson's *White Rage*, recounts the horrific violence that made America the nation that it is today. Slavery, lynchings and racial terror of all kinds filled the South with stories of brutality. Racial apartheid, strongly enforced, was the weapon of choice to control the perceived threat from hordes of dark savages, the masses of newly emancipated Black people. A complete separation of the races was seen as vital to keep African Americans in their place and to avoid polluting pure White civilization. Education is the perfect example of a self-fulfilling psychosis: White people imagined Black students to be inferior, and then created the conditions to prove their racist delusions. Battles over integrating schools were not fought so that Black youngsters could make friends with White kids. Contrary to popular belief, Black children weren't feeling inferior because they were taught in Black schools, but were often just trying to gain access to White schools simply because they were closer to their homes. This was the case for Linda Brown of the Brown vs Board of Education ruling which established that racial segregation in schools was unconstitutional. There is plenty of evidence that the teaching in Black schools was of the same standard or even higher than in White schools.[11] But it was true that Black schools received much less funding, so they were always at a disadvantage. In 1930s Atlanta there were eighty-two Black students per teacher compared to thirty-five White students per teacher. In 1946, White students received $80 more per head in funding, a chasm so wide it meant that 85 per cent of African American students could only attend school for half a day.[12] After the Brown vs Board of Education ruling the South dragged its feet for as long, and as hard, as it could to avoid polluting their racist utopia. There is so much mid-twentieth-century imagery demonstrating the depths of the psychosis of Whiteness, but I will tell the story of Minnijean Brown-Trickey of the Little Rock Nine because it is so harrowing that it is impossible to not see the underlying psychosis at play. I had the honour of interviewing Brown-Trickey for a feature in the *Guardian* over sixty years after the events and the trauma was still very clearly with her.[13]

The year was 1957. Brown-Trickey was one of the first Black students to attend the plush, well-resourced Central High School in Little Rock, Arkansas, alongside eight other Black students, who together made up the famous Little Rock Nine. Minnijean jumped at the chance to put her name down for the school as it was closer to her house than the Black school and had much better facilities. But the sixteen-year-old was completely unprepared for the rage and hostility she and the others would face. On their first day they were met with a mob of around a thousand angry Whites, desperate to stop them entering the school. The venom, violence and verbal abuse was so irrational and uncontrolled that she could only describe it as 'crazy'. Hearing her tell this story, it became clear that what she was describing was a mass psychosis, one that had gripped the entire crowd, and most of the town too. The students had no choice but to turn back that day. For the nine children to be able to enter the school they needed a 1,200-strong contingent of National Guard troops, who were mobilized by President Eisenhower. Because the violence had seeped into the school too, each child had to be accompanied by their own National Guard escort all day long. The cost of this was astronomical; it cost $3.4 million (over $30 million today), just so that a handful of Black kids could go to a White school.[14] The armed guards didn't end the verbal or violent abuse entirely, nor did they stop the spit. The spit meant that the students had to store a change of clothes in the classrooms of friendly teachers, as they were coated in it each day. It was clear from talking to Brown-Trickey that she was still suffering the effects of her torture. She moved to Canada after university and never spoke about the traumatic experience again, not even to her children. It was only when a programme about the Little Rock Nine happened to be on the television that she sat down with her daughter to watch it and explained who she was. In a perfect demonstration of the deluded dystopia she found herself in, Brown-Trickey was expelled from the school for calling a girl 'White trash'. Brown-Trickey had been hit in the back of the head with a sock filled with padlocks and couldn't stay silent any longer. Only three of the Little Rock Nine made it to graduation under these dire conditions. Public opinion was so set against the presence of Black children in the school that 70 per cent of White people in Arkansas voted to shut down the entire public school system for a year rather than continue with the integration 'experiment'. Yes, they really would rather their children didn't go to school at all than have them go to school with Black people. The terror that the Little Rock Nine and their families experienced was the full force of the Southern Wolf. But racial segregation in the North was just as strongly defended as it was in the South.

During his election campaign Joe Biden had to sidestep his hostility to school bussing in the 1970s, alongside attempting to erase his distinct history of cosying up to racist politicians and personally producing racist policies. Due to severe racial segregation in housing the only way to integrate the schools was to bus kids to schools outside their neighbourhood (of course, it was always racialized children who were given the opportunity to be educated with White children). Biden was the most anti-bussing Northern Democrat and feared that it would lead to his children 'growing up in a racial jungle'.[15] Bussing was a major issue; many White parents wanted to maintain the racial purity of their classrooms and keep the iconic ghetto out. Boston was at the epicentre of the protests, the same Northern, liberal Boston that was so far away from the plantations it could pretend it was the precise opposite of the snarling Southern Wolf. But conveying Black children to school by bus had to be court-ordered in Boston in 1974, sparking violent protests, and buses carrying African-American children were pelted with rocks and eggs. South Boston was the cradle of White resentment and Jean White, a bus safety monitor during that time, recalled 'signs hanging out of buildings, reading "Nigger Go Home". Pictures of monkeys. The words. The spit. People just felt it was all right to attack children.'[16] Scenes reminiscent of Little Rock were replayed in the liberal North. Boston even had to mobilize the National Guard to quell the unrest. The iconic image from that period is a Stanley Foreman photograph taken in 1976, called *Spoiling Old Glory*, that shows a White Bostonian holding an American flag like a weapon, ready to spear an African American.

Symbolically, the day after bussing was enforced, no White children attended South Boston Public High School, but in the aftermath White parents did in fact take flight from public education. In 1974 more than half of the public-school population was White but by 2014 that number had shrunk to only 14 per cent, even though the overall population of the city has grown rapidly. White Bostonian parents rely on private education (there were 86,000 public-school students before 1974 and only 54,000 by 2014), and there has been White flight into the commuter belt, outside the city limits and beyond the reach of the racialized communities in the city.[17] Paying for education or living in the commuter zone is the Northern Fox version of racism. It never ceases to amaze me that some of the staunchest 'allies' of Black people see no issue with their decision to embark on a two-hour each way commute to ensure *their* children get the *best* schooling.

That racial segregation is a hallmark of Northern cities should not be a surprise. When African Americans migrated north they were met with a barrage of brutal racist violence that served to maintain the separation of the races. The Great Migration, in which millions of African Americans fled the South, began in earnest during the First World War, due to demand for labour for the war effort. Refugees from the Jim Crow South were not, however, welcomed with open arms by the supposedly enlightened Northerners. Tension erupted immediately, and 1919 saw a swathe of race riots across the country. Now, I know when I say 'race riots', you picture hordes of criminal, thuggish Black people, burning their own neighbourhoods and clashing with the police. But look again with rational eyes: you will see marginalized citizens erupting in urban rebellions against unjust living conditions and clashing with police forces intent on crushing the dissent.

By 1919 the Black population of Chicago had more than doubled in ten years, thanks to the Great Migration. Irrational fears, a hallmark of Black immigration, around jobs, crime and women bubbled under the surface. Seventeen-year-old Eugene Williams drowned in Lake Michigan when he accidentally swam into the White section of the lake (yes, *the White section of the lake*), and had rocks thrown at him. This sparked weeks of violence. Black people were angry and protested, and almost the entire police force was deployed to the Black section of town to maintain 'order'. While so many police were in the ghetto White residents took the opportunity to unleash their pent-up frustrations and started attacking, beating and shooting unsuspecting Black folk in the rest of the city. The police continued to focus on the uprising in the ghetto, giving the White racists an almost entirely free reign for terror. The National Guard were mobilized to stop the unrest, but only after twenty-three African Americans had already died, along with fifteen Whites.[18] Unrest swept the rest of the country, both the North and the South, marking a new era in race relations, one where the formerly enslaved were fleeing the brutality of the South only to face the violent resistance of the North.

The imaginary segregation line in the Michigan Lake that Eugene Williams was unlucky enough to 'breach' demonstrates just how deep the pathology of Whiteness went in the US. That swimming in the same water as Black people would contaminate White people was an idea that was deeply held and defended in the North as well as the South. In 1950s Cincinnati, when Black residents were given access to public swimming pools, angry Whites threw nails and broken glass into the water to keep them out. In Pittsburgh, African Americans were only permitted to swim in public pools in September, giving the city 'sufficient time to properly cleanse and disinfect' the pool 'after the Negroes have used it', in time for the next summer.[19] Objections to sharing the same water as Black people were so widely held that it was common practice across the US to drain public swimming pools if just one Black person had polluted the water with their body.

In the North some of the first battles were over where Black people would be able to live. They wouldn't, of course, be allowed to pollute the nice White areas with their deviant presence. When the African-American doctor Alexander Dunbar attempted to move into a White neighbourhood in Detroit he was greeted by a thousand-strong mob and forced at gunpoint to sign his property over while the police looked on, a story that was recounted thousands of times across the North.[20] I emphasize the fact that he was a doctor because his class gave him no protection from racist abuse. Despite his occupational standing, he represented the iconic ghetto, the slum, and could never escape the irrational fears reserved for all Black people. Detroit worked hard to maintain its strict racial segregation and Dr Dunbar was forced to live in the Black Bottom neighbourhood, which had a population ten times greater than its housing could support. Detroit is just one case study in how the ghetto was created by a racist America, which forced African Americans into overcrowded, dilapidated housing and cut them off from jobs and opportunities. For a forensic examination of how the government, banks, businesses, homeowners and White residents colluded to create and maintain the racial segregation we still see today, read Keeanga Yahmatta-Taylor's excellent *Race for Profit*.[21]

GHETTOIZATION

'The ghetto' as an icon for Black dysfunction has become increasingly important. Southern Wolf-style racial prejudice has been outlawed and, to some extent, banished from mainstream sensibilities. In our shiny new post-racial world you can't call someone a nigger, but you can be wary of someone because of their postcode. Culture is now used as an acceptable code-word for racism and the culture of the ghetto is one to be feared and avoided. This is one of the reasons why investment in maintaining the ghetto accelerated in the post-civil rights era. When someone tells you that life is better for African Americans you need only two words in rebuttal: mass incarceration. Since the 1980s the prison population of the US has ballooned to historically unprecedented proportions and incarceration rates for African Americans are now higher than they were for Black people in apartheid South Africa.[22] The so-called war on drugs has seen countless people, mainly Black and Brown, given lengthy prison sentences for non-violent drug offences. The iconic ghetto was at the root of this, the fear of Hillary Clinton's young Black 'super-predators' who needed to be brought to heel.[23] In 1986 a gifted young basketball player named Len Bias, reputedly the next face of the NBA, died of a cocaine overdose the day after he was selected to play for the Boston Celtics. His death sparked a moral panic over the use of cocaine. Legislators competed to be the toughest on drugs, introducing mandatory minimum sentences and laying the framework for the prison industrial complex.[24] Racist disparities in sentencing became embedded in federal and state laws; infamously, there was a hundred-to-one disparity between the sentencing of those possessing powder and crack cocaine. This meant a five-year mandatory minimum sentence for possessing less than a quarter of a teaspoon of crack cocaine, whereas anything less than a loaf of bread of powder cocaine and you would be treated much more leniently. Crack was a much cheaper version of the drug and it flooded into African-American communities. Powder cocaine, on the other hand, was (and remains) a drug for the wealthy, a recreational drug for the White elite, leading to this racist disparity in sentencing. Len Bias's death, though it was used as a catalyst for these laws, was caused by an overdose on *powder* cocaine. The delusional nature of Whiteness was on full display: he was Black and therefore represented the iconic ghetto. The panic of the supposedly Black-led crack epidemic had already gripped the nation's psyche, so Bias's death was used to criminalize the wrong drug. The problem still looms large; when Barack Obama addressed this disparity, in the Fair Sentencing Act in 2010, he only reduced the ratio to eighteen to one; the very definition of better than nothing.

Crack cocaine did have a devastating impact on Black communities. Crack and the militarization of the gangs who distributed it caused increased rates of murder in poor Black communities that have been sustained to this day. But the idea that crack is a Black drug is a deluded fantasy. Black people are far more likely to be arrested for drug offences than Whites, but are no more likely to use or distribute narcotics, including crack. We must wonder how crack came to plague poor Black communities in the first place. As the hip-hop group Dead Prez explains, 'We don't own no boats and planes. We just cop it from papi, bag it in the cellophane.'[25] Remember that crack comes from cocaine; the same importers bring it into the country. By heavily penalizing those distributing and selling the crack version, emphasis is placed on criminalizing low-level street criminals. But it gets worse: the tale of how the crack epidemic exploded in the 1980s is so twisted that it sounds more like a conspiracy theory than the truth.

In 1982 Congress cut off financial support for counter-revolutionary *Contras* in Nicaragua. The Central American nation, with a population of just over three million at the time, had a Marxist government and Nixon's regime was terrified of Marxists being so close to the US and so funded a reactionary counter-revolution. In 1983 they invaded the even smaller nation of Grenada, in the Caribbean, with a population of fewer than 100,000, to depose the Marxist regime led by Maurice Bishop.[26] The fact that mighty America was terrified of Marxist governments in tiny nations in its proximity speaks to the depths of the psychosis of Whiteness. Once the CIA cut off the money in Nicaragua, Nixon was so keen to fund the oppressive, fascist insurgents he supported that he allowed the CIA to raise funds for the group through trafficking cocaine into the US. No prizes for guessing which community was the target. As the historian Carol Anderson explains, support for the *Contras* included help from the CIA 'to transport 1,500 kilos of Bolivian; diverting hundreds of thousands of dollars in "humanitarian aid" to indicted narcotics traffickers; and refusing to pass the names of known drug runners on to the appropriate authorities'.[27] Not only were the CIA paving the way for floods of drugs into the country, but they also facilitated the import of the military-grade weapons that poured onto US streets and claimed so many lives. So when Reagan launched his war on drugs he was hyperventilating about a crisis that he was largely responsible for. This is the power of the psychosis; it distorts reality, shaping the world into its own deluded image.

The parallels with the criminalization of poor Black inner-city communities in Britain are striking. Picture the number of times you have seen Black people play criminals on your television screen. *Crimewatch* has put food on the table for more Black actors than probably any other TV show. We even have our own genre of British 'hood movies and an equivalent gritty urban music scene. But what is often overlooked is that the same processes of segregation have shaped contemporary Britain.

ESCAPE TO THE COUNTRY

Inner-city areas of London, Birmingham, Manchester and other major cities are now dominated by racialized minorities, but this is a relatively recent demographic shift. Prior to the Second World War Britain kept her dark subjects at arm's length, thousands of miles away, in the colonies. Slavery, Jim Crow and openly racist policies were undeniably foundational to the US nation, but in Europe they could pretend that their Whiteness was legitimate. When mass migration began in earnest in the 1950s, exactly the same processes emerged as had already happened in the US. Colonial immigrants were restricted to the lowest-paying jobs and forced to live in the inner city in overcrowded and polluted neighbourhoods. I have interviewed a number of activists from this period and housing is a recurring topic. Multiple families shared houses built for one household. It was not uncommon for tenants to share a bed, swapping over between day and night shifts. Until 1968 there were no laws in Britain banning racial discrimination in housing, and 'no Blacks, no Irish, no dogs' signs were ubiquitous. Immigrants found it very difficult to get mortgages from banks and had to wait years before qualifying for social housing. Black people could only find housing in certain areas and, just like in the US, segregation became embedded into the political discourse. The Conservative politician Peter Griffiths won the Smethwick by-election in 1964 with the unofficial slogan 'If you want a nigger for a neighbour, vote Labour'. Smethwick Council had been refusing housing to immigrants and was by no means alone. In Birmingham in 1963, when the council tried to open a boarding house for Caribbean workers in then middle-class Northfield, the chorus of 'Not in my back yard' was so loud they relented and put it in the notorious area of Handsworth, which, as we have seen, then became associated with racist moral panic around so-called mugging.[28]

Britain continues to be hallmarked by White flight, best summed up by Malcolm X, who warned that 'as soon as you move out of the Black community into their community, it's mixed for a period of time, but they're gone and you're right there all by yourself again'.[29] These neighbourhoods now predominantly populated by racialized minorities were once exclusively White. On an anecdotal level, in Birmingham my primary school was mostly White, but by the time my son enrolled the only White students left were a handful of Eastern Europeans. We like to pretend that Britain is a multicultural utopia but in reality it is a deeply segregated country. Almost half of all Black people in Britain live in London alone, but most of the countryside is over 90 per cent White.[30] Just like in the US, there is stark racial segregation in the UK's cities. In Birmingham, the inner city is three-quarters Black and Brown, while the middle-class suburb Sutton Coldfield is over 90 per cent White. You are almost as likely to see a White person on my bus in Birmingham as I was in Dorchester in Boston.

White middle-class people are the most self-segregating group. They move as far away from minorities as possible and are proud of it. The liberal *Guardian* newspaper ran a special on the best places to live in Birmingham and highlighted Sutton, Moseley, Edgbaston and Kings Heath as the most desirable neighbourhoods.[31] They are also the Whitest. Kings Heath is the only one with any real diversity, but this diversity is also highly contained and avoidable, if you choose. A friend moved to the UK for work and rented what was supposed to be a flat in Moseley. It was actually a subdivided Victorian house, where her 'bedroom' was the first-floor landing. Her rent was more than my mortgage on my three-bedroom house. She lived there because two colleagues (for safety, let's call them both Karen) had emailed a list of desirable and no-go areas. The dirty little secret of the housing market is that it is completely racist. A 'diverse' area (which is a code-word for there not being many White people there) is always going to be cheaper to live in. There is less demand; White people simply won't buy houses there. Black and Brown equals the ghetto, so they stay well away. This is one of the reasons that residential segregation is so persistent. Even though I am a relatively high-wage earner, the gulf between the value of my own house and a similar one in a predominantly White suburb is so enormous I couldn't afford to move even if I wanted to (just to clarify, I absolutely do not want to). Housing market racism also goes a long way towards explaining the staggering racial wealth gap in Britain, as most capital is held in houses. But there are some perks to the racist housing market: where I live is probably the best area in which to raise a family and is certainly the best value for money in the city. We have good-sized houses with driveways, leafy avenues, large gardens, good schools, parks and excellent transport and commuter links. Houses are half the price they would be in a predominantly White area. I made a promise to my late wife that I will only reveal the neighbourhood I live in when it is time to sell up; perhaps I can trigger some White guilt-driven demand.

White flight has become so extreme that staying within the city limits is seen as 'slumming it'. When the Asian population of the White suburb Sutton Coldfield went up slightly, I somehow found myself in conversations where people were complaining that the area had 'changed' and was no longer the most desirable neighbourhood in the city. The goal now is to escape to the country, to the lily-white commuter villages away from pollution, crime and Darkies. In a fit of peak psychosis of Whiteness the *Daily Telegraph* launched a list of 'Britain's most liveable and affordable rural property hotspots'. Flitch Green, in Essex, came in at number one, where average house prices were an enormous £399,789 in 2021.[32] 'Affordable' by this metric meant house price in relation to average wages, which are extremely inflated in the London commuter belt by White people with money fleeing the city. A quick check on RightMove reveals that best you can get for less than £400,000 in Flitch Green is a three-bed terraced house. To buy the equivalent of my current house would cost well north of £600,000 (more than double the price of my home). Let's send a big thanks to the *Telegraph*.

In what some demographers are welcoming as a sign of reduced racial segregation, we are also seeing the inverse of White flight: White settlement in the inner city. But this gentrification is more like the missionaries on the ghetto bus than a genuine attempt at integration. In the era of post-industrialism, where manufacturing jobs have gone overseas and the inner city is no longer the fulcrum of the city, industrial units stand empty and cities need to find new ways to bring in revenue. We are living in the age of the consumer city. Factories are being knocked down and replaced with shopping centres or art complexes. The inner city used to contain polluted, overcrowded accommodation for manual workers; now, it has become prime real estate, as the city centre expands to accommodate the demands of retailers, offices and wine bars.

Birmingham City Council plan to massively expand the 'city core', cannibalizing predominantly Black and Brown communities like Nechells, Hockley and Ladywood.[33] Thousands of housing units have already been built, with more planned in the city centre neighbouring deprived minority communities. They attract predominantly White residents who can afford the inflated house prices. My current workplace, Birmingham City University, is part of this gentrification process, having moved to a shiny new (but too small) building on the edge of the city centre. My walk from the train station takes me through Nechells, one of the poorest and most 'diverse' neighbourhoods in Europe. It stands in the shadow of the university and the development of High Speed 2 (HS2), the super-fast train service to London that will make Birmingham part of the capital's commuter zone. I might as well be walking through a memory; the housing and people will soon be shifted out to make way for the new residents of the area.

Ladywood, on the other side of the city, where 80 per cent of the children lived in poverty a few years ago, is being transformed by gentrification. Developers are taking over a section of the neighbourhood ringed by a canal, offering luxury townhouse 'island living' at prices none of the current residents can afford. It may look as if the neighbourhood is mixed on the census, with the increase in White residents changing the demographic numbers, but it is a strange kind of diversity. London is of course at the forefront of the gentrification game, leading the way with obscenities like the 'sky pool' in a luxury flat development, where swimmers in a transparent pool linking two skyscrapers can look down upon a borough where half of all children live in poverty.[34]

Perversely, the diversity of the city has become a corporate attraction. Being multicultural becomes a unique selling point, and the range of restaurants and festivals a city like Birmingham hosts are part of its brand. Through the distorted lens of the psychosis of Whiteness we see the regeneration and integration of cities, not the reality of ethnic cleansing and retrenched racial inequality. The inner city of the future will be replete with plush parks, clean air zones (funny how pollution is suddenly dealt with when the demographics change), offices, the best restaurants and bars . . . and mostly White people. So-called diversity will be pushed to the margins and invited into the city core, for the most part to do the service, cleaning and security jobs that keep the city running.

SEPARATE LIVES

Britain is deeply segregated because the White middle class use their financial power to maintain the exclusivity of their neighbourhoods. But you couldn't guess this by the panic around segregation that regularly bursts into the mainstream press. In 2016, Member of the House of Lords Dame Louise Casey released a government-sponsored report into integration, grabbing headlines while warning that segregation was at 'worrying levels' across the country and that there was a failure to integrate.[35] Always consistent, *The Sun* led the panic with its headline 'GHETTO BLASTER. Mass immigration to Britain has changed it beyond recognition and turned communities into ghettos'.[36] Casey was alarmed that there were 24 wards in 12 local authority areas where 40 per cent of the population identified as Muslim and 20 wards with the same proportion of those of Indian descent. God forbid! The report neglected to mention that there are thousands of council wards in the country where 90 per cent of the population is White. If any of these fears were really about segregation then they would be focused on the monocultural suburbs and not the inner cities that are so demographically mixed they are unironically termed 'super-diverse'. The diversity is so 'super' that it is the source of moral panics, police surveillance and is usually hallmarked by steep inequalities. Casey was simply following a standard line, one well-ploughed by British politicians.

Enoch Powell, voted the fifty-fifth greatest Briton of all time at the turn of the twenty-first century,[37] is infamous for his 1968 'Rivers of

Blood' speech (delivered in Birmingham, of course). He mourned that witnessing the mass immigration of Black and Brown people from the colonies was 'like watching a nation busily engaged in heaping up its own funeral pyre'. There was something entirely incompatible about the 'alien' people, and he thought it was 'insane' to let migrants settle and bring their families. For Powell, opening the doors to the dark hordes would bring only discord and would end in a race war. Listening to Enoch's dystopian nightmare, in which he declared that the 'black man would have the whip hand over the white man', I am genuinely surprised that he was not admitted to a psychiatric ward the moment he stepped off the stage.[38] The country is composed of only 13 per cent of racialized minorities today, and in 1968 there were so few of us here that a state of delirium induced by the psychosis of Whiteness is the only rational explanation for his passionate ramblings. Powell was terrified that immigration would pollute the British way of life, a theme picked up by Thatcher in 1978, when she warned that Britain was becoming rather 'swamped by people with a different culture'.[39] The thinly veiled racist rhetoric of the Conservative Party was part of their brand, but also caused them to be dubbed the 'nasty party', something that Tony Blair seized on in the elections in 1997. New Labour supposedly embraced modern, diverse and multicultural Britain, but it did not take long for Blair to learn his lessons from Thatcher, his true political mentor.

In 2001 Bradford, Oldham and other northern cities erupted in violence after White far-right extremists rampaged through largely Pakistani and Bangladeshi communities. The provocation unleashed tensions in these predominantly Muslim communities, who became the angry face of the so-called 'riots'. Blair was quick to condemn the violence and commissioned Ted Cantle, a former chief executive of Nottingham Council, to investigate the roots of the problem. The Cantle Report spelled the beginning of the end for the British experiment in multiculturalism, the concept of a nation made up of what Labour peer Lord Bhiku Parekh dubbed 'communities of communities',[40] who embraced their differences as well as their similarities. Cantle blamed the violence on the 'series of parallel lives' that White and Asian youth were living up north.[41] I am paraphrasing, but according to that report the far right's racism was only possible because those poor working-class Whites who sparked the violence lived in their run-down council houses completely isolated from their Muslim neighbours. They just hadn't had the chance to get to know each other. Asian youths were venting their frustrations with racism and marginalization, but through the lens of the psychosis their problems could be explained by living with too many other Muslims, clouding their eyes to the wonders of Britannia. Cantle recommended scrapping multiculturalism, which he saw as encouraging segregation by supporting the growth of different ethnic communities. Instead, he recommended embracing 'community cohesion', an agenda that sought to bridge the divide and bring everyone together. This was done mostly by the state-funding initiatives that brought different groups together rather than targeting money at supposedly insular communities. One television programme of that time captured the spirit of the moment by bringing Muslim and White youth together to break down the divide; one White kid was shocked that '*They* eat pizza!' Whilst there is a certain romance to believing that such moments can build connection and community between different groups, they fail to understand the systemic nature of the problem. Both the White and Asian young people who were out on the streets were living in highly economically marginalized communities and the White extremists were hitting out based on resentments towards Black and Brown people that have a long history in the nation. I'm sure twenty years on everyone is looking back at the violence, reminiscing on how silly they all were, over a XXL Margherita. These are delusional-liberal notions of social change, but there is something deeply sinister behind this agenda as it locates the problems of society at the door of individuals and communities.

It doesn't take much to read between the lines of who the 'parallel lives' accusations were targeted towards: Muslims, who self-segregate and don't integrate correctly, meaning that poor uneducated Whites have little choice but to think they are aliens. The recommendation in the report that immigrants ought to make a 'statement of allegiance' to Britain really gave the game away because it located the attitudes of those coming into the country as the source of the problem.[42] Matters only got worse in 2002 when passing a Britishness test became a requirement for citizenship. The questions were so obscure and irrelevant that three-quarters of the existing population would fail it; a real-life example of what we often say, that we have to be twice as good to get half as far.

The Cantle Report was published after 9/11, which had dramatically increased the fear of the Muslim enemy within. It marked a shift in the racialization of Islamic communities. After so-called 'home-grown' suicide bombers attacked London in July 2005, it was confirmed that Muslims were a dangerous, self-segregating race, who represented a threat, not just to Britain, but also to the nation's cherished way of life. Rather than considering whether the issue of British-born people blowing themselves and others up because they hated everything the West stood for might be a failure of the nation, Blair of course framed it as a foreign evil that had been allowed to fester in segregated communities. As usual, the blindingly obvious issue of economic marginalization was ignored, but there was an even bigger elephant standing in the room. After 9/11 Blair had become Bush's lapdog, trailing behind him in invading Iraq. More than anything else, the bloody images of children being cut down by British bombs was a major recruiting factor for July 2005.[43] It is not an overreaction to wonder if the bombing would have happened at all if Britain had not invaded Iraq. But rather than accepting a little responsibility for running a country that marginalized Muslim youth and launched illegal wars that provoked a tiny minority over the top, Blair's delusional blinders kicked in. He specifically argued that we should 'reject . . . their false sense of grievance against the West'.[44] To Blair, it was a battle of ideas; he argued that 'we need, in the face of the challenge to our values, to re-assert also the duty to integrate, to stress what we hold in common'.[45] Not only was proper integration the only solution but it was necessary to do so 'at the point of shared, common unifying British values'. This is ironic because if we understood the legacies of the empire it would go without saying that there is little more British than launching a terror campaign in pursuit of a supposedly religious ideology. But in Blair's view, Britain is the moral force for good in the world that the Islamic extremists should learn from.[46]

Racism, sexism and xenophobia are three of the most quintessentially British values, but Blair was so deep into the psychosis of Whiteness that he could, with a straight face, believe that Britain was in a moral position to give lectures. Somehow, he imagined that 'fair play' had something to do with how a small, insignificant island with few resources came to dominate a quarter of the globe.[47] But the psychosis makes the irrational seem reasonable. Blair painted himself as a hero in his twisted history, when writing in 2007 for the magazine *Foreign Affairs* that the threat of Islamic extremism was 'not a clash between civilizations; it is a clash about civilization ... the age-old battle between progress and reaction, between those who embrace the modern world and those who reject its existence'.[48] Where does a nation forged on an empire built on slavery, genocide and colonial brutality fit into that history?

Blair also created the Preventing Violent Extremism and Terrorism strategy, commonly known as Prevent, targeting funding towards Muslim communities to counter so-called radicalization. The programme got off the ground in earnest in 2007 when the government sent money to local councils with more than 5 per cent Muslim populations, and by 2014 over £200 million been spent on initiatives to keep the Muslims out of the clutches of the mad mullahs.[49] If only Prevent were as benign as spending money on pointless programmes like #knifefree chicken boxes, but there was a much darker side to its agenda. More than 300 police posts in counter-terrorism were created, and alongside them an increased web of surveillance was implemented. Birmingham, yet again, is a good example of how the 7/7 London bombings in 2005 sparked surveillance of Muslim communities that reached *1984* levels. In Sparkbrook and Washwood Heath, two neighbourhoods that probably made Dame Casey, who opined about racial segregation, feel dizzy, three million pounds of Prevent money was invested in 150 cameras that tracked all the cars coming in and out of the area. That kind of web of surveillance was completely unprecedented, essentially making everyone in the area suspects. The public was meant to be reassured that the cameras were there to 'monitor a population seen as "at risk" of extremism' as though they were doing a public service to the very community they were racially profiling.[50]

When David Cameron was elected Conservative prime minister in 2010 he ramped up the rhetoric. He declared that what he called 'state multiculturalism' had 'encouraged different cultures to live separate lives, apart from each other and apart from the mainstream ... we've even tolerated these segregated communities behaving in ways that run completely counter to our values.' The use of *we* tells us a lot. Cameron grew up in the tiny village of Peasemore in West Berkshire. In 2021, 95 per cent of the residents of the entire county were White, so there is no doubt that in the 1960s, 1970s and 1980s he lived in one of the most racially segregated communities in the country. He went on to study at Eton and then Oxford, two of the most mono-cultural educational institutions in the nation and this means he was nurtured by the *we*, not the *they* who are so estranged from the purities of British life. Cameron's self-segregated upbringing is completely ignored in the panic about separate lives. His government made it a legal requirement for schools to respect the 'fundamental British values of democracy, the rule of law, individual liberty, and mutual respect and tolerance of those with different faiths and beliefs'.[51] In 2015 this became a duty to 'promote' this fantasy set of values. I have young children; when I visit their schools and nurseries, the psychosis of Whiteness is visibly present. There are displays of posters with the monarch's face in the middle, surrounded by the set of supposedly British values. The cognitive dissonance makes me sick. Any time there is a royalty-related celebration my children somehow manage to catch a stomach bug. But again, there is a more sinister side to this insanity. Schools have a legal duty to refer children to be 'de-radicalized' if they perceive them to be displaying early signs of extremism. From 2012 until 2016 1,839 children in England and Wales under the age of 15 had been referred for de-radicalization, and over 400 of these were under ten.[52] In 2016, the police were called after a ten-year-old Muslim child wrote the word 'terrorist' in a piece of work describing their house. He had confused it for 'terraced'.[53]

It would perhaps be easy to laugh at the absurdity of this, like so many examples of the psychosis of Whiteness in action, but this ridiculousness is in fact essential to the ongoing brutality of White supremacy. The segregation we currently see in both the US and the UK is almost entirely the result of White people with money fleeing or erecting barriers to keep out those who they have imagined are inferior and dangerous. As a result deprived inner-city communities predominantly composed of Black and Brown people produce just enough real-life imagery to stoke the psychosis of Whiteness's delusions. Lacking genuine experience of the 'Other', White hallucinations about racialized communities are further reinforced. There is no 'tolerance', no 'fair play' in communities that use their financial power to isolate themselves from the rest of society and then use racist delusions about those in the dark ghetto to justify their own privileges. Segregation is both a cause and effect of the psychosis a feedback loop amplifying the delirium.

Nightmares about being swamped and overrun by the dark hordes go to the heart of the psychosis of Whiteness and are why it so often erupts in violence. There is an irrational fear that White people are those who are in danger, the same tropical *neurasthenia* that plagued those who moved to the colonies. This is a central ingredient of the psychosis: an inability to treat the 'Other' as anything but the stereotype they perceive them to be, allowing racial oppression to continue. First we were savages, who required brutal discipline for our own good. Now we are culturally deficient, unable to control our bodies and in need of hostile policing to protect us from ourselves, and society. This is the reason that the idea of abolishing the police or the prisons is, for many, unimaginable, even though there is no evidence that more police means less crime and by all measures mass incarceration in the US is as astronomically expensive as it is ineffective. Without prisons and policing jungle-dwellers would tear society apart. They must be controlled, no matter the methods or the cost.

Irrational fears are a hallmark of the psychosis of Whiteness, no less so than the idea that racialized minorities haunting Western nations represent an existential threat to the homeland. As migration from the colonies has taken place over the last few decades in Britain, we have become used to the idea that White society needs to make sure we don't take control of the nation. In settler colonies like the US, where millions of the indigenous people were slaughtered and Africans enslaved, these fears are one of the foundation blocks of society.

5

We're Losing the Country

The death rattles of the Trump presidency were as violent and obscene as his time in office. On 6 January 2021, after it was clear that Trump would not be defying the constitution by staying in office, a collection of his White supremacist supporters stormed the US Capitol. Watching footage of senators running for cover reminded us all of how thin the line between nightmare and reality is. If this was pitched as a movie, it would have seemed too far-fetched. Politicians, commentators and the public struggled to explain the scenes; they were simply incomprehensible. A US president had been suspended from social media because he tweeted support for a racist mob invading the US Capitol building while Congress was in session. There is no part of that sentence that can be understood rationally. Forget Trump and the mob for a moment: it should be unimaginable that thugs could enter Congress while politicians were working there. It was a stark contrast to the over-policing that occurs any time a group of Black people descend on the nation's capital to protest. Terrifyingly, White privilege extends to insurrectionary mobs waltzing into Congress. You know you have fallen down the rabbit hole when Jay Kay, lead singer of Jamiroquai, had to go on record to insist he was not one of the mob. He had been mistaken for a rioter adorned in a Viking-horned racoon-skin hat who perched himself in the vice-president's seat at the centre of the Senate Chamber.[1]

The Capitol riot represented the breaking of a fever that had been burning for years. Trump's presidency was made possible in no small part due to the election of Barack Obama, the first Black president, who became a lightning rod for White racial resentment. Long before the nightmare of President Trump was realized, Trump led the racist 'birther' movement, falsely charging that Obama had been born in Kenya and therefore was not eligible for the presidency.[2] These racist lies made an impact on those he needed to get the Republican nomination: according to one public poll, more than half of Republican primary voters in 2011 believed that Obama was foreign-born, and only 28 per cent thought he was a so-called natural-born American.[3] Given Trump's historic lack of credentials, lukewarm support from his party, and overwhelming incompetence, without Obama his ascendency would probably have been impossible. It is difficult to understand how a majority of White women in America voted for a president who boasted about 'grabbing women by the pussy' other than as a course correction for White supremacy. The unfortunate reality is that Obama reminded much of the White population of what America really stands for. Old-fashioned racism is a comfort blanket.

The 6 January mob was angered by the irrational belief that the 2020 presidential election had been stolen from them. Trump's support in the US had always been rooted in the idea that the country was being taken away from the White majority. When accepting the Republican Party nomination in 2016 he struck an apocalyptic note, highlighting the 'the terrorism in our cities, threaten[ing] our very way of life', meaning the Black Lives Matter protests, the 'crime and violence that today afflicts our nation' in cities like Washington, Baltimore and Chicago [niggers], 'the number of new illegal immigrant families' crossing the borders [spics], that the 'manufacturing trade deficit has reached an all-time high' (offshoring industry to poor darkie countries) and 'one international humiliation after another' (some of those poor darkie countries were embarrassing the great US of A).[4] Clearly it was the niggers', immigrants' and globalists' fault that so many in once-great America were being left behind. This rallying cry was persuasive enough to get him elected and to nearly being re-elected, even after he presided over one of the most calamitous responses to the pandemic on the planet, one that undoubtedly cost tens of thousands more lives than was necessary. When it was clear that his mishandling of the Covid pandemic was hospitalizing his designs on a second term in office he played his White supremacist politics perfectly: he responded to the unprecedented protests for racial equality in 2020 only to condemn peaceful protest and triple-down on his attempts to be seen as the 'law and order' candidate.

For many the killing of George Floyd was a watershed moment, a prompt to re-examine the racist nature of society, at least superficially. But for Trump the protests Floyd's murder sparked were the perfect opportunity to rally his base. He gave a speech in the White House Rose Garden calling protestors 'terrorists' and then used the National Guard to release tear gas to disperse BLM protestors so that he could pose with a Bible in front of St John's Church.[5] He led an attack on critical race theory and concepts like White privilege, banned federally funded education programmes from using them, and vowed to 'defend, protect and preserve [the] American way of life, which began in 1492 when Columbus discovered America'.[6] A critical examination of the racist foundation of the nation represented an existential crisis for Trump's America, which depends on the wilful forgetting of both the past and the present. That so much of his appeal was based on 'what was lost' goes to the heart of a much larger fear, one that keeps White America (and the West more generally) up at night. The Capitol riots may nominally have been about Trump losing the election but they were also part of a larger belief that the good White Christian majority were losing the country to dark, alien forces.

Appeals to 'Make America White Again' have become common in the post-civil rights age. Many White people honestly believe they are the ones being discriminated against. The year after Trump was elected the majority of White Americans believed that they were disadvantaged because of their race.[7] The minor gains that have been made by a lucky few African Americans have sent some White people into a state of panic. Affirmative action policies have in fact disproportionately benefitted White women, but that has not stopped White racial resentment. Demonstrating delusional thinking, White women are often the fiercest critics of a policy that benefits them. Abigail

Fisher was the first applicant to sue a college, the University of Texas, over affirmative action. She argued that she had not received a place because African Americans were favoured as part of the university's admissions policies, even though there was no direct evidence that she would have made the cut had the policies not been in place.[8] Affirmative action will probably never happen in Britain, but I have heard derisive 'affirmative action hire' remarks upon my elevation to professor thrown at me more times than I can remember. There is a genuinely held, widespread belief that we receive advantages due to (a mythical) special treatment under the law. This is one of the reasons that the term 'White privilege' rubs so many up the wrong way; there is a delusional belief that the opposite is now true. Amongst Republicans, 77 per cent believe that seeing racial discrimination where it *does not* exist is a bigger problem than confronting the realities of oppression, and 31 per cent think that civil rights have gone too far.[9] NBA legend Kareem Abdul Jabbar wasn't exaggerating when he said that more White people believe in ghosts than in racism.[10] The extent of these delusions becomes even clearer when we look hard at the reality of our societies. Critical race theory came about because of a distinct lack of any progress on issues of racism, despite gains won by the civil rights movement. African Americans are worse off now than they were before the 1960s, when mass incarceration, continued poverty and the post-racial climate (where people have to be convinced that the problem of racism exists) are taken into account.

THE NEW RACIAL SCIENCE

'Racial science' refers to the dubious assortment of methods and techniques used to prove that the so-called White race is superior. The dead White men who created the body of knowledge the world is built on had various racist theories that supported White supremacy, and 'science' stepped in to provide the evidence necessary to the support their claims. Phrenology, the measurement of skulls, IQ tests, eugenics, biased slavery research (as in the case of Samuel Cartwright):

one doesn't have to look too hard to find supposed evidence that White is right.[11] Until the Holocaust this was all just seen as science, as rational and objective data about the inferiority of backwards races. That six million Jewish people were slaughtered based on these set of ideas led to a rethink and racial science became somewhat taboo. But cultural racism in supposedly scientific work is still prevalent. Researchers are still coming to the conclusion that Black people are poor because of their low morals, an inadequate work ethic and a propensity for violence. Although research is clear that there is no genetic basis for either race or White supremacy, researchers are still linking poverty to genes and IQ. In fact, James Watson, credited with discovering the double-helix structure of DNA, was stripped of his honorary titles in 2019 by the Cold Spring Harbor Laboratory in New York, which he had led for years, because of his racist views. He once said that he was 'inherently gloomy about the prospect of Africa ... because all our social policies are based on the fact that their intelligence is the same as ours – where all the testing says, not really'.[12] IQ tests simply measure how well you can navigate the educational priorities of Western countries. They are deeply culturally biased and international comparisons of IQ are worthless.[13] The most obvious indication that IQ is bogus is that you can study for and improve your results, but if IQ is innate, this shouldn't be possible. Old racial science is still very much with us, but there is also a new version, one that takes a different approach towards the same end. The old racial science aimed to prove White superiority, thereby supporting racist policies. But remember that we are in a new post-racial age. The role of the new racial science is to support the myth that we have moved beyond racism. However, maintaining the racist status quo means proving that it is really White people who are now being discriminated against.

In Britain we are experts at pretending racism doesn't exist. Instead, we blame everything on class. Panic around the failure of so-called 'White working-class boys' is so dishonest it can only be labelled racial science. We are presented with evidence that says White boys who are entitled to free school meals are underperforming the most, and least likely to go to university. This wisdom has become so taken for granted that the government, along with schools and universities, is tripping over itself to fawn over these so-called White working-class boys. The university that pays my bills (at the time of writing) used to be located in a poor, 'diverse' community and more than 50 per cent of its student body comes from a racialized minority. They recently invested one million pounds in a centre that reaches out to communities who are cut off from higher education. Of course, when it came to building the centre they ignored the myriad impoverished 'diverse' communities (including the one they fled) and set it up in a traditionally 'White working class' neighbourhood. Forget orange: poor White is the new Black.

The British government's response to Black Lives Matter has been to deny there is a problem with racism and to attempt to stop future protests with a draconian policing bill that makes the minimum sentence for defacing a statue harsher than the minimum sentence for rape. As part of their White supremacy offensive the government created the Commission on Race and Ethnic Disparities to report on discrimination.[14] They declared their intent from the outset when they chose Tony Sewell as the head of the commission, a discredited Black researcher who has been pedalling culturally racist arguments about Black school achievement for decades. Back in 2010, Sewell wrote in the national newspaper *The Guardian* that 'more than racism, I now firmly believe that the main problem holding back black boys academically is their over-feminised upbringing'.[15] Apparently, it was feckless fathers abandoning boys to their smothering mothers that caused Black boys to fall behind. We will cover the ~~Sewage~~ Sewell Report in more depth later in this book, but for now we will simply concentrate on the report's analysis of White, so-called working-class boys; its central thesis is the perfect example of the new racial science.

Class is a contested category anyway, but in schools it is almost impossible to measure. Not every student can be surveyed about income, background and cultural tastes, so eligibility for free school meals is used as a stand-in for class. To qualify for free school meals a child's parents must be receiving benefits and earn below a certain threshold. I have a PhD in sociology but I must have misread Marx's division of society into two classes: I thought there were owners and workers, not those who qualify for free school meals and those who don't. Other definitions of class take household income, type of job, cultural tastes and other categories into account, but the school system does not give us any real data on class. So there is no evidence that White 'working-class' boys are doing disproportionately badly; those peddling this myth are selling snake oil. What the data does tell us is that if you qualify for free school meals, no matter what your ethnicity, your GCSE results will be poorer. Surprise, surprise: in a capitalist society, having less money is a disadvantage. You'd think that for all the nation's love affair with Dickens's novels we would have been prepared for this shocking revelation. When the Education Select Committee released a report in 2021 claiming that 'White privilege' was in fact the 'opposite' of what was going on in the schools, they were either lying, fooled or deluded.[16] The data demonstrates that racialized minorities are more likely to be on free school meals. Only 14 per cent of White students receive them compared to 28 per cent of those of Black Caribbean origins. It is a privilege to be far less likely to need the school to feed you at lunchtime. But racialized minorities are significantly more likely to be 'working class' in any case, due to racial discrimination.

While it is true that White boys on free school meals attain lower grades at GCSE level that Black Caribbean boys on average, any honest analysis would recognize that even in a vacuum you cannot compare 14 per cent of one group with 28 per cent of another. But when you add the experience of racism, the comparison becomes even more absurd for Black Caribbean families. Free school meals are based on household income and racism is a key reason that a far higher proportion of Black Caribbean families qualify, as they are more likely to be in low-paid, public-facing roles, the same ones that made us more susceptible to die from Covid-19 and have increased our likelihood to qualify for food aid. Outside of income one of the key indicators of success in school is your parents' level of schooling.

But the 28 per cent of Black Caribbean families on free school meals will include those with high levels of education who either can't get a job at all or are in a low-paid job below their skill level due to racism. These are not barriers White families have to face, hence the lower proportion of students qualifying. It is utterly irrational to compare these groups because they are simply not like-for-like. Were we to look at the most disadvantaged 14 per cent of Black Caribbean students it is highly unlikely they would outperform their White counterparts. But the only measure we have for school performance is access to free school meals, so any nuanced, complex analysis is impossible.

I am not arguing that poor White people have it good in either Britain, the US or anywhere else; they do not, of course. But the problem with the new racial science is that rather than locating the blame within an exploitative class system, it is instead shifted on to all the imagined help that those with darker skins are receiving. The reason that the GCSE statistic is constantly mobilized is because it is one of the only bits of data that can be distorted to fit the necessary racial science conclusions. The Sewell Report lists statistics that show groups like Black African (42.9 per cent), Pakistani (41.3 per cent) and Bangladeshi (50.3 per cent) children achieving strong passes at GCSE level at roughly the same rate as or outperforming White children (42.5 per cent). But next to these results is the data for A-Level results in the same table. I was shocked to see that in this mere two-year gap all three groups had fallen significantly behind: only 6.1 per cent of Black African, 7.3 per cent of Pakistani and 7.8 per cent of Bangladeshi students received three As in their A-Level results compared with 11.1 per cent of White students. Just 3.2 per cent of Black Caribbean students can say the same. The media is fascinated by the failures of White working-class boys at GCSE level, but A Levels are far more important: they are the gateway to university, and therefore potential access to higher-paying careers.

Since the 1990s there has been a panic around GCSE attainment, resulting in uplift in some groups' performance. Pakistani and

Bangladeshi students were previously achieving well below White students, but parents and community members have focused on enriching their children's schooling through extra-curricular activities like tutoring, becoming governors and even creating Islamic faith schools. In 2014 there was a supposed scandal in Birmingham over rumours of a 'Trojan Horse Jihadist plot to take over Birmingham schools'.[17] In keeping with the psychosis of Whiteness, this originated in an anonymous fake letter to the head of Birmingham City Council claiming that extremists had created a five-step process to taking over schools that had a predominantly Muslim intake of children. This involved taking over the governing body and introducing Islamic principles into the school. The tactic had supposedly already worked in five Birmingham schools. A national panic broke out, even though the letter was discredited almost immediately as containing no evidence to support the allegations. Leaders of Birmingham City Council dismissed the letter as a hoax. Even so, when the letter leaked to the press it set off a national storm and the government stepped in. Michael Gove, Minister for Education at the time, insisted that the plot must be taken seriously and continued to insist in 2022 that there was 'a sustained effort to change the character of city schools'.[18] So the government stepped in and the five schools were investigated by the Department for Education on the basis of a letter that had already been deemed a fake. Two of the schools had recently been reviewed and deemed to be excellent but following these new investigations they were put into special measures on the false basis that they had made the schools adhere to Islamic principles. Complaints included separating boys and girls in assemblies; inviting extremist speakers; and removing headteachers who were too secular. School inspectors had gone into the schools and found none of these problems, and in fact two of the schools had some of the best exams results in the country. But when they went looking for problems based on a manufactured letter, they suddenly found extremists lurking around every corner. In reality, parents and the local community started taking a direct interest in how their children were being educated. The whole point of governing bodies is to

ensure this kind of involvement with schools. Due to stark racial segregation, mostly caused by White flight, the schools were
overwhelmingly attended by Muslim children. It may well be true
that this meant some conservative Islamic principles were brought
into the schools, but, contrary to popular opinion, this is not the
same as supporting extremism. Considering the number of single-sex
faith schools there are in the UK it is deeply contradictory to balk at
separating boys and girls in assemblies. There was nothing dangerous about the schools; they had created environments where students
who had struggled at GCSE level were doing extremely well. In testament to the delusional nature of the whole affair, one school was
criticized for instituting Islamic assemblies for their overwhelmingly
Muslim school population because they 'had not received permission
from the Education Funding Agency for an exemption from providing a broadly Christian act of worship'.[19] Surely we should be
questioning why Christian worship is the legal default for school
assemblies, not challenging the right of a school to cater to the population of its school? British schools have been put on a path to
privatization over the past ten years under the guise of making them
more accountable to their communities – but only if they're not too
Islamic, it seems. Lost in the furore was that these schools were all
examples of communities engaging with schools to improve outcomes for their children. Rising GCSE attainment in these
communities was due to the efforts of parents and communities and
should have been celebrated. Since the schools in the scandal were
purged of the so-called 'plotters', they have never again reached the
same heights of attainment for their children.

Contrary to the groans of the White grievance industry, there has
not been massive investment in improving the attainment of Black
and Brown children, nor any well-funded, systematic attempts to
specifically address the structural racism in the school system. Suc-
cessive government approaches to addressing inequalities in schooling
were tokenism at best and, at worst, cultural racism. The only genuinely funded attempt to tackle racial inequalities in attainment was
when the New Labour government introduced the Ethnic Minority

Achievement Grant (EMAG) in 1999. This was money for local education authorities ring-fenced for the problem of ethnic minority 'underachievement'. But the programme was little more than liberal window-dressing. The budget was paltry to begin with and frozen over the years. By 2011, when the Tory-led austerity government got rid of EMAG its budget was 200 million pounds for the whole country. That might sound like a lot, but actually represents 0.6 per cent of spending on schools. There was not enough money for any ground-breaking initiatives and most of the money was spent on learners whose second language was English.[20] This is in keeping with an approach to tackling the issue that largely excludes those minorities who don't speak perfect English, going back to a time when Caribbean migrants were deemed to be less intelligent because of their use of patois.[21] The meagre funding meant a focus on programmes of mentoring, where Black people are brought in to raise the aspirations of the obviously male-role-model-lacking poor Black boys growing up with no men in the house. When mentoring is provided as the solution, they are blaming us for the problem. It isn't the children or their families that need to be fixed, it's the schools. This patronizing focus on 'problem' children and their communities is evident from official guidance on 'effective use of EMAG' published by the government in 2005. One of its best practice case studies was of a school that instituted a 'weekly behaviour focus for pupils'. The children were encouraged to 'line up quietly', and of course to remember to take all their equipment to school. The senior managers in the school would get their hands dirty and randomly stop children in the corridor and ask if they knew what that week's behaviour focus was. If they were correct they were rewarded with a chocolate bar.[22] I guess we should be thankful that the school wasn't handing out boxes of fried chicken as incentives, but I doubt you feel any better about the use of your tax money. If this is best practice I honestly dread to see what the worst looked like.

Other empty gestures include ritualized performances of Black History Month. Schools aren't even required to engage with it and many don't, and many of those that do would have been better off

THE PSYCHOSIS OF WHITENESS

not bothering. My son's school held a competition for Black History Month where the children had to give a presentation about an historical figure. My five-year-old son made a PowerPoint presentation about Malcolm X, but lost out to his friend who drew a picture of Marcus Rashford. I'm a United fan so I have a lot of love for Rashford but he is definitely not an important figure in Black history. Neither is Idris Elba, but that didn't stop the school plastering his face on their Black History month poster. It was only thanks to my son's mother that I didn't write a public letter.

Taking education into our own hands has been the only successful intervention, and it is this that has led to the improved exams scores of Pakistani and Bangladeshi children. Until the 2000s Black Caribbean communities were leading the charge on both education reform and in creating alternatives to fill the deficits in the system. We created our own supplementary schools, where we would teach Maths, English, and the Black Studies the schools entirely left out, on Saturdays and after school. Education was the central pillar of British Black Power, but community mobilizations and supplementary schools have since declined as we have increasingly relied on the system to address its inherent racism instead.[23] We used to understand that school was a hostile environment but now we imagine it can be reformed. It really is no wonder the situation has not improved.

The most delusional aspect of the new racial science is the notion that White so-called working-class boys are losing out *because* of all the support for the Darkies. The Education Select Committee report was called the 'The Forgotten', implying that White working-class boys have been left behind to languish. This is nonsense: as we have already discussed, any gains are illusionary. Those groups who have caught up at GCSE have slid right back down two years later at A Level. If you look at other measures it is clear that the picture has not improved: for example, Black Caribbean children are twice as likely to be excluded from school.[24] White boys on free school meals' lower grades at GCSE don't hurt their chances of being employed when they leave school, either. Racism ensures that they outperform their Black peers on the measure that really counts.[25]

The collapse of even a glimmer of progress once students reach A Level points to a larger problem, one that is often masked in the university figures. Handwringing over poor White boys' lack of access to university is based on resentment of the increasing numbers of racialized minorities who have gained access to the sector. Black students are now over-represented in higher education, a remarkable position given that one generation ago universities were almost the exclusive preserve of rich White men. But as is so often true, this so-called racial progress is a mirage. For one, the available data is being abused.

Analyses like the Sewell Report rely on the same free-school meals delusion as school-exam results do. Perhaps even more alarming is that neighbourhood deprivation data has been mobilized to 'prove' that White kids are missing out the most.[26] But due to racial housing segregation this data is so misleading that it is irresponsible to use it to examine anything. Racialized minorities are predominantly found in the inner cities of a handful of major metropolitan areas, meaning that it is very difficult to find a neighbourhood dominated by any particular group. There are places with few White people, but they are incredibly diverse and, as we have already seen, there are vastly different schooling outcomes for different groups. For the most part the only ethnic group whose data you can isolate to analyse is that of White people. It is impossible to honestly compare neighbourhoods populated by poor White people with the diverse neighbourhoods where most of us live. Compounding the issue is that due to racism in housing these areas are not just diverse ethnically, but also by class. It isn't as simple as moving to a 'better' neighbourhood if you have a good job; my own neighbourhood is incredibly mixed in terms of class, housing doctors and professors as well as those living on housing benefit in houses of multiple occupancy. Neighbourhood data relies on the idea that people in a given area have similar levels of income, but this is simply not the case. The so-called scholars using this data are well aware of its uselessness, but ignore it. A 2019 report from the National Education

Opportunities Network sparked headlines thanks to its conclusion that poor White students were the most marginalized in access to higher education. But the authors recognized that their work 'does not allow much to be learnt about London' due to metropolitan neighbourhoods being extremely mixed in terms of income.[27] Remember that almost half of all Black people live in the capital, so it is utterly impossible to draw any meaningful conclusions on racism with a methodology that does not include the city. The new racial science depends on exactly this kind of sleight of hand.

The evidence for poor Whites being left behind in the university sector is a fantasy of those who focus on one statistic to the exclusion of all others. Black students may be over-represented in university but they disproportionately attend so-called post-1992 institutions, like the one currently paying my salary. Access to the university sector was widened in 1992, when it was recognized that far more young people needed to receive degree-level education to build the knowledge economy the country required. But the dirty secret is that there was little attempt to make the existing elite institutions more diverse. Instead the government created a whole host of new universities to meet the demands of the poor unwashed masses. That legacy lives on and Black students are still far more likely to attend a less prestigious institution than White ones. University league tables are a testament to White supremacy: the most diverse universities sit at the bottom of the rankings and elite White spaces like Oxford and Cambridge are firmly entrenched at the top. When I started university in 2002 there were more Black students at the 115th-ranked London Metropolitan University than there were in the twenty prestigious Russell Group universities combined.[28] It is no coincidence that I have only ever worked in the post-1992 sector; the segregation of Black staff follows similar patterns to those of students. We are disproportionately located outside elite institutions. I do not want to run universities with lesser reputations down. In my experience, education is often better outside the hallowed halls of the elite institutions and post-1992 universities are usually more supportive environments for Black students simply because they more accurately reflect the demographics of the communities they come from. They are also where more critical and engaged work is often done. Our Black Studies degree simply could not exist in the Russell Group. We have six Black members of staff in the same department, all producing work on Black life. Good luck finding that critical mass in ten elite universities combined. I prefer the sector, as I believe it gives students better education and experience and I can't imagine working in the Russell Group. But in a racist employment market the brand of your degree matters more than its content, in keeping with the delusions of the psychosis. If you believe that studying in the elite bubble of Oxbridge, which is more like Hogwarts than your average ex-polytechnic, makes you well prepared to understand and improve the world then there is little point in me trying to convince you otherwise. The truth is that Whiteness, in both curriculum and pageantry, is a key part of the allure of a university degree. Every time I sit through the brass band and have to process in to a graduation, wearing ridiculous garb, walking behind someone carrying an actual sceptre, I can only shake my head. My university only became one in 1992, but feels it has to embrace the grand traditions of the elite institutions. We expect the best education to be the Whitest one and ape the traditions of the sector to ensure that we, and our customers, truly belong. But we have a two-tiered system where Black and poor students are disproportionately located in less prestigious institutions, and unsurprisingly Black graduates are less likely to be employed at all as a result of this, let alone in graduate positions.[29]

Once in university, no matter where it is placed on the league tables, racial discrimination is more pronounced than in schools. Some racialized groups outperform White students at school level, but when it comes to university there is a pronounced gap in attainment between White and non-White students. Simply by virtue of not being White, you are significantly less likely to receive a good degree ranking, across the sector and across all universities.[30] From 2019 to 2020, 87.1 per cent of White students received a 2:1 or above, while only 77.2 per cent of non-White students achieved the same. The gap is even more pronounced for Black students, with only around 70 per cent hitting that mark. White students are almost twice as likely to achieve the top mark of a first-class degree than their Black counterparts.[31] The hierarchy of White supremacy is alive and well in the headquarters of much of its ideology. As Chris Rock once put it, in response to complaints that White people are being left behind: 'If you're losing, who's winning? Cos it definitely ain't us!'[32]

Black student participation in higher education is evidence of how we have been deluded into believing that if only we can gain the right qualifications we can educate ourselves out of racism. The programme 'Aim Higher', which ran from 2004 until 2011, was one of the only sources of government support aimed at students progressing to university-level education. It sought to raise the aspirations of under-represented students and encourage them to go to university, through activities like summer schools and mentoring by current university students; the idea was to role-model under-represented students into believing that university was for them.[33] When I was a university student I did this myself; I was paid a miserable hourly rate to encourage a version of my younger self to work hard and dream of racking up university debt. But like school interventions, the very notion of Aim Higher was that it was the kids who were broken, not the racist infrastructure that kept so many of us out of higher education. The idea that communities whose families migrated into the country so that their children could have access to better educational opportunities needed more motivation just shows the racist assumptions underpinning these interventions. We are more aware of the value of higher education; we already know we are driving in the race for success with the handbrake on. Our aspirations do not need raising, we need the playing field to be levelled so we are no longer at a disadvantage. The increased participation of Black students in university has nothing to do with government intervention, it's thanks to the knowledge that we don't have the privilege to shun higher education. We have no safety net to fall back on.

Aim Higher was also aimed at under-represented groups from deprived backgrounds, including White students. There has been no serious specific intervention to help racialized minorities access higher education or to support them in university or the school system. Money is targeted at those with fewer economic resources, not towards those who face barriers due to racism. Free school meals are a deprivation-based measure and so is the pupil premium, which gives schools money for each child receiving free school meals. Programmes like the Education Maintenance Allowance, which sent payments to students with low incomes to help them stay in further education, were cut by the great austerity government that began its destruction in 2010. Efforts to widen participation, like the creation of post-1992 universities, were targeted towards those on low incomes, as are maintenance loans (which used to be grants) and hardship funds. There are billions spent annually supporting deprived (mostly White) students in schools and universities and no government has ever seen racism as a separate problem worthy of addressing. Stormzy paying for a handful of Black people to go Cambridge doesn't count.

From primary school all the way to university racism shapes the outcomes of racialized groups. The progress that has been made is largely illusionary and the genuine successes that have been achieved are thanks to the tireless work of communities on the ground. The notion that too much focus has been placed on racism, leaving poor White kids behind, is as ridiculous as it is dangerous. There is no crisis of the White working-class in the school system separate from issues facing all children from a deprived background. White children are not struggling in schools because of the colour of their skin. In a racist society, that is a privilege. But the psychosis of Whiteness produces even more bizarre claims of threats to the White population than claims of the crisis of the so-called White working class.

WHITE GENOCIDE

The arch far-right-wing American media pundit Ann Coulter caused a stir in 2007 when she criticized President Bush's immigration policy. Drawing on the fears of many Americans, she pointed to demographic changes: reporting that, in 1960, 90 per cent of the nation was White, but 'the Census Bureau recently estimated that Whites already account for less than two-thirds of the population and will be a minority by 2050'. This existential crisis was, she argued, caused by mass immigration and immigrants' high birth rates compared to the White population. Such rhetoric is par for the Republican course. What made the piece stand out from the usual muck was her pronouncement that 'if this sort of drastic change were legally imposed on any group other than white Americans, it would be called genocide'.[34] It might seem quaint now, but back in the more reserved 2000s invoking 'White genocide' was typically reserved for the KKK and neo-Nazis. Coulter claimed her place in the right-wing-media hierarchy by setting a new low in the debate and pioneering making fascist discourse mainstream. Since then Tucker Carlson has well and truly popularized the term on Fox News and President Trump unofficially endorsed it when he declared that there were 'good people' on the neo-Nazi side of the Charlottesville rally. Trump's entire political appeal is based on an almost audible dog whistle; the idea that White people are being erased from the United States. The idea of White genocide is, of course, delusional, but more worrying is that the principal argument behind it, the demographic erasure of Whites from the United States, has been accepted as common sense. I have read, or heard, that the US will become a so-called majority-minority country, where White people are overrun by ethnic diversity, countless times. This discourse usually reaches fever pitch around election time as the Republicans panic that White voters are running out and they either need to broaden their appeal to Black and Brown communities, or make efforts to ensure they cannot get to the polls. By now you should not be shocked to learn that suppressing the non-White vote has become a central plank of the Republican Party strategy, through voter ID laws, closing of polling stations and erecting as many barriers as possible in states where the party controls the voting booths.[35] The term majority-minority is of course oxymoronic but the idea that it will soon come to pass is based on a completely distorted understanding of both race and of the history of Whiteness in the US and the wider world.

Proclamations of a non-White future for the United States depend entirely on viewing the Latinx population as people of colour. They are the largest immigrant group and have one of the fastest-growing populations. But, in keeping with the way the psychosis of Whiteness functions, this notion ignores the histories of immigrant groups once they step onto American soil. Latin America includes demographic groups who are descended from European colonialists (hence 'Latin'), much like those who 'settled' in the United States and became the White majority. But countries like Brazil, Ecuador, Columbia (named after good old 'Genocide Christopher') and Argentina are all European settler colonies built on White supremacy. Brazil had the largest enslaved population by far.[36] When the descendants of European imperialists who benefitted from White supremacy in their homelands cross the imagined border into the United States, they somehow cease to be White and are transformed into oppressed 'people of colour', both officially and in the public imagination. It is not that many Latinx can pass for White, they *are* White, in just the same way that the majority of people in the United States are. Rather than embrace the label of 'people of colour', 58 per cent of Latinx identify as White, rising to 65 per cent for those born in the US. Only 14 per cent identify as an established visible racialized minority (American Indian, Black or Pacific Islander).[37] There is a large group of 36 per cent who identify as some other race, and given the nature of these categories it is likely that this group would include a significant proportion who could pass for White. Speaking Spanish does not exempt you from Whiteness; most Europeans' first language is not English, but they are still White.

It should not be a surprise that Jair Bolsonaro, a right-wing racist populist in the mould of Trump, rose to power in Brazil and was its president between October 2018 and January 2023. Although over half the population identify as Black, Brazil is one of the most racially segregated countries in the world and all the features we associate with institutional racism in the West are rampant there. Half of all those taken in chains from Africa went to Brazil and it has been a White supremacist republic ever since. Brazil was the last country to abolish transatlantic slavery, supported apartheid South Africa, and has a rate of police murdering Black people that would make the Statue of Liberty blush. Brazilian police kill at nine times the rate of US law enforcement and 84 per cent of those who die are Black.[38] Bolsonaro's family are a mix of Italian and German immigrants and he headed a reactionary, racist administration. But in the people-of-colour logic, if he were to migrate to the US, he would be part of the new so-called majority-minority. It is clearly delusional to include straight-up White folks like Bolsonaro as people of colour but the majority of Latinx are of mixed heritage and have European, Indigenous and/or African ancestry, making things more complicated. Even so, automatically including all Latinx as people of colour ignores the process of becoming White that was central to the forming of the American nation.[39]

Whiteness is not a fixed category and there is no perfect biological link to Western Europe that defines a person as White. Like every other identity, it changes, depending on the times and the needs of a given society. Jewish people are a good example of a group that can switch in and out of Whiteness, to deadly effect. Defined as less than human by the Nazis who exterminated six million Jews, they are now the settler colonialists-in-chief of Israel and have been given the full support of the West's (and Whiteness's) power. The Irish, too, have been incorporated into the racial hierarchy of the USA. As British colonial subjects, for centuries the Irish were not extended the protections of Whiteness. Millions fled to the US to build a better life, but they had to earn their way into being accepted into Whiteness, to become White, in other words. They did this in large part by embracing White supremacy and committing racial violence with gusto in the race riots that scarred the nation.[40] The Irish and many other migrants find that there is a very important difference between the xenophobia that most immigrants face and the racism of White supremacy. After one generation White migrant communities fold into the mainstream, essentially disappearing. Even in the UK, where 'no Blacks, no Irish, no dogs' signs continued to be seen well into the 1990s, in large part due to the Troubles, the Irish community no longer faces routine discrimination. The White and light-skinned Latinx melt into the American mainstream in the same manner. Two decades ago, studies found that Latinx communities were closer to White ones in terms of education, health and other outcomes than we would expect, given the stereotypes about those communities.[41]

As the largest Latinx ethnic group Mexican Americans have long been a frame of reference for the incorporation of Latinx into America. The Chicano Movement emerged in the 1960s and aimed to resist discrimination against Mexicans by fighting for self-determination. They embraced an anti-racist, Third World approach, and made multiple links to African-American political movements, particularly Black Power groups.[42] But outside of the romance of so-called people of colour coming together, there is a darker history of Mexican incorporation into the American mainstream, one that depended on erasing African bloodlines and on appeals to Whiteness.[43] In the 1930s Mexicans were legally classified as White for a brief period and benefitted in ways that African Americans never could.[44] The conservative faction of the Mexican-American community leadership worried about being flooded with 'poor, uneducated and dark' Mexican immigrants who would prevent them blending into Whiteness.[45] This should not be a shock, given the racially coded nature of American society. The boundaries of Whiteness are elastic and shape-shift to include groups who would previously have been considered non-White.[46] Like every other light-skinned immigrant group, assimilating into Whiteness has been a key strategy for many Latinx communities.[47] But anti-Blackness was not a new concept for Mexican immigrants either.

Under Spanish rule up to half a million Africans were enslaved in Mexico between the sixteenth and the early nineteenth century and a racial caste system was installed, incentivizing Mexicans to 'marry lighter' in order to seek success in a White supremacist society.[48] After the Mexican War of Independence of 1810 to 1821 the formal caste system was abandoned, but pigmentocracy continued, and the Black population was effectively erased when their category was dropped from the 1921 census. Only in 2015 did 'Black' return as a group to be counted, and 1.2 per cent of the population identified with their African roots. Blackness was made invisible in the identity of the country so completely that Afro-Mexicans have been deported because the authorities do not believe there are any Black people there.[49] Puerto Rico has a similar history and a continuing presence of anti-Black racism,[50] meaning that when immigrants make it to the US it doesn't take them long to learn the racist rules of their new society.

An honest assessment of the history of both the United States and its Latinx populations would conclude that the most likely outcome is that White Latinx will blend into Whiteness after a few generations, like other ethnic groups. When I visited New York I was excited to see Little Italy as I love gangster movies. I pictured the images from *The Godfather* and couldn't wait to take in the sights and the sounds. It was one of the most disappointing trips I've ever taken. By the turn of the twenty-first century Little Italy had been reduced to just a couple of streets. Italians were no longer marginalized and confined to a particular corner of the city. They had proved their Whiteness and moved onwards and upwards into the American delusion. There is no good reason to think that those descended from the Spanish will fare any differently.

On a superficial but telling note, White Latinx have already dissolved into Hollywood. For example, Emilio Estevez, the son of a Latinx father and Irish mother (in a case of immigrant stories converging) was cast as all-American anti-hero Billy the Kid in the 1988 movie *Young Guns*, and Estevez's father is none other than Martin Sheen, who has become the archetype of the American president from his time on the TV show *The West Wing*. At first I thought perhaps Estevez was not actually Latinx and that in a Hollywood hipster fugue state Sheen had given his kids Mexican names. I had to do a double-take when I read that Martin Sheen is a stage name. His real name is Ramón Antonio Gerardo Estévez. Talk about dispersing into Whiteness. *The West Wing* cast a White Latinx as president and no one noticed. This is even more marked because when Sheen's President Bartlett's presidential terms come to an end he is replaced by Jimmy Smits's Matthew Santos. Without a hint of irony the show made a big deal out of the first Latinx president ascending to the White House, despite it being more of a passing of the baton. Sheen has recently declared that assuming a stage name is his 'greatest regret', and he uses his birth name in every other facet of his life.[51] But it was likely the best career move he ever could have made and it allowed him to blend in seamlessly. This assimilation of White Latinx into White society is more than just symbolic. Some of the discourse around White Latinx educational and societal progress mirrors that of the hard-working immigrant narrative of the European migration in the early twentieth century,[52] in stark contrast to the discourse around African-American innate failure.

It is important to note that becoming White will not grant all Latinx the benefits of the American delusions of Whiteness. US society remains organized around disparities of wealth and class, regardless of colour. While self-defined White Latinx fare better in relation to key social indicators like education and employment than those Latinx who describe themselves as any race other than White, they remain worse off in relation to White Americans.[53] Millions of Latinx in the US live in barrios, which have similar social conditions to African-American ghettoes. The containment of African Americans and Latinx in depressed urban ghettoes makes the upward social mobility seen by other immigrants less likely. African Americans are grossly over-represented in the criminal justice system and the same is true of the Latinx population to a lesser extent. Immigrants, particularly those from Latin America, have also become a central target for the far- and centre-right. Trump's signature campaign promise was to 'build a wall' between the US and Mexico, and he constantly raised the spectre of Latinx criminals threatening the homeland to titillate his base. In the current, heightened anti-immigrant climate it is certainly possible that a distinct Latinx identity will prevail against the pull of Whiteness. Due to some parallels of experience, there is a history of shared struggle between African Americans and Latinx communities, like the collaboration of militant groups the Black Panthers and Brown Berets.[54] This is why many see drawing out the differences between African-American and Latinx communities as a 'divide and conquer' strategy of White supremacy,[55] and why there are calls for Latinx to 'embrace a non-white identity'.[56]

As progressive as it may seem to imagine that some Latinx will embrace the anti-racist struggle, we must remember that the very notion that all Latinx are not White is a production of the psychosis. These delusions even seep into our efforts to overcome inequality. Through the rose-tinted lens of the psychosis, it might sound reasonable for the Latinx, who are for all historical and contemporary purposes White, to jettison the social advantages that position brings and struggle for the rights of so-called people of colour. But shake off the delusions and it quickly becomes apparent that there is as much chance of that happening as there is of Fox News hyperventilating about *The West Wing*'s affirmative-action president. For all the existential crises about minorities becoming the majority, or even the optimism that this might lead to powerful coalitions, the data tells us that the future is White.

TURKEYS VOTING FOR CHRISTMAS

Despite White supremacy being as intact as ever, the existential fear of the White majority being replaced remains. That is the power of the psychosis of Whiteness: it continually feeds the paranoia of the White population, fuelling the racial barbarity necessary to maintain the system. In the UK, mass immigration into the mother country after the Second World War has sparked the same fears of being 'swamped'. There have been similar pronouncements about the future as in the USA, and cities like Birmingham have actually become majority-minority. Author Lionel Shriver, described wonderfully on Twitter as the 'Waitrose Katie Hopkins', recently stirred the White genocide pot. In an article in the August 2021 issue of the *Spectator* she decried that a third of all births, and 80 per cent of those in London, involve a foreign-born parent. This led her to conclude that 'for Westerners to passively accept and even abet incursions by foreigners so massive that the native-born are effectively surrendering their territory without a shot fired is biologically perverse'.[57] The magazine tried to avoid accusations of racism by using the title 'Would you want London to be overrun by Americans like me?', but we are not stupid (hopefully). American immigration to Britain is minuscule and we know exactly who she was really talking about. Perhaps the low point in mainstream discourse around this theme came in 2008 when the BBC ran a series of documentaries called *White* which explicitly asked whether immigration had harmed the White working class. The advert for the series could have been taken directly from a far-right website. It depicted a White male face being written on in a variety of foreign languages in black ink by a series of dark-skinned hands, while the nationalist song 'Jerusalem' played in the background. As the man's face became covered in Black ink, 'Britain is changing' was written across his chin. Eventually, his face was entirely covered in black and as he closed his eyes, he blended into the dark background, with the caption underneath asking, 'Is white working-class Britain becoming invisible?'. To make sure we got the message, one of the documentaries took a sympathetic look at Enoch Powell and the impact of his Rivers of Blood speech. It concluded with an account of the 7/7 terrorist attacks as the culmination of Powell's warning that blood would run in the streets as a result of multiculturalism. For all of the problems of social media, there is no way the BBC would have got away with this blatantly racist week of programming if they had had to deal with Black Twitter back then.

In 2008 fears about immigration had reached fever pitch. There had been increased immigration from the European Union after poorer countries from the east were added to the bloc and their citizens were given freedom of movement across member states in 2004. Immigration from the EU had risen significantly and the immigrant population in Britain rose from 1.4 million to a peak of 3.7 million in 2017.[58] The increase in immigration set off a panic in the right-wing press and supposedly progressive figures like then-Prime Minister Gordon Brown promised his government would ensure that it would be 'British workers, for the British jobs'.[59] Fears around immigration created the careers of extremists like Nigel Farage, whose United Kingdom Independence Party (UKIP) had been seen as little more than 'fruitcakes, loonies and closet racists' until that point.[60] Mass EU immigration fuelled a desire for UKIP's only real campaign agenda: leaving the union. Enough ink has already been spilled on the rise of right-wing populism and the eventual referendum in 2016 when Britain voted to leave the European Union, but I'm going to focus on the aspects that demonstrate the power and delusions of the psychosis of Whiteness.

Anti-immigration feeling in Britain has always been tied to racist fears of Black and Brown people. Eastern Europeans coming to Britain is nothing new: while Powell was frothing at the mouth about Darkies, millions of Eastern Europeans were also entering the country for work. In an irony only lost on those in the grip of the psychosis, one of the Labour politicians with the toughest views on immigration, so much so there were rumours he was going to defect to UKIP, is Simon Danczuk. He is just one of the millions who have melted away into British society after their parents migrated from Eastern Europe. Farage's UKIP produced a poster for the Brexit campaign that pictured a line of Syrian refugees, strapped with the tagline 'Breaking point'. It is clear the Black and Brown 'Other' are feared, because of our ability to apparently change the country beyond recognition. But Eastern European migrants are overwhelmingly White, which is why uncontrolled immigration from Europe fitted the British pattern of encouraging White immigration, while restricting movement from the former colonies at the same time. One day I am certain evidence will leak out that a key driving force behind EU expansion was the wish that Eastern Europeans would migrate to the west. It would be the perfect tonic to bolster the falling White population (due to low birth rates when compared to Black and Brown migrant communities) and would usher in a younger, White demographic. Between the 2001 and 2021 censuses, the number of people born in Poland living in Britain increased twelve-fold, from 58,000 to 743,000. For Romania the increase was even larger, from 7,631 to 539,000, seventy times the number in 2001. These are now the countries where the second- and fourth-highest number of people born outside of the UK come from.[61] India, Pakistan, Bangladesh and Nigeria remain in the top ten, but most of the list comprises of countries where the majority of people are White. In my hometown of Birmingham, one of the majority-minority leaders, there are parts of the city where there would be almost no White people without Eastern Europeans. EU immigrants gave Whiteness a foothold. If the aim is to 'Keep Britain White', then restricting EU immigration was a grave mistake. The main blunder of the Remain campaign was not pointing out that the immigrants Brexit would prevent entry to were White. If that realization had kicked in, the result would probably have been different.

Although all White people receive privilege from being White those benefits are not shared equally. Part of the reason that Whiteness is maintained by delusions is that poor and working-class Whites are often duped into supporting people and initiatives that go against their interests. W. E. B. Dubois argued that poor Whites in the Reconstruction period in the South were bought off by the 'psychological wage' of Whiteness, even though uniting with poor Black workers would have been better for their economic interests.[62] It may sound patronizing to argue that poor Whites vote against themselves due to the delusions of Whiteness, but history has shown this has happened repeatedly. Neo-liberalism was voted for during the Reagan and Thatcher eras, largely predicated on anti-Black racism and hostility to immigrants, who were thought to be undeserving of the shared social-safety net.[63] The rich became richer and those at the bottom struggled to get by. The roots of the Brexit crisis were planted when social democracy was abandoned during Thatcher's reign. Public services were neglected and wages declined, resulting in a scrap for resources at the bottom. After the financial crisis in 2008 gave David Cameron's government the excuse to usher in austerity, opportunists like Farage argued that the reason for a long wait to go to the doctor, or for a lack of good school places or for social housing was too many bloody immigrants. In truth it was people like him, rich bankers who had taken an ever-increasing share of the pie, who were to blame for the rot of formerly successful working-class towns. The EU is the largest single market in the world and the economic benefits to membership were innumerable. Only the rich stood to benefit from the lack of regulation that came from leaving the union. Brexit is a supercharged neo-liberalism, applying the finishing touches on the project Thatcher began. But vague promises of 'taking back control' (of the borders) were enough to sway voters. The Remain campaign misread the mood by appealing to logic, while Vote Leave did all they could to stoke the psychosis. Immigration was undoubtedly the biggest driving factor behind Brexit but the areas that were most in favour of leaving were the ones with the fewest immigrants.[64] The debate was never about a rational assessment of the evidence but was instead based on appeals to fears that were rooted in the existential dread of Whiteness.

The hangover from Brexit led to the most blatant example of turkeys voting for Christmas in recent British history. In 2019 Boris Johnson had forced his way into leadership of the country and his appeal to the voters was simply that he 'would get Brexit done', ensuring that the so-called 'will of the people' was carried out rather than derailed. No matter that he is a cartoonish buffoon, that he is 100 per cent a privileged elite White male, born into wealth extracted from the poor, he became a populist representing the blue-collar Brit. A relatively close election was predicted, but with Brexit dominating the debate Johnson's party won in a landslide, dismantling Labour's red wall of solidly working-class seats in the north, areas that would previously rather have burnt their towns to the ground than see them represented by Conservatives. This was the great Brexit pay-off: northern, almost exclusively White towns accepting the 'psychological wages of Whiteness', at the expense of installing the living embodiment of all their political problems into power. Only delusional thinking can explain why so many supported their class enemy to take the country out of an economic bloc that benefitted them financially.

The US is no stranger to this phenomenon. Trump was delivered the presidency when the Democratic blue wall of largely White blue-collar states in the Midwest collapsed in 2016. A majority of White voters supported The Donald in both elections because, for all his obvious failings, he was the comfort blanket of White supremacy. This argument usually starts with economics, which are simple:

Trump is in the same camp as Johnson, a spoilt rich kid whose policies will make people like him better off at the expense of the rest. Just to reinforce the point about White Latinx, in 2018 we could add Bolsonaro to this list, creating an unholy trinity of White supremacist-lite leaders. But Trump's handling of the Covid-19 pandemic should have led to him being dragged from the White House. His slow response, refusal to support mask-wearing and general mismanagement is estimated to have caused more than 100,000 unnecessary deaths in the USA.[65] This is more than the number of American soldiers who died in the Korean and Vietnam Wars combined, and is around the same number of US deaths as in the First World War. Putting aside the dead bodies, Trump appeared on television suggesting that research needed to be done to see if drinking bleach or shining bright light inside patients' bodies would be a cure for Covid-19. Yet in the subsequent election the *majority* of White people voted for him to remain in charge of the country. Choosing Whiteness over health is very on brand for the US.

There is no country in the world more in love with guns than the US, where firearms outnumber people. For someone born in a country where handguns are illegal the idea of people being able to buy a semi-automatic weapon at a supermarket is a nightmare. More guns means more violence and up to 40,000 deaths a year are linked to gun violence in the US.[66] Suicide accounts for most gun deaths and White men are by far the most likely to end their own lives at the barrel of a gun. Although women in the US are three times more likely to *attempt* suicide, men are the most successful at it because they tend to use guns. Just 3 per cent of suicide attempts without a gun are successful, compared to 85 per cent involving a firearm.[67] From the outside this seems like a simple problem with an easy solution: restrict access to guns and save thousands of lives, White lives at that. But the gun is paramount in US society due to White supremacy. The myth of the frontier, of the threat from the natives and of slave rebellions, runs deep and continues in the form of fears of urban disorder and marauding Mexican gangs. When school kids get slaughtered by firearms the gun lobby's solution is not to ban guns but to arm teachers and send kids to school with bullet-proof backpacks. Being fed the staple image of the iconic ghetto reinforces the perceived need for decent, hard-working citizens to defend themselves. So even though White men are five times more likely to be killed by their own gun than by some-one else's, they defend their unfettered right to carry firearms to the grave. The delusions are so ingrained that there is a congressional ban on funding research into the negative health outcome of gun owner-ship. They don't *want* to see the facts.

In his book *Dying of Whiteness* the psychiatrist Jonathan Metzl writes about the states which vehemently rejected Obamacare. In a country where 62 per cent of bankruptcies involve medical bills, you would think there would be an urgent desire for affordable health-care. But Metzl sat through countless meetings in various Republican stronghold states and heard people reject Obamacare time and time again because they could not tolerate the idea of taxpayers' money being spent on racialized minorities, even though it would also save their own lives. The failure of Tennessee to support Obamacare was 'on a continuum of the leading causes of manmade death' in the state.[68] A recent report estimated that through historic neglect of the healthcare system, Trump's dismantling of Obamacare and tragicomic handling of the pandemic, up to 461,000 unnecessary deaths have occurred in the four years of Agent Orange's presidency.[69] Again for those at the back: The. Majority. Of. White. Americans. Voted. For. Trump. Both. Times. (Yep, if Black and Brown voters hadn't turned out in their millions, we would have had to endure another four years of The Donald.)

The left has been taking a knife to a gunfight for the last forty years. While the left has been making rational appeals to self-interest and data, the new right has emerged, fully embracing the psychosis of Whiteness. Making sense is illogical when irrationality is the nature of the debate. When people are willing to sacrifice themselves and their families at the altar of Whiteness it is time to wake up to scale of change that is necessary.

Paranoia is a hallmark of the psychosis of Whiteness. The irrational fear of being overrun by dark hordes is ever-present in the delirium necessary to maintain racial oppression. The fear of loss, of being erased by the natives, goes back to the beginning of Western society. The need to dominate and control the globe led to these feelings of unease, of always being afraid that the tables would turn, and that the savages would seek their ultimate revenge. The fears remain ingrained in society and that dread is what drives the necessary social policies to maintain the status quo. Always feeling superior, yet also under threat, provides the fuel to treat those who are Black and Brown with the necessary levels of disdain to oppress them. There is no point trying to combat the irrationalities with facts, because Whiteness is impervious to them. The abject fear of loss is the nervous energy that sustains the psychosis.

Demonstrating the irrationality of the psychosis, severe delusions of grandeur run alongside this paranoia. Whiteness as a concept is rooted in the idea of White supremacy, the idea that, as Enlightenment philosopher Immanuel Kant put it, 'the White race possess *all* the motivating forces and talents'.[70] Such grandiose delusions have led Whiteness to be described as a form of narcissism, hallmarked by pathological self-importance and the need to devalue those who are different.[71] There is probably no better example of a narcissistic personality than Trump and he also perfectly demonstrates the fragility that Whiteness is rooted in. Narcissism is at heart driven by a fear of being shamed and exposed as inadequate. Those irrational fears of White genocide or losing a grip on the country are directly connected to the delusions of grandeur that are a feature of the psychosis of Whiteness. Through its distorted lens White people are the centre of knowledge and culture, with the moral duty to act as custodians of the entire world. Nowhere is this more on display when it comes to culture, and the belief in the entitlement to define, hoard and possess the world's heritage, as we will explore in the next chapter.

6

Cultural Misappropriation

The Edo Museum of West African Art is due to open its doors in 2024 in Benin City, Nigeria, to much fanfare. In partnership with the British Museum, more than three million pounds has been raised for the state-of-the-art building, situated on the site of an archaeological dig to find more treasures of the once vast and powerful Kingdom of Benin. The new museum will host a display of the infamous Benin Bronzes, a collection of artworks pillaged from Benin in 1897 when the British destroyed the city. Thousands of pieces of the priceless art and heritage are scattered across the West, on display or in private collections, in countries like Britain, Germany, the USA, Austria and Sweden.[1] This will mark the first time in over a hundred years that the Benin bronzes will be on display in the place they were made. Returning these stolen goods to their homeland is the culmination of years of activism. The director of the British Museum, Hartwig Fisher, declared that the project 'will surely become one of the most significant museum initiatives in the coming decades'.[2] Unfortunately, as we have already learned, all that glitters is not gold, and this is certainly true in the case of the supposed return of the Benin Bronzes.

Fisher's excitement is a classic case of 'getting high on your own supply'; the British Museum's relationship to the Benin Bronzes is deeply problematic. As the nation's predominant trophy case for looted artefacts, the British Museum houses almost a thousand Bronzes. The Benin Dialogue Group was founded in 2007, bringing representatives from countries who stole the goods with Nigerian officials to try and achieve their restitution. The creation of a museum in

Benin City was agreed upon and announced in 2019. But, as it seem-ingly did for all issues relating to racism, the killing of George Floyd infused a jolt of energy into the proceedings and plans for the Edo Museum of African Art were unveiled in 2020. But the devil really is in the detail.

Although the museum aims to house a permanent collection com-prised 'of the most comprehensive display in the world of Benin bronzes',[3] it does so without the items actually being returned to it. The Bronzes on display will be a rotating selection of pieces *loaned* from various Western institutions. They are having their cake and eat-ing it, holding on to stolen goods while receiving a PR boost by helping the poor Africans to glimpse at least a little of their own heri-tage. This ludicrous compromise shows the power that Western institutions hold in the museum world. It also demonstrates that their primary excuse for hoarding the artefacts – that backwards Africans cannot be trusted to look after their own heritage – is just a smoke-screen. Frustration over the continued hubris of the heritage sector has been palpable, with Nigerian visual artist Victor Ehikhamenor exclaiming, 'We shouldn't have to ask, over and over, for what's ours'.[4]

The Benin Bronzes represent just one story of colonial theft but it contains all the elements that allow the West to feel comfortable hold-ing on to stolen goods. They start by denying, or at least downplaying, how the artefacts came to be in Western hands in the first place. Trade is typically the excuse used, the claim that Westerners legally pur-chased goods and then shipped them over to their respective mother countries. But even when this was the case, it takes a special short-sightedness to ignore the racial power imbalances created by imperialism. Europeans plundering the continent with guns were never entering a free marketplace. Museums functioned as tools to demonstrate superiority over the rest of the world, to boast about possessing better collections than rivals, and as a testament to the cul-tural superiority of the West. There were no limits on the depravity of methods of collecting to boost the nation's symbolic esteem.

There should be no way to avoid the immorality of the plunder that led to the presence of the Benin Bronzes in Western museums. In 1897

Vice-Consul General James Robert Phillips and a handful of British officials set off with a small expedition to overthrow the Oba (King) of Benin. It is testament to the psychosis of Whiteness that they believed they had the divine right to depose the ruler, and they ignored the warnings from the Oba, who made it clear that any attempt to dethrone him would result in their deaths. When the Oba's forces ambushed the expedition they killed nine British officials and the British response was typical. First there was a hyperventilating frenzy, whipped up by officials and the press, of outrage that the natives had dared to defend themselves. The defeat was labelled a massacre, committed by rabid savages running rampant. In response the full force of Britain's colonial army, and its supplies of automatic Maxim guns, was unleashed on Benin. The army, backed up by the press, pretended that this was done on humanitarian grounds in order to prevent the savages from, amongst other things, supposedly making human sacrifices, but in reality it was a punitive expedition, a show of strength to put the natives in their place. Benin City was burnt to the ground, the natives were subdued with horrific violence and the vast majority of Bronzes exhibited today were stolen in the aftermath of this terror. Within the British Museum the display gives a nod to this violent history, but assures the visitors that only 203 of their stockpile came from that punitive exhibition (as they were donated to the museum by the government in 1898). We are meant to be reassured that the rest of their pieces were sourced from private collections, as though those were not also almost certainly plundered from Benin. Looting artefacts was not just about personal gain for the thieves; it also reinforced the logic of White supremacy by putting the treasures of Benin into the hands of the White people, who were thought to be pre-ordained to own them. The historian Dan Hicks argues that, by displaying these objects, 'museums were co-opted into the nascent project of proto-fascism through the looting of African sovereignty'.[5]

In 2021 the British Culture Secretary Oliver Dowden argued that the Benin Bronzes 'properly reside' in British museums, continuing the well-established tradition of cultural imperialism. Demonstrating the delusional thinking necessary to hold such a view, he accepted that the Bronzes were 'acquired at a time of rampant colonial expansion in Africa' but added, 'in circumstances that I am not going to defend or condemn with the values of the twenty-first century'.[6] By that logic we can't condemn slavery, genocide, the denial of women to vote or any other atrocities committed in the past, as they were simply a product of their time. This is what I call the 'Jimmy Savile defence'; but molesting children was *always* indefensible, as was massacring civilians, burning down cities and looting cultural artefacts. The 'It was a different time' argument ignores the fact that there were plenty of people who thought the actions of the British abhorrent, not least those cut down by the bullets of their automatic weapons.[7] But in the psychosis of Whiteness the only perspective that matters is that of the White people with guns, and they thought it was fine, so we would be wrong to judge them with our modern lefty values.

Western museums are desperate to hold onto their stolen goods, and they justify this on the grounds that they are the best places to showcase the cultural heritage of the world. But only a small proportion of the artefacts are ever on display. Only around one hundred of the almost one thousand Benin Bronzes in the British Museum are able to be seen by the public. The rest are gathering (presumably high-tech) dust in storage. This problem is replicated across the heritage sector. Malcolm Gladwell has discussed the Metropolitan Museum of Art on his sometimes-excellent podcast *Revisionist History*.[8] Suffering financial straits, in 2018 the Met cut staff and introduced visitors' fees for non-New York residents, causing outrage. Gladwell found himself puzzled as to how an institution that holds more than two million objects and some of the most expensive art in the world could possibly be in financial difficulties. He discovered that the collections the museum owns are excluded from their financial accounts. Billions of dollars' worth of exhibits somehow do not count on the balance sheet, leaving the Met free to cut staff and charge visitors while at the same time refusing to sell any of its collection. In 1991 a public hearing of the Financial Accounting Standards Board was investigating the accounting practices of the heritage sector and officials rightly questioned how the sector could be treated so differently from any other corporation. In response, C. Douglas Dillon, then Chairman of the Met, gave evidence and proudly declared that it was pointless to try and account for their treasure trove because it would be impossible. He gave an example: the curator of the Islamic art collection would only ever be able to see a fraction of the Met's Islamic rug collection (one of the largest in the world) because most of it was in storage and far too expensive to move. Imagine having too much loot to be able to count it and using that as a defence. The vast majority of the Met's collection, which includes one of the biggest deposits of Benin Bronzes in the world, will continue to sit in warehouses and will never see the light of day, let alone be seen by visitors. Gladwell likens the museum to the dragon, Smaug, in *The Hobbit*, who sits upon a city-sized pile of treasure, incinerating anyone who comes close. Smaug has no need for the trinkets but hoards them anyway, claiming that he has the power, and therefore the right, to own these riches. However, in another demonstration of the psychosis of Whiteness, Gladwell fails to connect this 'Might is right' hoarding to the logic of White supremacy and instead falls down a pop-psychology rabbit hole about the pathological dimensions of collection. But the link should be abundantly clear. The right of possession, of domination, of hoarding loot, cannot be separated from the colonial mentality that developed the collections in the first place. White society is presumed to be the highest expression of culture, and therefore Western museums are seen as having the right, if not the duty, to loot and hoard artefacts from around the world.

Even if museums wanted to return objects, the law is designed to maintain White cultural supremacy. The British Museums Act of 1963 essentially makes it illegal to return artefacts for moral reasons. Museums are permitted to sell or give away items only if they are duplicates, if they were made after 1850 and the museum possesses a photo of it, or if they are deemed 'unfit' for the museum and of no use to students.[9] Ironically, under the law, the most successful case for returning cultural artefacts would be to embrace the racist ideas that say we have no history or culture worth studying, and that therefore the Bronzes and similar artefacts have no value. If that doesn't convince you that psychosis is the only metaphor to understand the state of things, then perhaps nothing will. But by arguing that the 'proper' place for looted objects is in the West, the museum sector holds onto these treasures because of their educational worth, thus implicitly making the case that they are valuable. The British Museum has steadfastly refused to return the Mokomokai to the Maoris in New Zealand. The Mokomokai are preserved heads belonging to the Maoris, with complex *moko* facial tattoos that denote significant ancestral links, and remain deeply sacred. But the British Museum argues that their value as 'sources of information about human history' outweighs any claim Maoris have over the skulls of their ancestors.[10] The notion that Western museums have a monopoly on the curation of human history displays the delusions of the psychosis of Whiteness. The art historian Alice Procter explains that, in the West, 'an object and culture only comes into being when it is touched by a White man'.[11]

The British Museum has repeatedly resisted calls to return stolen property, defending its right of possession through its claim to be 'a museum of the world, for the world'. Chris Spring, its former African collections curator, explained that looted artefacts should remain in the museum because:

> we need to remember London is a global African city, arguably the biggest African city in the world, if you think of all the different people. It's really important that people of African heritage living in the UK and in Europe can see cultural artefacts of their own heritage.[12]

A perfect illustration of the psychosis, which also produces delusions that multiply perceived diversity! Only 13 per cent of London's population is Black and 60 per cent is White, so how on earth anyone could describe it as an 'African city' at all is beyond me, let alone the 'biggest' in the world. Lagos, the capital of Nigeria, which is making demands for return of the Bronzes, has almost double the population of London and houses almost five times the total Black population of Britain. Apparently just living in the West means that you have a vastly disproportionate right to view art and history! But the aspect that made me laugh (or cry) the most was the idea that Black people are flocking in their droves to the British Museum. If the aim is to showcase African artefacts for Black people in Britain, the British Museum is one of the very last places to put them.

MUSEUMS ARE WHITE SPACES

As a now middle-class professor it may surprise you that I spend as little time as possible in museums. I do fondly remember looking at dinosaur bones as a kid, and it was exciting to see Egyptian mummies. But when I realized I was staring at corpses robbed from an African grave any excitement I felt quickly eroded. I recall visiting as an adult an exhibition about Olaudah Equaino in the Birmingham Museum during the bicentennial of the abolition of the slave trade in 2007. A massive fake polar bear took centre stage and made a lasting impression on me. I wondered why on earth the fact that Equiano saw a polar bear was of any interest at all, let alone a central feature of this exhibition. Aside from that I have only been in my local museum a handful of times, once in particular because Sky News wanted to do an interview about something race-related in 2018 and thought that an exhibition of local legend Vanley Burke's photographs would make a good backdrop. The adverts had hyped up the display, but as I went looking for the exhibition, I walked up and down the one corridor they had reserved for the handful of images they chose to display a number of times, not realizing it was the *whole* exhibition. Burke has taken thousands of pictures of the Black experience in the city but the museum had decided to completely marginalize his work within their walls. While I was in the building I thought I should also check out their 'The Past Is Now' exhibition, curated by local Black and Brown young people. They had done their best to represent the legacies of the British empire but were only given a small room to explore the theme. The tokenistic and marginalized nature of both exhibitions demonstrated the deep-seated problems with that particular museum and with the sector in general.

The first steps through the door of the Birmingham Museum and

Art Gallery are an introduction to Whiteness. One of the first things any visitor sees is a gallery of portraits of an array of dead White people, in contrast with one of the most diverse cities in the world just outside their doors. In fairness to my hometown, the museum has admitted that there is a problem, and are part of a project called We Don't Settle that aims to rethink their collection by asking young, racialized minorities to work with the heritage sector and plot a new way forward. I am part of the research team on the project, which has shown that there is no excuse for maintaining the status quo and has empowered young people to curate meaningful exhibitions and work in the museum. Unfortunately, the feeling of alienation that I feel in museums is not limited to my hometown, or even to the UK.

I have a daughter who has grown up in the United States, in Philadelphia. Like many US cities Philly has a large African-American population, who make up the biggest demographic. Much like my hometown, Philly is a hard, industrial city that has depended on Black and Brown folk for its place in the world. Black US culture had an impact on my expectation of the city. I grew up watching *The Fresh Prince of Bel-Air* on repeat and will go to my grave with 'in West Philadelphia born and raised . . .' etched in my mind. Legends of the Philly music scene like the Roots and Jill Scott, and even modern practitioners like Meek Mill, give the city its own vibrant sound. Black academics have used the city as a laboratory: from classics like W. E. B. DuBois's study *The Philadelphia Negro*, to more recent works like Elijah Anderson's *Code of the Street* and Nikki Jones's *Between Good and Ghetto*. If you spend a week in the North or parts of West Philly, you could go the whole time only seeing Black people; a testament to how segregated and how vibrant the community is. My daughter loves art, so I was excited to take her to the Philadelphia Museum of Art, especially when I checked the catalogue online and saw that they had a picture by her favourite African-American artist, Jacob Lawrence. But monuments to the psychosis of Whiteness greet you before you even set foot in the museum.

We ran up the steps to the museum along with a number of tourists, celebrating at the top, in homage to the famous scene in the boxing movie *Rocky*. This moment is so iconic that there is a real-life statue to the fictional character greeting you at the end of your climb. If *Rocky* were set in a two-horse town with no sporting legacy, one could possibly understand the statue's presence, but the city has such a strong boxing tradition that being a 'Philly fighter' is a brand all of its own. Two of the best to ever do it, Joe Frazier and Bernard Hopkins, laced their gloves in the city of brotherly love, but the African-American legends have not received anything like the royal treatment afforded to the fictional White boxer. The *Rocky* statue was gifted to the city in 1982 after it was made for one of the movies. There was debate about whether to accept what was essentially a movie prop, and for years it was placed outside one of Philly's sports arenas. But since 2006 it has had permanent pride of place atop the so-called 'Rocky' steps outside the museum, in the perfect delusional practice of life imitating art. Joe Frazier did finally get a statue in 2015, forty years after he won the heavyweight title, and sadly four years after he died. His statue was placed at the sports arena, the same place that was not deemed lofty enough for the tribute to the imaginary Rocky.[13] Part of the reason the film, and the character, was so popular was because he was the great White hope in a sport that for decades had been dominated by Black athletes. And it turned out that the pride-of-place monument to a White figment of the imagination was, sadly, the perfect introduction to the Philadelphia Museum of Art.

If I felt uneasy walking into my hometown's museum, when my daughter and I stepped through the doors of the Philadelphia Museum of Art, I felt physically sick. The design is no different to that of any European art museum, sporting the fake columns and calicos of the Renaissance. Most of the exhibitions are related to different European periods of art, and we really might as well have been in Europe, given the artwork on display. The African-American section was so small and uninspiring that I would have preferred not to have seen it at all. We spent about an hour looking for the Jacob Lawrence painting before being informed that, although they owned the picture, it was not on display. Like the majority of the Benin Bronzes, it was collecting dust in Smaug's pile of treasures. I had planned to stay for the whole day, exploring the breadth of African-American art, but we left after a couple of hours (most of which was spent looking for a painting which was in a cupboard). With the knowledge I have, I should not have been at all surprised that a US art museum would magnify the Whiteness of the European. After all, the US is just Europe on steroids, and given the settler colonial nature of the society, artificially creating White supremacist culture is even more imperative. Europeans can fall back on the weight of their traditions, whereas the US is built on erasing indigenous ideas and replacing them with imported White ones.

We must accept that museums were never meant for us. The emergence of museums was tied directly to colonial theft and the parading of loot to enhance Western prestige. So-called 'high culture' was always meant to be the exclusive preserve of the rich and, by default, the White. The museum sector has turned cities like London into crime scenes, monuments to the colonial violence upon which its collections depend. But the history of Western museums and colonial displays goes deeper than the looting of objects. Our bodies, too, both dead and alive, were to be presented to the inquisitive public for their entertainment, and for so-called scientific enquiry. Anthropological exhibitions displayed skulls of Africans and depicted different races to prove the irrational racial theories of White supremacy by arguing that different head measurements correlated to varying degrees of intelligence. But even this did not satisfy the curiosities of Western consumers. Thousands of visitors flocked to see human zoos where people were put on display for the visiting public. Watching an African family be exhibited was considered a legitimate activity, a day out with the children. We were not seen as fully human and as such we were considered to have no rights that needed to be respected. We were savages, animals, so different from rational and beautiful White people that we could only be comprehended through the lens of supposedly scientific study.

In 1851 the Crystal Palace was opened: a spectacular glass structure showcasing the Great Exhibition, sharing the wonders of the

British empire with the public through exhibits from around the world, including the Koh-i-Noor diamond (pilfered from India). The exhibition was wildly successful and an estimated six million people visited it. Once the building was moved to South London it continued to host colonial exhibitions and in 1895 it presented 'Africa at the Palace', where visitors were invited to see Somalis on display. There was nothing unique or even unusual about this. Across Europe and America such exhibitions were commonplace. London, Hamburg, New York, Oslo, Brussels and countless other cities housed these exhibitions and today there is a website called Human Zoos where you can see old advertisements for the exhibits.[14] The Paris World Fairs of 1878 and 1889 drew 28 million visitors and included 'Negro villages' for public consumption. Two and a half million people visited the Bradford World Fair in 1804 where a hundred Somalis were paraded, who were then forced to tour around Europe demonstrating wrestling and spear throwing.[15] Human zoos were money-making ventures and there were even stories of African performers who pretended to be from different parts of the continent, acting out whatever tribal fantasy the productions required.[16] Perhaps the most painful story that emerged from the human zoos is the case of Saartjie Baartman, a South African woman who was paraded around Europe as a spectacle, from 1810 onwards, due to her big breasts and buttocks. She was seen to represent the embodiment of Black female savage biology, in contrast to the perfection of the White woman. She was dubbed the 'Hottentot Venus', the vision of deviant Black sexuality. Even death did not end her ordeal. The French 'scientist' George Cuvier

> spread her legs, studied her buttocks and cut out her genitals, setting them aside for preservation. After Cuvier and his team of scientists finished their scientific rape, they boiled off the rest of Baartman's flesh. They reassembled the bones into a skeleton. Cuvier then added her remains to his world-famous collection.[17]

Her remains were put on display in Paris until 1975 and it took until 2002 for her body to be returned to the Xhosian people of South

Africa. When we consider the deluded (and frankly, perverted) nature of the history of cultural misrepresentation of colonial people, it should be obvious that we must leave the idea that the West is run on 'rational' thought at the door. Even attempts to try to deal with painful and sordid history end up compounding the problem, because the museum sector cannot break out of the framework of the psychosis of Whiteness.

BOYCOTT THE HUMAN ZOO

At the 2014 Edinburgh Festival the White South African Brett Bailey's *Exhibit B* made its debut in Britain, having previously toured in South Africa and Europe. The show involved taking Black local performers and arranging them in tableaux designed by Bailey to evoke memories of the human zoos of colonial times. The performers stood statue-still while the audience walked around them, serenaded by a choir. Imagine a couple in tribal gear, a woman chained to a bed as a sex slave for her colonial master, a man with a shackle over his face, and a replication of the grotesque display of Saartjie Baartman, a naked Black woman paraded in a cage because of her 'extraordinary' breasts and bottom. The stated aim of the show was to 'provoke audiences to reflect on the historical roots of today's prejudices and policies', and it received excellent reviews in the press for its supposed confrontation of racism.[18]

The existence of, and positive critical response to, *Exhibit B* is evidence of how the psychosis of Whiteness distorts how we see the world. Strip away the noble sentiment and the endorsements from the liberal establishment and you are left with the reality of the piece: lifeless Black bodies on display for the public, and the centrepiece Hottentot Venus, an interchangeable naked Black woman in a box for all to see. In truth, rather than challenging the racism at the heart of the human zoos, Bailey recreated it; he exploited Black bodies in the service of so-called art. The psychosis presents the work as inoffensive, and, moreover, transforms it into a heroic piece of anti-racist work. It is delusional to argue that a White man putting a naked Black woman in a box is anti-racist.

Black flesh (Black female naked flesh, in particular) is frequently exhibited for the world to see. As one performer in Edinburgh asked, 'How do you know we are not entertaining people the same way the human zoos did?' An artist in the show in Poland, Berthe Njole, experienced a group of men 'laughing and making comments about my boobs and my body. They didn't realise I was a human being. They thought I was a statue.' They returned and apologized after the show, but this hardly mitigates the reality of objectification; apparently, if she were a statue, it would have been okay to laugh.[19]

We must question what it is about the Black body that is of such interest to the director and the audience. It is not simply a record of history, connecting people to the past; there are plenty of periods that require re-examination and artistic representation, so there must be something of *particular interest* in the Black body that caught the attention of this director. Objectification is a standard trope of mainstream popular culture. It is at the root of how the White population understands their relationship to Black people. Liberals get to feel the 'discomfort' of their colonial history while fawning over the naked and prostrate Black body. There are better and much more appropriate ways to remind people of the history of human zoos without recreating them in the flesh.

Even if we accept the stated noble intentions of this work we cannot overlook the reality that Black bodies were being used to convey a message to White audiences. Objectification is a strategy used to evoke guilt and discomfort in those with a colonial legacy. Exhibit B reproduced the idea that Black people are passive agents, mere conduits to make White people speak to each other. Bailey himself admitted that his methods for the performance were 'very difficult to get right . . . the performers are not asked to look with any anger at all. They must work with compassion.' The Black actors were not speaking for themselves – they were a mouthpiece for the director's deeply disturbed message about race relations.

Exhibit B is a microcosm of the problem with critical Whiteness studies, where the aim is to reach into the souls of the White public and transform them into anti-racist allies. One of the performers in the London show, Stella Odunlami, argued that *Exhibit B* was important because 'it denies the spectator and the performer the luxury of hiding. It forces us to examine the darkest corners of our mind. It is brutal, unforgiving and unapologetic.'[20] This confrontation with White audiences is key to the idea of knowledge being redemptive. However, we have to be cautious of the power given to White people as the mechanism for change, and *Exhibit B* is a perfect example of the dangers of it.

Sometimes the messenger defines the message. Brett Bailey was described by Jan Ryan of UK Arts International (who also supported the project) as being 'a South African who has grown up in an environment which has repressed the majority of its people'. That is clearly disingenuous: he is a South African who grew up *as part* of the minority that oppressed the Black majority in the country. This destroys any legitimacy he might have had in terms of the representations of Black people he chose to portray. Bailey putting on the exhibition is akin to a German organizing a piece of 'performance art' featuring Jews dressed in prison garb, numbers tattooed to their arms, locked in a contrived concentration camp. Thankfully that idea is simply unimaginable; it would be censored without a second thought. The fog of the psychosis prevents people from seeing the horrors that have been experienced by Black people in the same way, and at the heart of this episode is the sorrow that no one organizing this exhibition managed to see the most obvious parallel precisely *because* of this devaluation of Black life, suffering and experience.

Being trapped in delusional thinking means that a person is unable to accept that their dysfunctional view is irrational, as was evident in the campaign against Exhibit B and the arguments (or lack thereof) advanced in support of it. The hip-hop artist and author Akala captured the nature of the psychosis:

Some of these reasonings may even appear sound at first glance, until we examine them in the context of the actual world we live in, not the fairy world of a certain kind of White liberal – and their Black and brown servants – the same world inhabited by humanitarian imperialisms and post-racial posturing.[21]

His use of the seeming oxymoron 'humanitarian imperialisms' indicates the irrational nature of the world we have to inhabit, where the only way to understand it is to use two words that should be incompatible. The campaign to stop *Exhibit B* in London was led by local activist Sara Myers, who complained of being talked down to by the Barbican when they initially addressed her concerns. She asked academics to write to the board explaining their objections to the piece. We wrote an open letter, signed by over thirty scholars in the UK and abroad, clearly citing our complaints to the Barbican. We received a two-paragraph response that accepted we had differing views, but stating that they did not think that the piece was racist because it had been displayed elsewhere. They later wrote a page-long response to the campaign, which again made no effort to engage with the actual arguments advanced about the problems with the show. Throughout the campaign they didn't engage with the issues raised at all.

Exhibit B was briefly discussed on *Newsnight* on 25 September 2014, and it was a particularly distorted portrayal: a sanitized version of the exhibition was presented, ignoring the controversial naked imagery, and they even went to the extreme of putting a cardigan on one of the usually bare-naked exhibits. The reality of the show was never discussed, just the fantasy-led, more palatable version. The psychosis allows those inside it to create their own reality.

In debates about whether it was right to call for the cancellation of the show, censorship was the key defence of *Exhibit B*. In defending the exhibition, Trevor 'formerly of the Black community' Phillips argued that, 'I am in principle, opposed to the banning of artists' work, since for the most part, this power has always been used by the state and by oppressive regimes to deny a voice to minorities'. The censorship of art makes people uncomfortable for good reason. Freedom of expression is worth defending but the idea that art is beyond censorship is ludicrous. A cursory search of the internet will find a myriad artworks that are racist, anti-Semitic and homophobic, that should clearly not be allowed to be displayed in public. When art is offensive in its nature it is rightly censored; freedom of expression does not mean that people have the freedom to racially insult others. Anyone advocating that 'art should not be censored' should be campaigning for the Barbican to commission an exhibition of Jihadist 'art' celebrating the glory of 7/7 (I welcome Uncle Phillips's thoughts on this issue). The controversy around *Exhibit B* was never about freedom of speech, but about whether the piece was racist. Instead of engaging in that discussion, commentators simply cried for free speech, and compared the campaign to episodes like the one when Salman Rushdie received a fatwa for *The Satanic Verses*.[22] But there were no calls for Bailey to be killed for staging *Exhibit B*, just vocal condemnation of his artwork that dehumanized Black people.

The other defence put forward was that the public had a 'right' to see it and as Stella Odunlani, one of the actors, put it, to 'critique it for themselves'. What this argument misses entirely is that we only have the right to see that which is available to view. I have never seen a minstrel show, but I know they are racist. Absent from the discussion was why the Barbican and other funding bodies found it necessary to channel resources to *Exhibit B* when they have such a poor record of supporting home-grown Black talent whose work is genuinely anti-racist. The question of whether if Bailey were Black there would have been protests was raised; but the reality is that if he were Black the show would probably never have been funded in the first place. Bailey was allowed to set the agenda due to White privilege. He crafted the piece, ordered Black bodies into submission and was supported by the arts world in doing this. Seeing the show would be to participate in that privilege and legitimize the pacification of Blackness in that narration. We campaigned to have the show cancelled and there were similar actions in Paris and Toronto.

At one of the protests against *Exhibit B* I wondered how on earth it could be shown in a so-called global city. Reflecting on the psychosis of Whiteness, however, it makes perfect sense. The 'newly' globalized and cosmopolitan world is supposed to have transcended boundaries of race, creating cities as melting pots of diversity and tolerance. In these global cities art is given a special role, a signifier of cosmopolitan consumption. Art must be defended because the city's role is now primarily to showcase culture and entertainment rather than driving industrial development. Global cities cater to the cosmopolitan consumer, who is overwhelmingly White and middle class. In this sense the city, its centre and cultural areas in particular, are designed and structured by those in the grip of the psychosis. No one thought to ask how the Black inhabitants of London would react to *Exhibit B* because the Barbican exists in a reality where they simply do not matter or even exist.

In fact, the global city of London was the perfect staging post for *Exhibit B* but it was also the cause of its demise. The Black journalist Hugh Muir noted how the show received great applause and no protest at the Edinburgh Festival:

> But the Barbican is different. London is different, with 11% of its population of 8 million having origins in Africa or the Caribbean. Different worldview, different tradition of activism; altogether a different dynamic. One of many factors: geography doomed Exhibit B.[23]

A reaction from the Black population in London was inevitable but in the fog of the psychosis the Barbican could not understand that. That reaction, when it arose, was formidable.

The major lesson of the campaign was that only street demonstrations had a real impact. Rational arguments were ignored or reinterpreted, and had we relied on those alone the show would have gone on. There is no reasoning with Whiteness. But even the protests never shook the Barbican out of its psychosis entirely; the cancellation fit perfectly within their dysfunctional worldview. At the final protest on opening night the protesters crowded the entrance to the Vaults at the Barbican, an enclosed space where the noise from the crowd was amplified. The noise and passion of the protesters 'terrified' the Barbican staff, to the point that they ordered an evacuation of the building, sending the performers into a state of panic, who thought perhaps there 'was an imminent threat that could put our lives at risk'.[24] The psychosis turned a non-violent crowd of people chanting, singing and playing drums into a dark mob ready to storm the building and destroy the venue along with anyone in it. In truth it was not the campaign that stopped *Exhibit B*, but the irrational fear of the Black masses, *tropical neurasthenia* in the twenty-first century.

The heritage sector in the West cannot be separated from the racial violence it is built upon. Whiteness radiates through the collections and through the assumptions that lie at the heart of how we understand the space of the museum. White is right to the point of absurdity. Greek antiquity is a source of fascination because, in the racist logic of Western thought, it is the basis of civilization. Egypt is either ignored or incorporated into the Mediterranean in order to erase the African origin of the knowledge that flowed into Greece. Remember, it is the White race that created knowledge, so history must be bent to fit that sur-reality. One of the longest-running controversies of the British Museum involves the Parthenon Marbles, which were removed by Lord Elgin in 1801. The Greeks have long argued that the 2,500-year-old treasures should be returned to their home country, but have had as much luck as the Nigerians. Just like the Benin Bronzes, the Marbles' presence in Britain's national museum remains a symbol of Britain's cultural vitality. As the warehouse of the world for ancient treasures Britain retains pride of place in global affairs. But arguing that Britain is the best custodian for another country's cultural artefacts is deeply delusional, perhaps best illustrated by the time when the museum tried to clean the treasures in the 1930s. The Marbles were originally painted in bright Egyptian blue, a nod to the African influence on Greek civilization.[25] But over time the paint flaked off and they returned to a dusky off-white colour due to their material. Ancient Greece is obsessed over for its 'Whiteness', in both ideology and presentation. In the minds of the curators the original colour of the friezes must have been pictured as brilliant white; surely this would be the colour chosen by the founders of civilization? They vigorously polished the Marbles to restore this supposed whiteness and in the process, which included using wire wool, irreparably damaged the ancient artefacts of which they had unilaterally declared themselves the rightful custodians. Breaking Ancient Greek objects in the pursuit of whiteness/Whiteness is peak psychosis; these delusions are at the heart of the heritage sector.

Once again, we cannot argue our way out of this insanity. Even if the museums wanted to return the objects, British law does not allow it. Moreover, the reason that former colonies do not always have the capacity to care for their own cultural heritage is due to lasting economic damage inflicted by the racial global system. As one small act of rebellion, I hope that the Edo Museum of West African Art accepts the British Museum's loan of the Benin Bronzes, and then simply refuses to return them. Although I wouldn't quite rule out a punitive expedition from Britain to see her stolen treasures returned.

The heritage sector depends on the mirage that we have moved beyond the racism that built its collections. It is the perfect example of the problems involved in the idea that we are now 'post-race'. In the supposedly modern world empire is in the past and institutions can drop their inherited guilt and its associated baggage. This is the most true (and utterly confounding) in the case of the royal family, who revel in colonial nostalgia while pretending to have remodelled themselves in the new age. The marriage of Prince Harry to Meghan Markle was meant to mark the modernization of the family, finally dragging it into the twenty-first century. Thankfully, as we will see, it turned out to be the perfect cautionary tale about the danger of falling into the delusions of a 'post-racial' society.

7

The Post-Racial Princess

Meghan Markle and Prince Harry's appearance on the *Oprah Show* in 2021 heralded the end of the fairy tale that began when they started dating in 2016. Watching Markle explain that the racism she had experienced from the press and the lack of support she received from the royal family caused her to experience suicidal thoughts while pregnant was a reminder that, no matter how high you climb, you are still Black. For many Black people in Britain it was the first time we had ever felt connected to her, because she narrated an experience that is all too common. As the dub poet Linton Kwesi Johnson put it, 'Inglan is a bitch',[1] and we know all too well that this place will mad you. The couple had been chased off the island by the remorseless tabloid press who turned Markle into a pantomime villain. They painted her as the stereotypical Black woman: the diva who was manipulating Harry to go against his family. This was particularly remarkable because, as far as I could tell, she tried to fly under the radar as much as possible. In the entire time, from flirtation to pregnancy, I can't recall anything Markle had to say at all, let alone something interesting or even slightly controversial. In the absence of anything real, a constant drip feed of negative behind-the-scenes stories were published, about Markle being mean to her staff or making her sister-in-law cry (although it turned out the opposite was true). Only a year after they were married, the couple became so exasperated with the press's treatment of Markle that Prince Harry released an official statement condemning the 'continual misrepresentations' of his wife.[2] Just six months later the couple announced they would be fleeing the country due to the venom they were receiving. That the spectacle ended so badly and so publically should come as no surprise. There is a greater possibility that the Queen really was a lizard than there was of Markle's marriage into that despicable family ever having a happy ending. But the speed at which it all came crashing down was alarming and demonstrates the extent to which the royal family and Blackness simply do not mix.

It was difficult for me not to say 'I told you so' (which is why I did say it, as often as possible) in the middle of the media storm, because I did not share in the delusions that saw their marriage as racial progress. In fact, the couple's divorce from the family was more of a teachable moment than their marriage, as it laid bare the realities of racism experienced even by those in high places. It also showed the fragility at the heart of the psychosis of Whiteness, sometimes in comic form. Hyperventilating about Meghan Markle became part of TV host Piers Morgan's public persona (and probably his personal time too). He led the hateful cheer squad, complaining about her supposed attitude and her disrespect for the Queen and the nation. When he was called out for his not-so-subtly racist rants by the Black weatherman Alex Beresford on *Good Morning Britain* he walked off the set and quit the show altogether. I guess the forecast for that day was 'stormy with a chance of White fragility'. As entertaining as it was to revel in such tantrums and as welcome as it was to have the media spotlight on racism rather than on delusions of racial progress, we shouldn't get too carried away with the spectacle of the couple's great escape.

The *Oprah* special was filmed on the Monticello estate of journalist Gayle King, and the couple remained keen to maintain the fairy-tale mirage. Although the pair have largely absented themselves from royal duties, Meghan has now ascended to the rarefied air of going by first name plus title, as in Meghan, the Duchess of Sussex™ (any more drama and we may end up calling her the 'princess formerly known as'). In the surroundings of a lush garden, Meghan described the racism she was subjected to by the British press, while rarely using the dreaded 'r word' (God forbid). The most memorable nugget from the interview was probably Oprah's open-mouthed horror when it was revealed that someone in the family had wondered what colour their baby would be, with Meghan assuming the family member hoped the baby would not be too dark. Perhaps the racism of the royal family was lost in transatlantic translation, because Oprah's alarm was entirely misplaced. Meghan is the only Black person in that family for a reason, and her father-in-law was a well-known bigot who was basically banned from public speaking because he couldn't be trusted not to offend people – I'd be more shocked if no one in that family had questioned the complexion of the children. In testament to the delusional nature of public discourse, much of the discussion following the interview focused on this supposed revelation and speculation abounded as to who it might have been. Once again racism was reduced to the overt expression of racial prejudice, rather than examining the larger institutional picture. This focus on racism only existing if someone uses a racial slur prompted the Society of Editors (of the British press) to condemn the couple for making accusations 'without evidence' and defending the press as 'certainly not racist', and with 'a proud history of calling out racism'.[3] It is absurd to present a blanket defence of something as diverse as the British press, an industry that includes everything from the odd left-wing newspaper to a whole host of right-wing tabloid rags. Some newspapers' only history of engaging with racism comes by way of promotiong it: supporting the Nazis, British fascists, racist politicians and taking deeply anti-immigration stances. But of course the British press as a whole is not racist.

While the anti-racist analysis sparked by the couple fleeing Britain was partial, it was infinitely more productive than the debacle surrounding the wedding. Meghan Markle's entry into the royal family sparked a wealth of press coverage and debates about the nature of racism in Britain. I saw first-hand how the press feasted on the marriage; I fielded calls for commentary from national as well as international news outlets. In fact, I first found out that Markle and Prince Harry were a couple when *Ebony magazine* in the US asked me to write a piece about the significance of the pair's relationship in

2016. The article responded to a piece in the *Daily Mail* in November 2016 that didn't even try to hide its racism, headlined: 'Harry's girl is (almost) straight outta Compton: Gang-scarred home of her mother revealed – so will he be dropping by for tea?'[4] All the stereotypes of Black urban poverty were rolled out to make it abundantly clear that Markle was alien to the privileged White life of the monarchy. The disturbing tone of press coverage led Prince Harry to release a statement condemning the 'racial undertones' of these stories.[5] But for all the negative treatment the relationship and Markle received, press coverage of the wedding was for the most part positive, framing the marriage as a mark of progressiveness in 'modern Britain'.[6]

In the run-up to the wedding I commented for a range of publications: *Guardian*, *The New York Times* and *Newsweek*, and I appeared on *Newsnight*, Channel 4, CNN, Canadian Television and Globo in Brazil. Sky News sent two different camera crews to talk to our Black Studies undergraduate students at Birmingham City University. The substance of all these discussions was essentially the same: asking to what extent the marriage improved race relations in Britain. The Monday after the wedding I found myself on *Good Morning Britain* debating with the writer Afua Hirsch – with whom I usually agree – about whether the 'Royal Wedding was a sign of Britain changing'. Hirsch was caught up in the representation politics of the event and its choir, its Black pastor and the feeling that they had brought Blackness to Westminster Abbey and the monarchy. I was busy celebrating Malcolm X's birthday at the time so all this was lost on me. They could have resurrected Martin Luther King to do the service, jumped the broom and danced the electric slide out of the church and it would still have been the Whitest of weddings. Hirsch argued that it was symbolically important for young Black people to see that the monarchy does not have to be exclusively White, precisely because the institution has such an important place in Britain's imagination of itself. Even the smallest change is seen as progress because it opens the door to a different discussion about race and identity. Hirsch was by no means the only Black commentator to find some hope in the new relationship.

In 2016, before marriage was on the table, the writer and socialite Lady Colin Campbell remarked on how unimaginable a royal having a relationship with a Black woman would have been twenty years ago, adding that 'the ethos of the age is acceptance and inclusiveness. The days when marriages were regarded as desirable only if people were of the same class and colour are gone.'[7] Black Entertainment Television (BET) heralded the relationship as a changing of the guard after the end of the Obama presidency, declaring that 'we may be leaving the White House, but we might be making our way into the royal castle'.[8] Symbolically, Obama's presidency and Markle's royalty are connected. They both provided visually different representation in roles that were previously bastions of Whiteness. But they also both show the limits that this kind of symbolic change represents. In the debate with Hirsh I referred to the notion that a Black princess would empower Black communities in Britain as nothing more than a dream, which earned me the accolade of 'party pooper' from host Piers Morgan. That is precisely the point of breaking down the delusions of the psychosis, to burst the fantasy balloons of progress and reveal the underlying racist fabric of society.[9]

Hailing a Black royal as a sign of a supposedly 'modern' Britain is in fact symbolic violence, part of a discourse designed to legitimize continued racial oppression by masking it. The idea that we have moved beyond race into a supposedly 'post-racial' world is one of the key delusions of the psychosis of Whiteness, gaslighting us into believing that the very White supremacy that continues to shape the modern world no longer exists.

POST-RACIAL DELUSIONS

The civil rights movement was based on the idea that gaining access to the system in order to reform it would deliver racial equality. Major victories were won in these endeavours: desegregation, voting rights, protections for African Americans and race relations legislation. The result is that the US now has some of the most progressive legislation in the world, including policies like affirmative action that are unimaginable in Britain. African Americans are also better represented in local, state and national government than Black minorities in any other Western country, and the election of Barack Obama was a testament to the foundation laid by the civil rights movement. Despite all these successes – in fact, the US civil rights movement may be one of the most successful in history at achieving its stated goals – it utterly failed to address the problem of racial inequality.

The March on Washington in 1963, immortalized by Martin Luther King's 'I Have a Dream' speech, was not only against segregation, but also for 'Jobs and Freedom'. Under the reign of the first Black president the unemployment rate of African Americans remained significantly higher than the average, while the proportion of Black people in poverty stayed at almost two and a half times higher than the rate of White Americans. In an astounding demonstration of racism and poverty in the US, half of all African Americans with jobs in New York City work in fast-food restaurants. Even when Black people have work it does not pay properly, a situation that contributed to the massive increase in food-bank usage of African Americans under the Obama administration.[10] In a far less well-remembered speech in 1968, King warned about the evils of underemployment, of people working 'full-time jobs for part-time wages'. The situation for African Americans was so bleak that he labelled it an economic depression, with millions on wages 'so inadequate that they cannot even begin to function in the mainstream of the economic life of the nation'.[11] This is still true today. A burgeoning Black middle and political class does not equal racial progress. CRT emerged out of the recognition of the failure to rebalance the scales, and the late Derick Bell offered the following warning about the illusions of civil rights gains: 'What we designate as "racial progress" is not a solution to that problem. It is a regeneration of the problem in a particularly perverse form.'[12]

Obama's reign in the US, like Markle's addition to the royal family, was symbolic. However, Obama was the leader of the country and had some power, however limited, to address racial inequality. The hope that he would make change was not completely delusional, even if it was entirely misguided. He certainly *could* have done more, even if eradicating racism is beyond the brief of the presidency. In the case of Markle, however, there was no avenue for her as a member of the royal family to make any substantive change to racism in Britain. Even the monarch only has symbolic power; the head of state in image only, rolled out to keep up the mystique of the British Crown.

The ceremonial nature of the former monarch's role was on full display towards the end of 2019. Since the British general election in 2017, following the Brexit vote, Parliament was deadlocked in disagreement over how the UK would leave the European Union. Prime Minister Theresa May resigned and Boris Johnson replaced her. Johnson was one of the faces of the Vote Leave campaign and promised to bulldoze Brexit through. One of the actions he took was to prorogue (suspend) Parliament for what he intended to be one month to halt opposition party schemes against his plans. Parliament was subsequently reopened two weeks later, after the Supreme Court found Johnson's actions to be illegal. But in order to suspend Parliament he had to get the Queen to use her powers of prerogative.[13] It should be alarming, in a democracy, that the monarch has the power to close Parliament, but her role was entirely ritualistic. The government instructed the Queen to suspend Parliament, and she had no choice but to act. In the end it was the courts who decided that his action was unlawful and reinstated the chamber. Her Royal Highness had no role in deciding upon the action or whether it was appropriate. As the Duchess of Sussex, Meghan Markle did not even have that ceremonial power, let alone access to any of the levers of power necessary to make substantive change.

Undoubtedly, having a prominent symbolic position and celebrity status gave Markle more power than the average subject of the Crown. Celebrity and fame are powerful forces in society and can mobilize publics and put pressure on institutions and the government to act. But this should not be conflated with direct access to power that can reshape people's lives. If the first Black president was not able (or willing) to attempt meaningful change then it was always a fantasy to expect the Duchess of Sussex to have that power. It is absurd to look to any member of the monarchy to make significant transformation of the nation. But the idea that the monarchy has actual power is dangerously alive, even in Britain. One of the hosts that replaced Piers Morgan on *Good Morning Britain* was the far duller Richard Madeley. It's tempting to see Morgan as the rabid Wolf and Madelely as the liberal Fox, but the former has no bite and the latter possesses zero cunning. I prefer my racism to be out in the open and Morgan certainly excels in that regard. On the other hand, Madelely is your bog-standard, passive aggressive, mediocre White man who thinks he is being clever when he really is not. The show itself is almost designed as a showcase for the psychosis of Whiteness and they regularly talk about race, but only in the most dramatized manner. In 2021, I found myself talking to Madeley about students at Oxford University who had voted to remove a picture of the Queen from their common room. That the students had a picture of the Queen on the wall in the first place was more of a news story than that they had finally decided to take it down. But through the distortions of the psychosis this became a feeding frenzy for the right-wing press, with the *Daily Mail* reporting that the 'Education secretary slams "absurd" cancelling of the Queen'.[14] One thing that I appreciate about shows like *GMB* is that there is no liberal censoring, so you can make it as plain as you can handle. I calmly explained that the 'Queen is the number one symbol of White supremacy in the world', so I understood why they took her picture down. Madelely's response was so delusional that I was speechless for a moment. He uttered the following defence of Her Majesty, confusedly wondering, 'How can that make any sense when this queen presided over the end of what was left of empire through the Commonwealth? She's dismantled the colonies, she's presided over their destruction.'[15] Even if we believed that Britain benevolently destroyed the empire to usher in a new era of racial equality (lol), the Queen would have been a passenger, a mere symbol who held no power. If the government had decided to put down the liberation movements with a nuclear African winter, she would have announced the policy in her Queen's speech on Christmas Day without skipping a beat and gone back to enjoying her roasted pheasant (or whatever it is that the aristocracy eat).

Making this full-throated defence of Her Majesty even more delusional, the royal family is one of the most direct links to the colonial era today and contains all the trappings of elitism, patriarchy and racism. The image of Britannia ruling the waves is wrapped in the majesty of royalty. That an almost exclusively White family, who have only very recently included any diversity in the form of Markle, can stand as a representation of the British nation should tell us everything we need to know about the power of the symbol of royalty. Their Whiteness is not a coincidence, it is the point. That is why it was still remarkable in the twenty-first century that a prominent member of the royal family married someone of mixed heritage. Far from Markle's inclusion changing the symbol, she is the exception that proves the rule. The continued press hatred she has been subject to is evidence of unease at her presence. Even after the couple withdrew from royal duties they remain at the centre of the media circus. Although, with Meghan's podcast, the Netflix series and Harry's all-too-revealing memoir, they do seem determined to stay in the spotlight.

Markle is the perfect example of the delusions of the 'post-racial' moment. She married into one of the most powerful symbols of Whiteness and colonial nostalgia, which underpins contemporary manifestations of racism. Her addition to the Windsor family photo did not change the role of the monarchy, nor its symbolic violence towards descendants of the former colonies, either at home or abroad. In fact, it is more likely that, just as in the case of Obama, the plan was to use Meghan to make new connections between the racist institution she represents and those Black and Brown people who are its victims. The only positive action that the royal family could take in regards to racial inequality would be to abolish itself. If having a Black face in the Whitest of institutions makes Black people feel more connected to the monarchy, then this is the worst possible outcome of Markle's inclusion in the family.

The sad reality is that racial equality in Britain is stagnating rather than improving. Racial disparities across all areas of social life continue, including police brutality and abuses of power, steep economic differences, health inequalities and unemployment.[16] And just as the structural problems continue, the past few years have also marked an increase in overt racism. Speaking in a generally positive piece about the wedding, the historian Ted Powell commented that it is 'difficult to overstate' the importance of a 'mixed-race' addition to the royal family. He continued that it was 'hugely positive for Britain, particularly in the wake of Brexit, the controversies of immigration policy and the Windrush scandal'.[17] The Vote Leave campaign has been credited with a rise in racist hate crimes.[18] The *Windrush* scandal was caused by the government's 'hostile environment' policy towards illegal immigrants, which has also affected countless migrants from the former colonies who migrated legally but had no documents to prove it.[19] People who have been living in the country for decades are suddenly subject to deportation and have lost their jobs because they have no proof of their legal status. It is no exaggeration to say that the current government is pursuing one of the most overtly racist policy agendas the nation has experienced in decades. The election of Boris Johnson to prime minister in 2019, with his history of calling Black children 'piccaninnies' with 'watermelon smiles' and comparing Muslim women wearing the veil to 'letterboxes', only emphasized the point.[20] There is a different, more aggressive feel to the racism that we are experiencing in the current moment. The notion that this context is why we should be thankful for Markle becoming a royal is exactly what Bell had in mind when he warned us about what we might designate as racial progress. Celebrating a Black princess may make us feel better, but it does not change any of the realities of structural racism, Brexit, the *Windrush* scandal, or the marked decline in public discourse. It is an illusion, worth only as much as a mirage on the horizon of a desert. By placing faith in an empty symbol, we take our focus off addressing the real problems of racism, which are as deep-seated as ever.

INTERSECTIONAL FAILURES

To understand why the progress represented by Prince Harry's marriage was a mirage, we need to consider the concept of 'intersectional failure'. Kimberlé Crenshaw, who coined the term 'intersectionality', uses it to refer to those moments when one form of inequality overrides the intersection with another, in ways that typically work against Black women.[21] Speaking at the Women of the World Festival in London in 2016, Crenshaw gave the example of the Black Lives Matter movement's marginalization of the women who have suffered violence at the hands of the police. Anyone who has paid attention to the movement can recall names like Mike Brown, Tamir Rice and Eric Garner. Rekia Boyd, Shantel Davis and Shelley Frey are less familiar. While it is true that Black men are killed at higher rates than women, Black women are far more likely to be subjected to such violence than their White female counterparts.[22] Crenshaw started the #SayHerName campaign in order to bring light to these cases, but has spoken about being shouted down on Black Lives Matter protests and how the mothers of the female victims have been pushed to the outer margins by the campaign.[23] Police violence is seen as a racial issue, not a gendered one, and therefore the focus is on the male victims. Black men as victims of state violence in the public sphere fits the narrative of the assault on Black men, who have been represented as savages in need of control since the enslavement of Africans. To understand the violence against Black women, who have often suffered in the private sphere, demands a different set of analyses. Intersectional failure is an inability to analyse through a lens that includes both race and gender, and the result is that Black women are marginalized from the discourse and from the struggle. Post-racial delusions about the royal wedding are also an example of such a failure.

The premise that the royal wedding was positive was based solely through a lens of race. Markle is Black and therefore changed the face of the family, representing the diversity of supposedly modern Britain.

What is entirely missing from this notion is gender. The princess narrative is deeply problematic from a gendered perspective, as are fairy tales about the shining prince opening their heart and kingdom to their true love. This idea becomes even more absurd when we consider the family she married into. The royal family is a deeply patriarchal institution in terms of structure, succession and presentation. In Prince Harry's statement condemning the press, a major theme was how he had seen them destroy the life of his mother, Princess Diana, who died in a car crash while being chased by the paparazzi. There are particular expectations of a royal wife and the British press will savage anyone who departs from these. If we saw past the post-racial fantasy of Markle, we would query a financially independent, outspoken and successful woman being subscribed into a role that confined her in gendered traditionalism. The idea that any woman marrying a man represents some kind of achievement sets back progressive notions of gender by decades.

Crenshaw's work on intersectionality emerged from CRT and Black feminist thought. An immovable part of the concept is that to see the world from the position of Black women offers unique insights due to their intersectional location. Intersectionality is a way of articulating how the experience of those at the junction illuminates social structures and relationships, piercing through the psychosis of Whiteness. Therefore the marginalization of Black women is particularly problematic because it disallows knowledge from the very standpoint that *can* reveal the myriad ways that institutions reproduce exclusionary practice.

The appalling *Daily Mail* article of November 2016 located her as alien not only because of her race but also her nationality. Aversion to foreigners joining the royal family aside, her American heritage is important to the discussion of race. Britain is terrible at recognizing its own racist history and racist present. There has been no real reckoning with the importance of racism to the nation. The situation in the US with regards to racial inequality is no better for this acknowledgement, but there is a robust public discourse about racism there. So robust that Britain often prefers to talk about racism through

America to distance herself from the problem. Britain's Black History Month is full of Martin Luther King and the US civil rights movement, and when the school curriculum does address slavery it focuses on the US rather Britain's own role in the Caribbean. While Britain has largely ignored decades of campaigning around police violence, George Floyd's murder thousands of miles away finally brought mainstream awareness of the problem. Accepting an African American into the royal family was far easier than doing the same for someone who was Black British.

The wedding itself was a prime example of this and Hirsh, in our debate on morning television, celebrated seeing images of Blackness in the last place we would ever expect to see them. But the pastor was African American, and the gospel choir sang 'Stand by Me', which has been used as an anthem of the US civil rights movement. Embracing African-American Blackness is far easier because the general public is more used to seeing these kinds of representations from Hollywood and it allows them to distance themselves from race issues by assigning them to the US. It is interesting to consider how representations of Black populations in Britain would have been received. It is also true that Markle's connection to the issues of race in the UK will not be the same as someone who grew up experiencing racism on these shores.

The most obvious way that Markle offers limited representation for Black women is via her skin tone. Colourism has always been a major issue, and having lighter skin can mean benefitting from a greater proximity to Whiteness.[24] No Black person escapes racism, but being light-skinned offers privileges: from being able to 'pass' for White to preferential treatment in the employment market and in other areas of social life. This remains the case today in terms of access to the public sphere – the Caribbean is a perfect example of a pigment-ocracy, where access to top jobs and politics is still eased by having lighter skin – and in relation to widespread standards of beauty.[25] Light skin is fetishized across the world, while dark skin, full lips and Afro hair remain demonized.[26] It is difficult to maintain the claim that Markle represents either Black women or an entirely new representation within the monarchy when phenotypically she is so distant from a Black aesthetic. The average young Black girl will not look at pictures of Meghan and see herself. This is in no way an argument that because she is light-skinned Markle is less Black. Blackness is defined by politics and not by skin tone. Some of the most radical Black activists have been light-skinned and some of the worst reactionaries have been dark in colour. But if the issue is about representation, a large part of that is visual, and Markle looks like an acceptable version of the light-skinned Black womanhood that is now commonplace in mainstream discourse. The general lack of consideration of Markle's mixed heritage in the rush to look for a progressive symbol is also noteworthy.

We should avoid solidifying the category of mixed-race into some kind of absolute. The majority of those descended from the enslaved are mixed to some extent. Designating someone as mixed-race because they have one White parent reifies the idea of race itself: that the mixing of two different heritages creates something new, different and remarkable. It also directly follows racial definitions from British slave plantations. The child of a slave owner and an enslaved African was designated a *mulatto*, from the word 'mule'. The reason why the word mule was used is a good example of how the psychosis of Whiteness prevented rational thought: in the eighteenth century, eminent philosophers, including Voltaire, believed that those of mixed heritage were infertile because two different species had mated, similar to the offspring of a horse and a donkey.[27] If only that had really been the case, perhaps the enslavers would have not raped Black women on an industrial scale because it would have meant they could not breed subsequent generations of the enslaved. Mixed-heritage children were considered Black, but not in entirely the same way as those without mixed parentage. Sometimes they were extended privileges, especially if they were children of the enslavers. The racial classification of the *children* of those of mixed heritage was determined by their non-mixed-heritage parent. If the other parent was Black, the children were classified as *sambos* and treated like the rest of the enslaved. Whereas, if the other parent was White, the children would be called *quadroons* and able to pass for White.[28] In thinking about the difference that Markle's inclusion does *not* make to the royal family, it is worth bearing in mind that Harry and Meghan's children would be considered White (or White-passing), according to the racial logic of enslavement. The so-called 'one drop rule' that classified those with a hint of African blood as Black does not apply in this context. Given the history of racial mixing and classification in Britain and her status within an elite institution, if Markle had stayed silent within the family she herself would simply have passed for White. In fact, following the couple's public departure from Britain she admitted that she only 'understood what it was like to be treated like a Black woman' when she started dating Prince Harry.[29] Ironically it was her entry into that terrible family that made her, and us, perceive her as Black, leading to her inevitable departure.

Highlighting a mixed relationship as progress is also an intersectional failure. In societies with mixed populations it should not come as a surprise that there are mixed relationships. Britain has long-standing mixed-heritage populations, particularly in port cities like Liverpool and Bristol, where those from Africa and the Caribbean working at sea would visit and settle. Following the end of the First World War in 1918 both cities also saw an increase in Black immigration from those who had served in the military. 2019 marked the hundredth anniversary of race riots in port cities, due in part to accusations of Black men having been 'stealing' White women.[30] Today, the fastest-growing ethnic group in Britain is those of mixed heritage. But neither the long history of mixed-heritage people in Britain, nor the significant population in the present reveal anything about the nature of racism. Brazil is often celebrated as a racial democracy because of its large mixed heritage, or *mestizo*, population. More than half of Brazil's population is of African descent, meaning that there are more Black people in Brazil than in any African country except Nigeria. But the reality is that Brazil is one of the most racially unequal societies in the world, and colourism and Whiteness shaped its political and economic system.[31] The only thing mixed relationships tell us is that when people live with different groups, colour is not a barrier to forming relationships. These interpersonal decisions are not indicative of changes to structural racism. Racism does not need strict boundaries or the prohibition of racial mixing in order to flourish. The version of racial oppression currently operating has developed beyond these old codes.

If we broke down any individual's relationship to society, no one would be a perfect representative of a Black feminist standpoint. That is precisely the problem with the politics of representation, it is not something that any individual is capable of. Markle is a Black woman, but it would be a grave mistake to argue that she can be a vehicle to understand the world through the collective position of Black *women*. As a Black woman Markle will receive certain treatment, but her experience (like that of any other individual) can never represent the position of all Black women. It is delusional to expect her to do so.

REPRESENTING THE ~~EMPIRE~~ COMMONWEALTH

One of the most troubling aspects that emerged from Meghan's *Oprah* interview was her sadness that the couple never fulfilled their ambition to build better relationships with the Commonwealth countries. The Commonwealth is a collection of fifty-four nations and has a combined population of over two billion people. All but two nations are united by one common feature of their history: once being part of the British empire. The largest empire the world has ever known had multiple ways of coordinating its possessions. At the 1926 Imperial Conference (a gathering of the prime ministers of the self-governing colonies of the British empire), the Dominions pledged allegiance to the British Crown, and were thereafter collectively known as the Commonwealth. Demonstrating the racism at the heart of empire, the semi-autonomous Dominions comprised Canada, Australia, New Zealand, Ireland, New Foundland, India and South Africa. All were White-majority countries, apart from the latter two, but India was represented by two White men (the Earl of Birkenhead, who was

Secretary of State for the colony, and his deputy, the Earl of Winterton) and South Africa explicitly represented the White minority's interests. Following the independence of several of the colonies in the post-war period, the modern Commonwealth was born, and the majority of former colonial possessions joined the club. We are assured that each member of the Commonwealth has 'equal' standing, but its original head was King George VI and since his death it has been Queen Elizabeth II and is now King Charles III, at the specific request of the former queen.[32]

Nobody has a clear idea of what the Commonwealth does, or of what the allure to the member nations is. Joining it is voluntary and it makes general commitments to trade and vague promises about human rights. In the run-up to Brexit there was an as-yet (and likely forever) unfulfilled suggestion that trade to the Commonwealth would be boosted.[33] The truth is that the only nation that benefits from the organization is the former mother country. The Commonwealth is a reminder of the once-great empire, a pretence that Britain still has some influence over the world. The global club is symbolic of Britain's lost place in the world; yet another hallucination steeped in the psychosis of Whiteness. On the one hand, the nation's desperation to retain a body that is a symbol of its own decline is comic. But on the other, the fact that nations remain in the Commonwealth demonstrates the remaining power of empire. Even Mozambique and Rwanda have joined, with no direct imperial connection to Britain, but both aimed to gain closer unity with East African countries (Kenya, Zimbabwe and Tanzania) that were British colonies. The fact that, in order to foster unity with other African countries, Mozambique and Rwanda were prepared to join the remnants of the British empire is testament to the lasting legacy of colonialism: and shows that although the political rule of imperialism was dismantled, economic colonialism remains deeply entrenched. The Commonwealth includes some of the poorest countries in the world, whose economies have been decimated and remain controlled by Western powers. Membership of the Commonwealth is voluntary and largely meaningless, but the necessity to feel part of the imperial club is due to the economic pull of the West in general and Britain in particular. The empire may have crumbled, but Britain still has a strong neo-colonial economic role that maintains the poverty of its former colonies. Whatever benefit there may be in the former colonies coming together, the fact that they do so in the shadow of the empire, led by the British monarch, should tell us all we need to know about the deeply problematic (and sycophantic) nature of the Commonwealth. By stressing its mission to strengthen 'human rights' in member states the Commonwealth also allows Britain to maintain the supposed 'civilizing' mission that was at the heart of empire.

In truth, the Commonwealth is little more than a rebranding of the old British empire, a more palatable version of global racism for the modern world. The Commonwealth Games are the perfect example of how the Commonwealth is simply PR. The Games revel in being 'inspired by the diversity and dynamism of the Commonwealth itself ... and its enduring commitment to human rights, democracy and the rule of law'.[34] How noble it is for the federation to take up the White man's burden through sport. The Commonwealth Games Federation has written historical delusions into their constitution, which states that 'the first flagship Commonwealth Games was held in 1930'.[35] Of course, this is untrue; the Commonwealth Games was not used as the title of the event until 1978. At their founding in 1930 they were called the British Empire Games, which is what they remain in all but name.

Birmingham, my hometown, hosted the 2022 games, which is somewhat ironic, given that most of the city's people are descended from colonial immigrants. I'll admit to being happy at the announcement at first, but only because we were promised better transport links and even had the prospect of a tram dangled before us. As it turned out, there was no tram and an unsightly (but useful) overpass was demolished to prettify the area where the games were to be held. The Alexandra Stadium for athletics is in Perry Barr, one of the most deprived and 'diverse' areas of the country, one that has been all but abandoned over the last couple of decades. Birmingham City University, my own employer, evacuated to the city centre in 2016, leaving a crater in the local economy. The blight of such inner-city areas is only amplified by massive investment in the city centre that has seen billions of pounds poured into it while the rest of Birmingham is left to rot. The old campus site could not find any investors and sat vacant for years until the Commonwealth Games stepped in and made it the site of a 500 million-pound development to create an athletes' village. But once Covid struck, the council scrapped works already in progress due to delays. Housing was eventually built on the site but rather than the family dwellings needed for the area it became flats needed for the Games. The fact that it took a colonial institution to bring any investment into a deprived area filled with children of the empire tells us all we need about modern race relations. The lustre of the Games being held in the city quickly wore off thanks to the upheaval caused by the building projects and the appointment of a board for the Birmingham Games on which nineteen out of the twenty members were White.[36] It was difficult to miss the historical symmetry of a white elephant infrastructure project being forced on a 'diverse' population by an imperial institution dominated by a collection of White do-gooders.

The existence of the Commonwealth is symbolic violence. It revels in the imperial history that has impoverished the former colonies to the point of continued subjugation. It is a throwback to an openly racist past and perpetuates a structurally racist present, just like the royal family. But, as I have already mentioned, one of Meghan's regrets in stepping back from royal duties was that she and Harry were stripped of the roles as president and vice-president of the Commonwealth Trust, which supports young people across the globe. In her *Oprah* interview she recognized how important the Commonwealth is to the monarchy and that as a mixed-race person she felt a responsibility to its 2.4 billion mostly Black and Brown citizens, explaining that 'growing up, as a woman of colour, as a little girl of colour, I know how important representation is; I know how you want to see someone who looks like you in certain positions'.[37] Imagine the dystopian reality where the monarchy embraced the Black princess and used her as the modern face of their imperial institution. During the couple's honeymoon period in the family there were stories given out in the press that they were thinking about moving to 'Africa' to bolster these links. Yes, 'Africa' – the stories were not more specific.[38] Thankfully, the psychosis of Whiteness stirred the press into the frenzy that made the couple flee their royal duties before that happened, because that is what it took to save us from them. Once they departed the family was left with Will and Kate to represent the brand and they could not have done a better job. When the future king and his wife toured the Caribbean in 2022 they thought it was a good idea to wholeheartedly embrace colonial nostalgia. The lowlights included recreating a photo shoot of Will's grandparents from the 1960s, waving from the back of a Land Rover and being snapped greeting smiling local children through a chain-link fence.[39] The pair were so stiff it was difficult to tell from the pictures of their visit to Madame Tussauds whether they were visiting or the actual exhibits. It was as if they were trying to be the opposite of relatable Harry and Meghan. The tour was so disastrous that it led to a number of the former colonies rethinking keeping the British monarch as the head of state and their membership in the Commonwealth.[40] But Will and Kate are the perfect figures to represent the reality of the monarchy, a relic that is cherished because it is evokes fuzzy feelings of colonial nostalgia. The anger that the tour stirred up is exactly what that terrible institution needs. The Commonwealth has no place in an anti-racist world and if Will and Kate's ambassadorship hastens its demise then let's hope they do a world tour soon.

Queen Elizabeth's death has (hopefully) hastened the decline of the Commonwealth and might cause former colonies to cut ties with Britain. The Queen was hugely popular for many in the former empire because they had been raised to revere her. I don't think I have ever met anyone who loved the Queen more than my Jamaican grandma. Countries like Jamaica were already considering cutting ties with the royals and the Queen's death may mark the 'end of an era'.[41] Earlier in the year some Caribbean nations questioned the leadership of the Commonwealth transferring to King Charles on his succession to the throne, with the Finance Minister of St Vincent and Grenadines, Camillo Michael Gonsalves, arguing that the royal link 'perpetuates some of the very unfortunate history of the Commonwealth'.[42] Unfortunately, the Queen's death will not have the effect of shaking those on the British Isles out of their delirium. Her reign went on for so long that people became familiar with her and she became a dependable fixture in their lives, so much so that people deluded themselves into believing they actually knew her. The collective grief that was shed when she passed was bemusing to witness. This woman was so far removed from common people that she wore gloves if she was ever greeting the masses. She never made waves, dutifully announcing whichever dastardly policy the government of the day were pursuing. She was Queen for my entire life and I cannot remember one single interesting thing that she ever muttered. We did not know her at all, we simply got used to her presence, the symbol. For many Black people in Britain she symbolized the racism that we had to deal with on a daily basis, especially because the fascists draped themselves in the Union Jack and embraced the Queen as their own. In my segregated neighbourhood I saw more flags in solidarity with Palestine than I did British ones flying during the nauseating celebrations of her seventy years on the throne. The reactions in my neighbourhood to her death were in such stark contrast to what was happening in so-called mainstream society that it truly felt like living in a foreign country. The media was wall-to-wall with positive coverage of the Queen and her legacy, to the point that it felt like Soviet-style propaganda. I got requests for comment on her colonial legacy from at least twenty journalists and they were all based outside the UK. I can think of no better example of the psychosis than people waiting in a queue for more than twenty-four hours[43] to walk past a likely empty coffin of someone they had never met and made no substantive difference to their lives. But that is the power of the symbol, through the delirium, the Queen became a valiant leader, the Britannia who ruled the waves in honour of the great nation.

Post-racialism is an essential feature of the psychosis of Whiteness; it addresses none of the issues of structural racism, and holds up cosmetic alterations of representation as signs of progress. In doing so, society fails to understand the nature of the problem or mobilize appropriate resources to tackle racial injustice. Celebrating Meghan's inclusion into the royal family is the perfect example of a post-racial delusion, illustrating how poorly the nation understands racism, and of the power of the desire to live in a fantasy instead of addressing the ongoing issues. Racism is deeply entrenched in Britain and the monarchy and its symbolic image are key vehicles for maintaining nationalisms based on nostalgia for empire. No addition to the royal family could fundamentally change the institution's complicity in maintaining racial inequality. Seeing Meghan's inclusion within the family as progress in race relations was a hallucination. Rather than representing a radically new development in supposedly modern Britain, the marriage was perfectly explicable in the context of the racist status quo. If we are serious about fighting racism, we should bury any delusions that Meghan bore any relationship to our struggle.

The promise of the Black princess was always tokenistic. The notion that Black people breaking through glass ceilings into the halls of presumed power represents progress is a key delusion of the psychosis of Whiteness. Black managers, CEOs and even presidents do not alter the underlying structure of racism. If we are to overcome racial oppression we urgently need to realize that diversity and anti-racism are different projects. There are certainly overlaps, and as a Black professor I do everything I can to bring more Black people into the institution. But I also recognize that dismantling racism requires more than just bringing in Black faces. Our presence is not resistance if we perpetuate the same set of deeply problematic practices. Unless we are radically overhauling the way that institutions work we are just putting Black faces into the PR brochures of White institutions.

But a particularly disturbing feature of the psychosis of Whiteness is how certain Black and Brown figures are used as tools to reinforce White supremacy. We must remember that the British empire was extraordinarily diverse and could not have functioned without an array of Black and Brown middle managers to control the colonies. This is no different today: some Black and Brown people are elevated into prominent positions and then carry out racist policies and circulate racist ideas, as we will discuss in the next chapter.

8

Black Skin, White Psychosis

The backlash that followed the Black Lives Matter summer of 2020 was swift, and in Britain it was led by the government itself. Prime Minister Boris Johnson laid the groundwork in a statement given in the aftermath of the BLM protests, reminding everyone that racism was an American problem, that George Floyd was killed 'thousands of miles away – in another country, under another jurisdiction'. After giving a token nod to the problems faced by Black communities in Britain, he praised the nation for making so much progress. He also took the time to stress, in the face of the overwhelmingly peaceful protests, that 'those who attack public property or the police – who injure the police officers who are trying to keep us all safe – those people will face the full force of the law'. Tellingly, he patted himself on the back for leading 'the most ethnically diverse government in the history of this country, with two of the four great offices of state held by a man and a woman of Indian origin'.[1] Diversity isn't always the enemy of racial progress, but there is probably no better example of the damage it can do than Johnson's government.

Priti Patel may have been the first racialized minority woman to occupy the role of Home Secretary, but she also thought the BLM protests were 'dreadful',[2] and defended the right of England football fans watching Euro 2020 to boo their own players for taking the knee, a protest which she dismissed as 'gesture politics'.[3] Patel hated BLM so much that she put forward a bill that might make those kinds of protests almost impossible, while also bringing in longer sentences for defacing statues.[4] Millions have been celebrating the supposed change in how we understand racism, brought about by the largest protests in British history, but Patel was going out of her way to make sure they could never happen again. Patel was also criticized for mass deportations which took place late at night, being seemingly happy to let migrants drown in the Mediterranean so they cannot reach Fortress Britain, and, if they do make it, deporting them to Rwanda.[5] There is a long history of anti-Black racism in South Asian communities and her focus on cracking down on BLM protest and much of her draconian immigration policy has targeted those of Caribbean and African descent. The delirium of Whiteness has produced disturbing results in India, where a combination of caste and White supremacy made Hitler's *Mein Kampf* a bestseller in 2014.[6] When groups of Black or Brown people adopt ideas of White supremacy, embracing their slightly elevated position on the racist ladder of value, it cannot be separated from the psychosis of Whiteness. But Patel has taken this a step further, by bringing in immigration legislation so restrictive that she had to admit her own parents might not have been able to settle in the country had she been in charge.[7] I would not be surprised if by the time this book is released Patel has deported herself: surely the only illogical endpoint of her delirium. When Johnson was forced to resign, Patel stepped down and was immediately replaced by the second South Asian female Home Secretary, Suella Braverman. The celebrations at seeing the back of Patel were short-lived, as Braverman somehow turned out to be even worse. She continued the policies of her predecessor and managed to reach even further lows. Despite the fact that Britain has some of the lowest numbers of asylum seekers in Europe, Braverman invoked the spirit of the far right when she told Parliament that 'the British people' would not tolerate the 'invasion' of immigrants crossing the Channel.[8] Her distain for asylum seekers was such that she ignored legal advice to book hotel rooms for the overflow of migrants in the Manston detention centre. The overcrowding led to dangerous conditions in the centre and led to criticism from Patel, who made it clear that even she was not that cold-hearted.[9]

In response to the challenge raised by BLM, the most Ethnically

Diverse Government of All Time™ doubled down on their strategy, appointing the institutional racism denier Tony Sewell to lead a commission examining racial disparities in July 2020. As you may recall from Chapter 5, Sewell has been making racist arguments about racial inequality for decades. For Sewell the problem isn't the system; it's the community, with the absentee fathers and weak-willed mothers leading their sons down a path of gang violence, drug dealing, prison and death. (Daughters are invisible.) Sewell can only get away with this blatant racism because he has skin in the game. He is one of the long line of Black commentators who have risen to prominence through being all too happy to put a Black face on White racist ideas. Although Sewell often likes to invoke the Jamaican national hero Marcus Garvey, claiming he is all about the Black community lifting itself up, the only similarity between the two is their dark skin.

Expectations for the report were low from the beginning, but I was surprised by just how terrible the eventual report turned out to be in March 2021. It denied that institutional racism existed, of course, blaming other factors, such as class, geography and cultural deficits, for the differing outcomes of minority groups. But the report also included a passage explaining that 'there is a new story about the Caribbean experience which speaks to the slave period not only being about profit and suffering, but about how culturally African people transformed themselves into a remodelled African/Britain'.[10] Glorifying one of the most brutal periods of human history was a new low, even for Sewell, but perhaps we should be thankful that we had the opportunity to transform ourselves through all the whippings and rapes. After the report's publication, scrambling to backtrack, Sewell invoked Bob Marley's 'Redemption Song' to claim that he had simply meant we should be proud that we did not lose our humanity in the horrific system,[11] not the first time he has contorted the legendary Marley to his own nefarious ends, once describing him as an 'alleged anti-colonialist'. Sewell must have either been drunk or hallucinating when he tried to explain Marley's line 'I have no education, I have inspiration. If I was educated I would be a damn fool' as a plea from the reggae star for some good old-fashioned colonial education.[12]

Marley was legendary because he rejected what the Rastafarians call the 'Babylon System' of education, and he thought that university was 'deceiving the people continually' and 'graduating thieves and murders'.[13] At least by mauling his words to such an extent Sewell inadvertently proved Marley right: one of the consequences of embracing the myths of Western so-called education is ending up a 'damn fool'.

Sewell was not the only Black person selected to dance to the government tune. In a group seemingly designed for a *Daily Mail* spread, only one of the ten people on the commission was White. The most ethnically diverse commission examining racism in British history declared that institutional racism did not exist. This was not accidental: it was the exact reason they were appointed. Diversity being used in the service of White supremacy is nothing new; it was a necessary feature of European empire building. The British empire subjected a quarter of the globe to the British crown. Genocide was not used to erase the natives, other than in settler colonies in the Americas and in Australasia. Instead they were ruled by remote control, with a small number of British bureaucrats inside the country in question, who relied heavily on local administrators. Without these collaborators, there is no way that the British or any other European empire could have succeeded. The British army in India, for example, was mostly made up of Indians subjugating their people for their White paymasters. The Amritsar Massacre of 1919, when British troops opened fire on an unarmed crowd and killed hundreds of civilians, is currently receiving some very late attention due to a strong Sikh presence in Britain. But many of the soldiers who slayed defenceless men, women and children were Sikhs in British uniform.[14] The same was true across the empire. The current crop of Black and Brown people promoting White supremacy are just following in the footsteps of the chiefs, administrators and soldiers who took a salary in the service of Western imperialism. The psychosis of Whiteness has never been reserved for those with White skin.

So profound is the conflict within those wanting to find success in White society that psychiatrist Franz Fanon dedicated his work *Black*

Skin, White Masks (1967) to understanding the phenomenon. He argued that the effects of colonialism were not just physical, but that they were also profoundly cultural and psychological, that by training the colonized to believe in White supremacy, it would break down their resistance. Fanon explained that 'after being a slave to the White man he enslaved himself. The Negro is in every sense of the word a victim of White civilisation.'[15] We were brainwashed to associate Blackness with immorality and savagery. As Malcolm X put it, White society 'taught you how to hate yourself, from the top of the head to the soles of your feet'.[16] For Fanon this hatred of Blackness created a 'neurotic orientation' that could be remedied in two different ways. If you accept that the 'Black man is the colour of the devil' then you lean into the stereotypes, becoming the inhuman terror keeping White people awake at night. On the US plantation this was the 'Bad Nigger', the hyper-masculine anti-hero who refused to be tamed. Think of the Hustler, Bad Bwoy, Gangsta, Thug, or of how the figure of the 'Pimp' is now revered in much of rap culture.[17] Psychosis is the only term that explains the celebration of a masculinity so toxic it glorifies violence and barbarity against Black men and women. I love hip-hop and grime, and am too old for drill, but so many of the lyrics and much of the imagery should come with a health warning. Spend too much time listening to stories of violence, drug dealing and sleeping with as many women as possible and you might actually come away believing that the 'iconic ghetto' really does define Blackness. The defence for the music highlights a much more serious problem: no matter how sordid the lyrics are, they represent a reality for some. Look at the murder rates in Black communities in the US, the Caribbean or even Britain. You are significantly more likely to be killed if you are Black, and it will probably be by a Black person *because* you are Black. Not in the sense that we are hunting each other in some kind of internal racist sport, but due to the fact that we have dehumanized ourselves to the point where Black life matters less even in our hands.[18] My father was a criminal defence solicitor and I will never forget him retelling his conversations with a 'Bad Man' from Jamaica. He had come to Britain and behaved as he would have done back home, executing two people on his travels. My father, always the political activist, asked him if he'd ever killed a White man; he couldn't even comprehend the idea. This is someone who had dropped countless Black bodies but could not even imagine taking a White life. Now, I am not advocating that we go out and take some Whitey scalps, but there is no point trying to dodge the uncomfortable reality that White supremacy has reached into our collective psyche this deeply.

If embracing the dangerous stereotype of Blackness is not to your taste, you can also take an alternative route when trying to embody anti-Blackness. Fanon explains that many have come to the realization that to 'order my life like that of a moral man, I simply am not a Negro'.[19] This is where the White mask comes in, the rejection of all things perceived to be Black to prove that you are not. I went through this delirium as an eleven-year-old. I knew Blackness was an important part of identity, so I denied that I was Black. I had only White friends, and embraced exclusively White culture, even the desire for White people's hair (although I'm glad to say this last one was short-lived). It felt like the only way to make sense of myself. If Black was bad but I was good, then I had to be White. Like converts to a religion, those who are trying to prove their Whiteness are always the most extreme. You may remember the song 'MMMbop', by the teen boyband Hanson. However, you probably don't remember that they had an album too, and at my lowest point I went into a record store and purchased it. My early teen years were not the easiest and I was routinely called names like Bounty Bar and Coconut, because both are brown on the outside and white on the inside. I used to hate both of those terms, but they were accurate. I was running away from my Blackness, trying to reach something I had been told was the ideal. My experience was not unique. Institutions remain dominated by Whiteness and there is a pressure to 'fit in', to prove you belong. For many, that means acting what we understand to be White. Importantly, this is not a conscious decision. People do not decide that they are going to abandon their roots. Society conditions us, bleaches us down to the soul. Fanon argued that before the Negritude movement, which embraced a positive conception of Blackness, 'the West Indian was a White man' because they had been so fully unmade by White supremacy.[20]

It is vital that we recognize that there is nothing 'White' about doing well at school, listening to certain music (though Hansen might be the exception), living in an area with lots of White people, or having White friends. Not every Black person is brought up in the hood, listening to hip-hop and dodging bullets. As discussed, the 'iconic ghetto' is itself part of the psychosis of Whiteness, so we must be careful how we define what is 'authentically' Black. At the same time, it is fair to point out self-hatred when we see it. Bleaching your skin is not a lifestyle choice, it is a dangerous result of embracing racist delusions. Similarly, if everything a Black person does is rooted in White culture, then it is right to question whether they have issues with their Blackness. This is nothing do with searching for some kind of cultural purity, but Blackness is a political identity meant to connect us so that we can overcome White supremacy, and we have to acknowledge that there are ways of being that run counter to the interests of Black communities.

HOUSE NEGROES, COONING AND TOMMING

When it comes to Black faces servicing White racism there are some important distinctions to be made. I rarely use the term 'sell-out', because it presumes that a person who was previously serving Black communities traded their politics for a few pieces of silver, although there certainly are instances where this is the case. My favourite hip-hop album is *Like Water for Chocolate* by Common, who used to be known as one of the most political and underground of artists. He went on to try and increase his record sales, working with Kanye West and doing movies, and the Black power vibes contained in my favourite album have since been replaced with a watered-down made-for-TV version of Black politics in his recent work. But it would be inaccurate to declare Kanye (or whatever he is going by now) as a sell-out. Aside from his one comment that 'George Bush doesn't care about Black people', he has always produced apolitical bubblegum music and was more interested in a mainstream audience than in any cause. Although I will admit that I didn't predict his recent turn to embracing Trump, hanging out with White supremacists and defending Hitler. Clarence Thomas was sworn into the US Supreme Court to replace the civil rights icon Thurgood Marshall and has spent the last two decades doing his very best to unravel all his predecessor's good work. But he is not a sell-out; he didn't buy in to the idea of Black liberation in the first place. I am not saying that figures like Thomas and Kanye are just out there living their best lives and are therefore beyond criticism. We can, indeed *must* criticize them, but it is important to be precise when we do so.

There are far too many Black people who have swallowed the lies of White supremacy and wholeheartedly support the racist political and economic system. Malcolm X explained this phenomenon when he drew a distinction between the house and field negroes on the plantation. He chastised those who worked in the house as being too close to the master, receiving lighter work and relative privilege due to their location. Malcolm argued that this proximity to the master and scraps from their table made the house negro cling to their elevated position. So deeply ingrained was this affection to their enslaver that 'if the master got sick, the house negro would say, "What's the matter, boss, we sick?" We sick! He identified himself with his master more than his master identified with himself.' Malcolm painted this picture of the house negro in stark contrast to the field negro, the masses who toiled on the plantation, caught the lash and felt the harshest brutality of slavery. Therefore, the field negro hated their enslaver with every part of their being, and

> when the house caught on fire, he didn't try and put it out; that field Negro prayed for a wind, for a breeze. When the master got sick, the field Negro prayed that he'd die. If someone come to the field Negro and said, 'Let's separate, let's run', he didn't say 'Where we going?' He'd say, 'Any place is better than here.'[21]

The field negro was the authentic Black position, because he or she understood the truth about the plantation: that the only solution was to get as far away from it as possible, rather than trying to reform it. Malcolm took this metaphor and applied it to his contemporary America, arguing that the same distinction was still in place, between those in the middle class with relative privilege compared to those in the ghetto. Just as on the plantation, the modern-day house negro wants to live near the master, to accept the scraps from the table and defend the racist system that keeps all Black people down. Listen to Malcolm's 'Message to the Grassroots' speech and he is clearly in disbelief at how any Black person can pledge allegiance to a country that hates them:

Imagine a Negro [saying] 'Our government'! I even heard one say 'our astronauts.' They won't even let him near the plant – and 'our astronauts'! 'Our Navy' – that's a Negro that's out of his mind. That's a Negro that's out of his mind.[22]

The house–field negro analogy is by no means perfect. Conditions in the house were often just as horrendous as those in the field, especially for Black women, who were in closer proximity to their enslaver and subject to sexual violence. But the power of the idea is that it emphasizes that, no matter what your relative privilege might be, you are still enslaved and subject to racism. This is where the anger towards those who pander to White supremacy comes from: they are going against all our interests.

Demonstrating the delusional nature of the current debate, there is an attempt to make the term 'house negro' a racial slur. I received abuse on social media and from right-wing journalists for defending the South Asian academic Aysha Khanom, who asked British commentator Calvin Robinson on Twitter, 'Does it not shame you that most people see you as a house negro?' After receiving complaints stoked up by the right-wing press, the Leeds Beckett University Centre for Race, Education and Decoloniality summarily dismissed Khanom, throwing her to the mercy of the baying mob. It is truly mind-boggling that a centre with 'Decolonial' in its title showed so blatant a disregard for such an important contribution to Black intellectual thought as the concept of the house and the field negro. The right-wing press went to the lengths of starring out 'house n****', as though it was interchangeable with nigger. (I'd given up the hope of a rational debate long ago, but the idea that terms created in the struggle for racial justice are racial slurs equivalent to those hurled at us when we were being hung from trees is not just absurd, but downright offensive.)

'House negro' speaks to the class dimensions in Black politics. If you can 'make it', then you can easily be blinded by the privileges of Whiteness that you have better access to. It should serve as a warning to all of us who have managed to achieve what Malcolm X called 'token integration'. There is no way (nor do I have any desire) to avoid the truth, that in terms of my location in society, I am a house negro. I earn more money than most people in the West and more than all but a tiny minority of the global population. I have been inoculated from the worst effects of racism due to my standing and relative economic privilege. I'm not even routinely stopped by the police. Because I have it better than most it would be easy for me to think that progress has been made, and that is exactly the stance that far too many in my position take. I have to work extra hard to fight off the delusions of the house negro mentality.

The concept of the field negro (who represents the masses) is helpful in this regard because Malcolm argues that the conditions they have to put up with should be the yardstick. Not the conditions in the house, but those suffered in the field. It should be obvious that little has changed for the mass of us when you realize that the Black male youth unemployment rate prior to the Covid-19 pandemic was double the rate of White young people's unemployment *after* the crisis devastated employment opportunities.[23] Not to mention the medieval conditions that many of those in the underdeveloped world face. By 2030, so-called sub-Saharan Africa will house 90 per cent of all those living in extreme poverty.[24] We don't need an audit of the state of the race, we need to accept that the race is in a state.

Just as important as diagnosing the pathology of the house negro mentality is the reality that, no matter how much money and prestige you have, you are still Black and therefore will experience racism. I may have it better than most, but the stress arising from working in one of the Whitest of institutions is sometimes unbearable. Since being promoted to professor it has only worsened. I am either treated as a potentially dangerous thug or as an uppity negro, depending on the situation. Malcolm X declared that the house negroes had 'lost their minds' if they thought they could ever truly be part of the American Dream. In many ways Malcolm is rejecting Dubois's state of 'double consciousness', that to be an 'American' and 'a Negro' is to be in conflict, with 'two souls, two thoughts, two unreconciled strivings; two warring ideals in one dark body, whose dogged strength alone keeps it from being torn asunder'.[25] The state of double consciousnesses only holds true if you believe that there can be a place for you in mainstream society. The house negro mentality arises from the constant attempts to reconcile the irreconcilable, leading to a delusional allegiance to a society that is against you. For Malcolm X the solution was simple: stop thinking of yourself as an American and that internal conflict melts away. You will never hear me describe myself as British. I am Black and *in* Britain and my commitment to this nation will never go any further than that. I am not burdened with the 'two warring ideals' and am free to try to overturn the status quo that is Britain.

'House negro' is a mechanism for identifying inauthentic Black identities based on their regressive politics. This is not a cultural criticism, but one that invalidates those with a house negro mentality from understanding the true nature of racism in society. There are many reasons that you may wrap yourself in the flag and find comfort in the delusions of Whiteness. More power to you if that is what you need to survive. But it does mean that you are incapable of understanding the problem and should keep your delusions out of any conversation about the solution. Remote interviews for television have opened a slice of our private lives up to the audience. I always sit in front of two full bookcases, in part to make sure I still have some privacy: the rest of the world does not need to see my personal life. I once found myself in discussion with Calvin Robinson, who regularly appears on TV arguing that racism doesn't exist. I could barely concentrate on whatever culture war we were engaged in because he was sitting in front of his Union Jack pillow with a picture of the Queen on the wall. House negro, please! Some people have no place in a serious conversation about racism. But that is precisely the reason that figures like Robinson have found such a lucrative niche in the media landscape.

In the recent past, minstrel shows were popular because they presented blacked-up actors and titillated White audiences by performing extreme versions of racial stereotypes. There weren't many roles for Black actors back then, so some would apply the boot polish, red lipstick and play the coon for the raucous crowd. Remember that not too long ago this was the only gig that the now beloved Lenny Henry could get on British television. Black commentators who are given airtime to make outrageously racist (and stupid) statements to rile the crowd into a frenzy is a modern version of cooning. My only reservation about appearing in the myriad so-called debates on mainstream television is that I am always a little uncomfortable about playing any role in a coon show. From 'Racism doesn't exist' to 'It's really all about culture', I've heard it all, even that my complaining about blackface in the twenty-first century was 'communism'. I don't try to convince those who are deeply gripped by the psychosis of Whiteness, but I aim to speak to the audience who are (usually) desperately seeking some rationality in the midst of the delirium. 'House negro' is a noun, but 'coon' should be used as a verb. It is an active decision to debase oneself by playing the (damn) fool to the gallery. The ~~Sewage~~ Sewell Report was an act of cooning on the part of Tony Sewell, as were his subsequent media performances. Being trapped in a house-negro mentality makes the allure of cooning seem more palatable, but these are two very different categories.

I should stress that it is not just the middle-class archetype who may be either a house negro or who coons. House negro is a classed position, and one of the only real differences between the plantation and today in terms of race relations is that there are more opportunities for people to leave the field for the relative comfort of the house. The reason we accuse rappers and sports stars of selling out is because they were often born in the field, but their success gave them keys to the house. It's easy to point the finger at those donning the cultural attire of the elite. The idea of the Coconut, the person who has Black skin but dons a White mask, and the house negro are distinct though often related positions. In fact, the house negro who is seen as culturally Black is more dangerous because they present with an aura of authenticity. The rapper Lil Wayne is a case in point: he may have started in the field, but rose firmly into the house, even taking the step of endorsing Donald Trump. He rose to prominence by cooning, presenting the hyper-masculine stereotype of the Black macho man that many White audiences wish to consume. Ever since Niggaz Wit Attitudes (N.W.A.) burst out of Compton, there has been a tried and tested blueprint for cooning your way into the house. Before you object too strongly, what else could you call Lil Wayne rapping the words 'I whip it like a slave', other than a coon show?

Although these pronouncements may sound like judgements, they are an indictment of the system rather than the individual. The realities of racism create the necessity of leaning into the delusions of the psychosis of Whiteness in order to be successful. It is no coincidence that the most successful rappers and RnB singers are those playing up to the stereotype of the gangsta or the hypersexualized vixen. These are the images that sell because they feed into the psychosis. I doubt that Lil Wayne or other rappers in his mould are intentionally cooning. They may genuinely believe that they are creating works of art. Understanding their roles as part of the psychosis of Whiteness removes the need to question their intentions; they simply cannot help themselves. It also explains why many in the field, who experience the brutalities of racism first-hand, embrace a house-negro mentality. It's comforting to believe you have the affection of the master, or in this case White society, or that you can share in the prestige of living in the Greatest Country in the World. We are in a more perilous place now than at any other time in history, because so many have been tricked into believing that we are making progress, that there is some substance behind the dreams we are being sold. Barack Obama became the poster child for these symbolic delusions when he became president in 2008 and in the process created a whole new category of Black identity.

THE WHITE HOUSE NEGRO

The prospect of a Black president seemed so preposterous in the run-up to the 2008 election that few people genuinely thought it would happen. We were not too far removed from Chris Rock declaring that the Republican retired army general Colin Powell had less chance of securing the 1996 vice presidential nomination than Rock did of winning an Olympic 'bronze in female gymnastics'. Forget being the president, Rock was certain that 'there will *never* be a Black vice-president', explaining that 'you know they say "never say never", well I'm saying never. There will never ever ever *ever* be a Black vice-president.'[26] When Barack Hussein Obama stood for election, I laughed at the idea over the dinner table. It seemed so ludicrous. So when it actually happened even the most seasoned Black radical activists got caught up in the moment. My mom, who is steeped in the Black Power movement, and who, along with my father, is the biggest reason for my politics, cried when he was inaugurated. The only time my mom chastizes me for anything I say publicly is when I criticize Obama because, even after his complete failure to put a dent in racism, she, like many others, is still holding out hope. That he has so much support is in large part due to novelty. Witnessing a Black president of the US is like seeing a unicorn in real life. That most of us were so blinded by the rise of Obama demonstrates the depths and impact of the psychosis. It distorted our thinking, even among those who should have known better, away from seeing what was, in retrospect, blindingly obvious. I never thought he would be elected, but I could see the damage that would be done if he was, all the way back in 2007. The rift between me and my mom over this has never really healed (especially because I keep picking at the scab). I took my cue from Tupac, who warned us from beyond the grave that 'although it seems heaven sent, we ain't ready to see a Black President'.[27]

The passing of legislation, the election of Black officials and the invites given to a few fortunate African Americans to join the middle class present the illusion of progress. After Obama's election 69 per cent of African Americans agreed that his presidency was 'the fulfil-ment of Martin Luther King's dream'.[28] The truth is that Obama was not, and never pretended to be, Black America's representative in the White House. From as early as 2004, in the speech that sparked his run for the presidency, he was clear that there was 'not a Black America and a White America and Latino America and Asian America – there's the United States of America'.[29] He followed through on this hallucination with a presidency bereft of policies to address racial inequality.

Obama played the aesthetics well, embracing hip-hop, Black celeb-rities, basketball, singing in churches and welcomed Black Lives Matter activists to the White House, but any substance was sorely lacking. Even at end of his presidency, when he had no excuse about trying to get re-elected, he couldn't even muster the bare minimum. Trump used his pulpit to pardon his friends and alleged co-conspirators. There were whispers that Obama might release the Black political prisoners still languishing in federal jail. But no, when the first Black president last left the White House there were still nine-teen Black radicals in federal prisons convicted of supposed crimes in the 1970s.[30] Worse still, when he did turn his attention to issues of racism, he managed to make matters worse.

Obama's response to the killing of Trayvon Martin was not to address any of the systematic problems of violence towards Black people, not to change any laws or insist on a civil rights prosecution against the child's killer ... but instead was to launch a mentoring programme. My Brother's Keeper (MBK) was created for Black boys with absent fathers, funded mostly by the private sector and with the full-throated support of the conservative right.[31] We can't even call this blaming the victim; Trayvon Martin was visiting his father when he was killed. Although MBK did nothing to address the issues behind Trayvon's killing, it drew widespread support because it fit the post-racial fantasy of the Obama presidency. It took an event rooted in systemic racism and drained all the significance of that racism out of it. The encounter was still presented in racial terms, just in a way pal-atable to maintaining the status quo, perpetuating the idea that race is only a barrier because of the culture of the oppressed. Single parent-hood, and in particular the failure of Black mothers to raise their male children, was mobilized as the explanation for the crisis of Black boys, which is a trope often used to demonize Black families.[32] This narra-tive of cultural deprivation fits the ethos of the American delusion that says, if some can make it, then it must be the fault of those left behind that they did not. The only indicator of racism that improved during Obama's reign was the Black unemployment rate, but even this was an empty stat, because in the same period food-stamp usage ballooned in Black communities.[33] What kind of employment leaves those in work unable to eat? But even after it was clear that Obama had failed to make any inroads into racial inequality, the essayist Ta-Nahesi Coates titled his book *We Were Eight Years in Power*, as if Obama's presidency were some sort of collective achievement for the African Americans he ignored and maligned.

I am not blaming Obama for his failure to address the problems of Black people. If he had promised us anything then he would never would have been elected. If he had tried to fight for any substantive reforms while in office he would probably be dead. Obama learned that the tightrope he was on could easily be cut when the Jeremiah Wright saga erupted on his campaign trail. Obama's former pastor was accused of delivering racist diatribes from his pulpit, and in response Obama showed his ruthless commitment to his mission and threw his friend under the bus, condemning the supposedly racist remarks and insisting that he, Obama, was a good negro who could be trusted. Racism in the United States tends to be more honest. The president's home is called the *White* House for a reason. The primary function of the president is to maintain the racist status quo, to both be defined by and feed the psychosis of Whiteness. Obama couldn't be a *Black* president and had no choice but to contort himself to fit into the role. Perhaps the low point of his presidency came in May 2016 when he visited Flint, Michigan at the height of the water crisis that led to a disproportionate number of Black families being poisoned by the water supply. The governor of Michigan was pretending that the water was fine while the residents had long stopped drinking the poison from their taps. When he arrived in the city the people were hopeful that surely Obama would signal hope and change. But those hopes were dashed when he toed the party line and even drank (well, wet his lips with) Flint water and declared it 'safe'; an indefensible act of cooning that should have shown us the nature of his presidency.

By the end of his reign many were jaded by the first Black president. But there were still plenty who had hope and a common refrain (one I even heard from my dad) was that once he was out of office, he would be able to use his platform in pursuit of Black liberation. Imagine Obama Unchained ripping off his shackles to settle the score and free us all from the plantation. Unfortunately, he has managed to be even more disappointing out of the White House than inside it. At least when he was president we could make excuses, but now we can all see through the emperor's new clothes and the truth of his naked ambition. He and Michelle started how they meant to go on, by immediately visiting billionaire Richard Branson's Caribbean island for some decadent relief. Since then they have settled into their lives as a celebrity power couple. In his role as wise old sage, Obama feels free to provide unrequested advice to activists about maintaining the racist status quo. At the end of 2020 he was criticized when he tried to lecture activists calling to 'defund the police', warning them that they might have 'snappy slogans', but these were bad politics as they risked alienating people.[34] It would be easy to write off Obama and his post-presidential celebrity and allow him to settle in as the Uncle (Tom) of the nation. But there is a deeper lesson to be learned from the case of Obama. He didn't sell out; he never made any promises. He isn't an Uncle Tom because he never pretended to represent the Black population. Credit to him for creating a whole new category of Black political identity: the White House negro, someone who danced, cooned, sang, shucked and jived all the way to the presidency.

UNCLE TOM LEADERS

We have seen many a Black leader who has led their people into the clutches of White supremacy. Africa and the Caribbean are full of them right now, a hand-picked elite who siphon off wealth for themselves and their Western paymasters. There are also those the West sent to lead us astray. Malcolm X described the Uncle Tom in this way:

> The slavemaster took Tom and dressed him well, and fed him well, and even gave him a little education – a little education; gave him a long coat and a top hat and made all the other slaves look up to him. Then he used Tom to control them. The same strategy that was used in those days is used today. He takes a Negro, a so-called Negro, and makes him prominent, builds him up, publicizes him, makes him a celebrity. And then he becomes a spokesman for Negroes.[35]

Importantly, the Uncle Tom is a figure distinct from the house negro and cooning is usually not a part of the repertoire. This is because an Uncle Tom is supposed to be able to lead the Black community down the wrong path. Uncle Toms can't be wearing a White mask or shucking and jiving their way through the culture wars, because no one would follow them. Caricatures like the right-wing media star Candace Owens, who delights in taking the most outrageously racist positions, are clickbait to a White audience, sending them into a tizzy. The Uncle Tom persona has to be credible enough for at least some Black people to fall for their charms. The person Malcolm X most frequently labelled a 'modern day Uncle Tom'[36] was none other than Martin Luther King, who no one could accuse of cooning. I'm sure Malcolm would have seen King as a house negro, with his relative privilege and strong belief that the United States could be redeemed, but he must have had enough of the field and rebellion in him to ignite the masses. Malcolm saw King as a Tom precisely because of this leadership, that he could lead Black Americans to march straight down the cul-de-sac of token integration. Malcolm X wasn't questioning King's Blackness, he was challenging how he used it to mislead the people. Uncle Tom is probably the most misused of all the terms which describe Black people who in some way collude with White racism because it is conflated with that of the Coconut or house negro, and with cooning, when it is a different and more dangerous position to be stuck in. A case in point may be none other than one of the most famous Black political leaders of the last hundred years, whose struggle against apartheid was an inspiration for the globe.

I stumped Piers Morgan on live TV by refusing to defend a Nelson Mandela statue in Trafalgar Square because he was a 'sell-out' and I wrote about the first Black South African president in my book on Black radicalism, *Back to Black*.[37] So it may not come as a surprise that the beloved figure turns up in this section of this book. Mandela was honest enough to admit that he sold out the revolutionary struggle in his own autobiography, where he explains that he unilaterally negotiated with the enemy and spent the last years of his incarceration under house arrest with his family.[38] I'm not sure that touring his comfortable family home would evoke the same emotions as the trauma tourism of travelling to his prison cell on Robben Island. I spent time in South Africa a few years after Apartheid and visited again twenty years later. Not even the psychosis of Whiteness should be able to prevent anyone from seeing how much of a failure the African National Congress (ANC)'s South Africa is. The Black poverty rate is over 50 per cent (compared to less than 1 per cent for Whites),[39] murders have risen to over 20,000 annually, and corrupt leaders and corporations are bleeding the country dry. Worse still, one of the most violent forms of the psychosis is the xenophobia that has gripped the nation. South Africa is the most prosperous country on the continent but its people are desperately poor. This paradox means that economic refugees from other parts of Africa travel to South Africa to find work, but are met with violent resentment from the locals. When a fifteen-year-old girl from the Democratic Republic of the Congo is hospitalized by her South African schoolmates because they didn't think she should have been eligible to run for class president then we should be able to see that the nation is firmly in the grip of the psychosis.[40] None of this is an accident. The post-Apartheid settlement was designed in the same image as the so-called decolonization on the rest of the continent. It was only a hallucination of Black political power while White domination of the economy has been maintained. Mandela was the piper who led the nation happily singing to its doom.

Mandela has a much better reputation than other Uncle Tom African leaders like Mobutu, who made no effort to hide his theft of billions from the Congo. Or Goodluck Jonathan in Nigeria, who engineered the looting of over one billion dollars from his country in a single transaction.[41] But Mandela was more successful at doing the master's bidding than the rest, because after he was elected in 1994 he was pivotal in cooling down the country most ripe for revolution on the continent. Due to the delusionary nature of White supremacy it seems that we need a White cartoon villain to organize against The Man. The Black Lives Matter summer of 2020 was sparked by images of the murderous cop in the nation presided over by the buffoonish Trump. In African countries, where the people dispensing White supremacy are as Black as those on the receiving end it can be more difficult to see the real problem. But South Africa was one of the few European settler colonies on the African continent and Apartheid created a system of racial segregation even more extreme than in the United States. Everyone could see the stark problem of racism and therefore the struggle to survive was defined as anti-White supremacy. The African National Congress made radical demands for the redistribution of land and wealth, and organizations like the Pan-African Congress Movement insisted on continental revolutionary links, with the liberation of Azania (South Africa) seen as a key step in the wider struggle for Africa. Had Azania erupted in revolution it would have spread quickly to Zimbabwe, which had a similar settler colonial history, and then across Africa. But Mandela made sure that the course of the nation and the continent was steered down the cul-de-sac it finds itself in today. It is a testament to the strength of the psychosis of Whiteness that Mandela, the continent's ultimate sell-out, remains extremely popular. If the South Africa of Mandela's legacy is a hell for the masses, the Black population, it is a perfect illustration of the psychosis of Whiteness in its purest form. White people there inhabit a different world, where they contort themselves to be comfortable in their privilege. When I visited South Africa in 2019 for Africa Liberation Day I saw the delusions that have become a reality first-hand. I had the displeasure of visiting Orania, an all-White settlement just over an hour away from the town of Kimberley, where the revolutionary leader of the Pan African Congress, Robert Sobekwe, died under house arrest. Orania was founded in 1991 by Carel Boshoff, who was the son-in-law of Hendrik Verwoerd, the architect of Apartheid. The settlement is Afrikaner- (meaning White) only and you can only move there after a successful application. At last count the population was more than 2,500 people and growing.

Access to Orania is restricted. Although there is no fence or gate, the locals around the settlement know that they are not welcome without invitation. I gained entry through a colleague, Dr Sabatampho Mokae, who lectures at one of only two universities founded since the end of Apartheid. He had visited previously after the community's former leader, Wynand Boshoff, organized a tour. In the first sign of just how distorted the situation in South Africa is, Boshoff, the grandson of Verwoerd, had recently been elected to parliament, twenty-five years after the fall of Apartheid. In fact his fascist party, Freedom Front Plus ('plus' emphasizing more racism), also had nine other successful election candidates, more than doubling their success in 2014.

Seeking legitimacy after their mainstream success, the Oriana movement had been on a PR charm offensive in the months before my visit. My guide was feeling confident and suggested that rather than pre-arranging a visit, we should just turn up and take in the sights. Bear in mind that Orania exists because it is on private land, and South Africa is one of the most violent countries in the world, where people have no problem shooting trespassers. 'Brave' and 'crazy' were some of words people threw out when they heard this plan.

As you turn into the settlement there is a large sign that reads 'Welcome to Orania', but it provoked the opposite feeling in my stomach.

Nazi-style propaganda images of families and pioneers are dotted throughout the town, building their twisted version of the future. I was flying out later that day so we visited on a Sunday morning when everything was shut for church. It was eerily quiet and we missed the opportunity to be refused service in the café.

Our first stop was the former house of Betsie Verwoerd, the wife of Hendrik. Since her passing Orania has turned the house into a museum and monument to Verwoerd. When I shared pictures of Orania on social media there was a chorus of outrage about how the ANC could possibly allow the town to exist. But the government has condoned the all-White settlement. In 1995, maybe in an attempt to strengthen his 'sell-out' credentials, Mandela actually flew into Orania on a helicopter to have tea with Betsie and gushed that his reception was 'as if I was in Soweto'.[42]

Almost everyone was extremely polite to us, so much so that it was a little discomforting. The only time we experienced open hostility was when a car stopped and the man inside said we looked 'lost'. The driver then proceeded to tell us that Orania was like 'South Africa used to be ... safe' before driving off with his family. We drove up a dirt road to see a monument Boshoff had shown my colleague Sabata. Within two minutes a security van sped up to us. Even the security guard was overly polite: when we explained that I was from the UK and wanted to see what South Africa was like, he let us take a photo of the security car and made sure we took his number in case we had 'any trouble'. But the most troubling scene was the monument at the top of a hill overlooking Orania. It featured a bronze bust of the town's logo and a little White boy pulling up his sleeves, flanked by busts of various male, Afrikaner heroes. I dread to think what takes place in this shrine to racism when the sun goes down.

Orania is not a relic of an old era, it is growing. They are building new houses and even a college and student accommodation. It seems that what 'South Africa used to be' is appealing to many. While we were taking pictures, our escort for the rest of our visit turned up. I had the misfortune of speaking to the Deputy CEO of the Orania movement, Pieter Groenewald, and his defence of his settlement is all the evidence anyone should need that Whiteness is a psychosis. He started as he meant to go on, declaring that he was an 'African, with white skin', and that an all-Afrikaner settlement was no different than a Zulu homeland.

Going on, he claimed that studies have shown that people are happier when they live 'with their own', and that the residents of Orania are simply trying to maintain their culture. Groenewald even tried to argue that his small eco-settlement was the solution to South Africa's problem. The state has failed, and therefore hyper-localism, where everyone works and builds a community together, is the way forward. While he tried hard to avoid saying anything racist, he was basically arguing that the Black-led state was corrupt, and that Black people spent their government subsidies on alcohol rather than on building strong communities. That's why the logo of the town is the White boy pulling up his sleeves.

To signify the depths of the psychosis, Groenewald complimented me on my T-shirt. I wore a Malcolm X T-shirt with the words 'Try Me' written on the front for my visit to the all-White settlement. He seemed to think Malcolm would understand. 'Black pride is exactly what you need,' he said, and likened it to the politics of Orania. If Malcolm X had been President of South Africa, he might well have visited with a helicopter, but it would not have been to have tea with Betsie.

As we drove out of Orania, with a car following us to make sure we left, it felt like we were leaving a different world. The residents exist in a protective bubble of Whiteness, where they can play by the old rules of Apartheid. On the way back to Kimberly we had to pass one of the poorest Black shanty towns I had ever seen. It was a brutal reminder of the reality of the situation in the country. The psychosis of Whiteness protects people from having to deal with their privilege and complicity in a racist system; Orania just takes that logic to an extreme. More troubling is that in an overwhelmingly Black country, with a Black political class, shanty towns like this are allowed to exist in the shadow of an all-White settlement. The sad truth of South Africa is that the whole nation is built on the delusions that have become the basis of reality. A country full of those with Black skin being defined by the psychosis of Whiteness.

Of all the barriers to breaking through the psychosis of Whiteness, Black and Brown faces feeding the delirium is perhaps the greatest. It is the classic case of being careful what you wish for when it comes to diversity. The unintended consequence of anti-racist protests has been unprecedented access to the house for those fortunate enough to be able to 'make it'. The sight of relatively successful racialized minorities feeds into the delusion that we have moved into a post-racial society. Racism can't possibly exist if Indians are achieving so well, or if there are lots of Nigerian private-school pupils (unfortunately, I have heard both of these arguments multiple times, from respected people). We are in a paradox, where our relative success hurts the chances of those in less fortunate positions because it reinforces the delusions that maintain the racist status quo.

Matters are made far worse by those who actively perform for White supremacy, cooning and Tomming their way up the ladder. You will find few better examples of the psychosis of Whiteness than the fact that the most racist rulings of the US Supreme Court are penned by the sole Black judge. Or that the British Home Secretary deporting desperate migrants to Rwanda was the first woman 'of colour' to hold any of the great offices of state. Or even that one of the most celebrated Black figures of the twentieth century sold out the revolutionary struggle and chose to have tea with the wife of the architect of Apartheid, in an all-White settlement. If we have any chance of piercing the psychosis of Whiteness, then we must always remember that the delusions of Whiteness disturb all of our thinking.

Epilogue: Out of the Rabbit Hole

After our journey through the psychosis of Whiteness it might be difficult to see the deeply optimistic message of this book. We have spent our time learning that the problem is even worse than we previously thought, that society is trapped in a psychosis that prevents any rational efforts to understand, let alone deal with racism. There is no reforming this system and Whiteness is the defence mechanism that ensures the racist status quo remains intact. But once you accept that we cannot educate our way out of racism you will be liberated from the hamster wheel of the anti-racism industrial complex. After the scales fall from your eyes you are left with a choice. The easiest route is to take the blue pill and fall back into the comfort of delusions. But the red pill will keep your eyes open to the uncomfortable nature of reality. Just like in *The Matrix*, the real world is harsh but the struggle is not out of reach, if only you first unplug yourself from the simulated reality.

The Matrix is a good place to start. The late philosopher Jean Baudrillard, whose writings on the blurring of reality with simulation are credited with inspiring the film, strongly disliked the movie. Turning down money to work on the sequels, he explained that '*The Matrix* is surely the kind of film about the matrix that the matrix would have been able to produce'.[1] He perfectly captured the feedback loop of many of the supposedly anti-racist books that are doing such good numbers in the post-George Floyd era. Too much of that literature is meant to make us feel better, troubling us enough to think that we are 'doing the work' without ever getting our hands dirty. We must inoculate ourselves against these delusions so that we can see the mirages for what they are. I am not saying that you shouldn't read any popular books on anti-racism or Whiteness. Thanks to Audible, that has been one of my main pastimes over the past couple of years. But we do need to understand their limitations. If the conclusion of an argument is that we need to educate White people out of the problem, then you need to depart before you get stuck at the dead end. We have been on the right side of the argument for the past 500 years and look where it has got us.

The only way to end the psychosis of Whiteness is to destroy the conditions that create it. We can build an alternative to this racist system, but we first need to believe that it is possible. We must avoid false prophets offering illusions of change. For instance, the rise of China and other Third World nations is not the turning point that many often assume. Their ascendance is predicated on embracing the system of White supremacy, not overturning it.[2] As a result they are in the grip of the psychosis of Whiteness as deeply as those in the West. Consider that skin bleaching is a multi-billion-dollar industry in India, one of the supposed miracles of the new economy.[3] White is right, even when you have to burn off your skin cells to achieve it. As for China, they are weaning their population *onto* milk.

Most of the world's population develops a lactose intolerance after childhood. Europe and her descendants tend to buck that trend, so if you are looking for a concrete example of White privilege then look no further than the ability to harmlessly enjoy a Frappuccino. Although the majority of the Chinese population are lactose-intolerant, China's milk consumption has recently jumped dramatically to become the third largest in the world. None of this is accidental; increasing milk production and encouraging consumption is part of the ruling Communist Party's strategic plan.[4] Apparently most children can drink milk without being made ill by it and by maintaining consumption into adulthood a tolerance can be built up across the population. You might well ask where the obsession with milk in a lactose-intolerant populace comes from, given that cattle are a significant contributor to polluting the atmosphere through deforestation, their feed and the gases they produce. Thirteen million cows are necessary to keep up with the growing demand from China; this is not sustainable development. China now aims to triple its milk production.

Chinese filmmaker Jian Yi, who has made a film about food production in the country, highlights the 1984 Olympics as the key turning point. It was the first time many Chinese people could see foreigners on TV, and they were amazed at their size and speed. He says that 'they concluded that Americans ate a lot of beef and drank a lot of milk and Chinese people needed to catch up'.[5] Since the 1980s, as China has grown wealthier, the government has been incentivizing milk production. President Xi Jinping has talked about creating a 'new China man' and it is in no doubt that the future ideal citizen of the country consumes dairy to bulk up like the Americans. Milk has become a status symbol and the number of Starbucks in the country has increased twenty-fold since 2005.[6] China is so deeply engulfed in the psychosis of Whiteness that the government is pumping billions into transforming its population to be able to consume a Western diet. The symbolism could not be more apparent; milk is actually white. This is about as far from a revolutionary alternative as we could get. China is a facsimile of Western so-called development, keeping all its worst abuses and excesses while pretending to be different because of its revolutionary past. The rise of China is the perfect example of how diversity is not going to solve our problems. Society cannot just *look* different, it has to *be* different. Seeing Black faces in high places might lift our spirits, but if institutions are racist then the colour of the person at the top is irrelevant. There is nothing wrong with diversity. Parliament and the workplace should reflect the society we live in. But we need to stop thinking that simply changing the crew on deck shifts the direction of travel, let alone the nature of the vessel. Instead, we must focus on the outcomes, not on the presentation.

More Black people in White spaces isn't the solution, and nor is trying to get White people to be reborn as allies. In terms of practical action, a good start would be to stop using the term 'ally' completely. As of right now. To reach out for an ally maintains the White saviour framework, where we need a helping hand to solve our problems. It is true that within White institutions you will need those in power to support you, but there are two ways to navigate this that don't invoke throwing up your hand for an ally. The most obvious one is to avoid White institutions; across the world we have a long history of Black-led organizations and this is ultimately one of the solutions if we want meaningful change. But as I have not yet left the comfort of my university salary it would be hypocritical of me to chastize anyone for maintaining the delusion that we can make these institutions work for us. The second approach, one that I am currently working through, is to utilize the concept of 'interest convergence' from (dare I say it) critical race theory.[7] As racism is a permanent feature of society, the times we can enact change are the moments when the interests of the White population converge with those of racialized minorities. Lincoln only agreed to emancipate the enslaved as part of the US Civil War because he needed those on the plantations to defect and join the cause of the Union Army to win.[8] Britain only agreed to end formal colonialism because nationalist movements meant that it was in their interests to hand over power. The limited police reforms we have seen in Britain only came about after the urban rebellions in the 1980s; the cost of doing nothing forced the government to act. The same is true of civil rights legislation in the US in the 1960s. At the time the US was assuming the moral leadership of the world in its war against communism, it came to be in the government's interest to stop the violent crackdowns of protesters in the South and support civil rights goals.[9] The protests themselves could make these interests converge also, by causing disruption, and boycotts were especially useful in this regard. The infamous Montgomery Bus Boycott of 1955 to 1956 made it in the interests of the bus company to end segregation, and the same was true in Bristol in 1963. We would be right to question the extent to which these examples led to substantive change. Although they changed the arrangement of the system, the framework stayed intact. But they were powerful movements that did lead to shifts, and none of them relied on educating White people out of their delusions. Converging interests is a far safer route to making the changes you want to see in your workplace than relying on a well-meaning ally. In fact, we managed to start the first Black Studies degree in Europe at my university because of interest convergence.

In 2017, when students had to start paying over £9,000 in fees, the university was falling over itself to start new courses to bring in more ~~customers~~ students. We sold Black Studies as unique, the only course on the market like it, and whereas once there were only stormy waters between us and the creation of this degree, the sea then parted, leaving us a clear path to running the course. I cannot say that any of the managers who supported the degree were allies; in fact, given my own experiences at the university, I can attest that the institution is just as racist as any other. But it didn't matter, they supported the course because it aligned with their interests and that is how you make change within institutions.

A related concrete action we can take is to immediately stop all unconscious bias training. If it is unconscious, then it cannot be trained out of someone. If that is your goal, you are just wasting everyone's time and your money. Bias, just like the psychosis of Whiteness, arises within the society we live in. Only in a society not defined by racism will you end the unconscious biases it produces. I am not saying we should get rid of equality, diversity and inclusion initiatives completely. Part of the reason that the psychosis is so firmly embedded is that the school curriculum operates on a principle of the 'epistemology of ignorance'. We only learn information that feeds the psychosis, meaning our deficits of understanding are immense. Whenever I give a talk at a company I use the opportunity to provide some education about the true nature of the world, information that is sorely missing from the school system. Of course this isn't enough, and it's likely that what I say is reinterpreted through the lens of the psychosis. But education is important: if we want to build another world, we first have to be able to imagine it.

One of the main lessons the psychosis of Whiteness can teach us is that we need to stop waiting for White people to transform the world. Black people have a long history of organizing without the blessing or involvement of White folks, but we must admit that lots of our activism has revolved around trying to influence White people, who have power in this system. Ultimately, if the aim of your work is to convince Western governments to change, then you are hoping to influence the White politicians and populations that support them. If you are advocating for the education and training of White people as a tool to transform institutions, then you focus on redeeming their wayward souls. If you feel part of an imaginary 99 per cent of the world, one that needs the so-called White working class to join the global struggle for revolution, then you are centring Whiteness even in your revolutionary dreams. One of the most dangerous delusions of the psychosis is believing that we are lost without White people. Stop waiting for, or trying to convince, White people. It is as useful as a rat chasing its tail. This lesson is just as important for White readers. People are not more likely to listen to your anti-racist sermons because of your skin colour. White supremacy is not like a courtroom, where we need advocates who can speak the language of the judge to get a fair hearing. Racism is more akin to the entire criminal injustice system; it creates the power imbalances where Black people are in the dock in the first place. If you want to help, then you need to work on over-hauling the system so that we are not the ones on trial.

The only solution to the problem of racism is revolution. The delusions of the psychosis of Whiteness are caused by the political and economic system of White supremacy and if we want to eliminate it we must go to the source. We need to stop individualizing the issue and end the liberal charade that if we could only educate everyone, we would all live in blissful union. Please do not put this book down believing that any individual can be cured of the psychosis, that when you turn the last page you are cleansed of your pathology. One of the more frustrating developments in people finding Black literature was how Reni Eddo Lodge's book *Why I Am No Longer Talking to White People About Race* became a fashion accessory for those who wanted to look woke. Ironic, not least because, despite the title, its main audience was White liberals who wanted to dip their toe into anti-racist waters. If this book becomes anti-racist decoration then we will have to apply Baudrillard's maxim: *The Psychosis of Whiteness* is a book surely only the psychosis could produce about the psychosis. As one of the most privileged people on the planet (not too fast, earning more than an average income in the West puts you in that bracket too), this is something that I always have to be wary of. To avoid that pitfall we must acknowledge that accepting Whiteness as a psychosis is an essential step, but only a baby one. I am not cured of the psychosis because I still benefit from the system that produces the delusions. It is like knowing the matrix is a simulation but not being able to unplug yourself from it. The psychosis is both a symptom and a defence mechanism for White supremacy. It is important to recognize it only insofar as that leads us down a path towards making transformative change. We must build alternatives to this political and economic system. To do so we need to come out of the fog and believe that revolution is possible.

So reject the soothing tones of the White supremacy self-help racket. Pleasure is the last emotion we should be seeking in a world where Black and Brown children die by the second so that we can indulge ourselves in our leisure time. The psychosis allows us to believe that the blood on our hands is really the sweat of our hard labour. When you break out of your delirium you should feel guilt, shame and distress. Do not push those feelings aside, embrace them and then get over yourself. It is not about you. We must collectively work to build a reality free from White supremacy. We cannot afford to rest until that goal has been achieved. The journey to liberation will be uncomfortable, so rather than ending this book by trying to reassure you, I challenge you to confront the demons that haunt our society.

Notes

PREFACE: THROUGH THE LOOKING-GLASS

1. Staff and agencies, 'Black and White Minstrels creator dies', *Guardian*, 29 August 2002.
2. I. Lewis, 'Lenny Henry says he was used as a "political football" after appearing in blackface minstrel show', *Independent*, 9 October 2021.
3. B. O'Neill, 'The madness of censoring shows like Little Britain', *Spectator*, 10 June 2020.
4. T. Nicholson, 'How did it take this long to put "Little Britain" in the bin?', *Esquire*, 11 June 2020.
5. 'Churchill was a racist, and comparable to Hitler, says academic', *Good Morning Britain*, ITV, 9 October 2018.
6. A. Saini, *Superior: The Return of Race Science* (Boston, MA: Beacon Press, 2019).
7. S. Tharoor, *Inglorious Empire: What the British Did to India* (London: Penguin Books, 2016).
8. M. Mukerjee, *Churchill's Secret War: The British Empire and the Ravaging of India during World War II* (New York, NY: Basic Books, 2010), p. 347.
9. R. Tingle, '"If he holds those views why is he living off the public purse?": Outrage as controversial taxpayer-funded black studies professor who says Britain is "built on racism" claims Churchill was a "white supremacist" in debate', *Daily Mail*, 12 February 2021.
10. K. Heren, 'Academic sparks Good Morning Britain debate over whether BBC should drop "racist propaganda" Rule Britannia from Last Night of the Proms', *Evening Standard*, 24 August 2020.
11. Yahoo Finance, D. Allot, '5 mind-blowing facts about Jeff Bezos' wealth', 27 July 2021.

12. M. O'Connell, '"A managerial Mephistopheles": inside the mind of Jeff Bezos', *Guardian*, 3 February 2021.
13. Ibid.
14. The Last Poets, 'The White man's got a God complex', from *This Is Madness*, Media Sound Studios, 1971.
15. C. Rock, *Bigger and Blacker*, HBO, 1999.
16. A. Asher, 'Far-right British activist Katie Hopkins challenges Biden to lock her up after claiming she's in US illegally', *Independent*, 26 October 2022.
17. H. Mance, '"Britain has had enough of experts," says Gove', *Financial Times*, 3 June 2016.

1: WHY PSYCHOSIS?

1. L. E. DeLisi, K. U. Szulc, H. C. Bertisch, M. Majcher and K. Brown, 'Understanding structural brain changes in schizophrenia', *Dialogues Clinical Neuroscience*, 8(1), 2006, pp. 71–8.
2. Wiregrass Georgia Technical College, LibGuides, DSM-5: Schizophrenia Syndrome and Other Psychotic Disorders, available at Schizophrenia Spectrum and Other Psychotic Disorders - DSM-5 - LibGuides at Wiregrass Georgia Technical College, accessed 16 March 2023.
3. K. Andrews, '"We were made to feel like outcasts": the psychiatrist who blew the whistle on racism in British medicine', *Guardian*, 13 January 2020.
4. J. Metzl, *The Protest Psychosis: How Schizophrenia Became a Black Disease* (Boston, MA: Beacon Press, 2010), p. xvi.
5. K. Andrews, *Back to Black: Retelling Black Radicalism for the Twenty-First Century* (London: Zed Books, 2020).
6. W. Bromberg and F. Simon, 'The protest psychosis: a special type of *reactive* psychosis', *Archives of General Psychiatry*, 19(2), 1968, pp. 155–60, 155.
7. Ibid., p. 156.
8. Ibid., original emphasis.
9. S. Cartwright, *Report on the Diseases and Physical Peculiarities of the Negro Race*, New Orleans Medical and Surgical Journal, 1851, p. 695.
10. L. Braun, 'Race, ethnicity and lung function: a brief history', *Canadian Journal of Respiratory Therapy*, 51(4), 2015, p. 99.
11. Ibid.

12. I. Beckley, E. Barnaby, Y. Timi-Biu, A. Sharma and T. Adeleye, 'Episode 1', *The Bias Diagnosis* (Amazon Audible podcast, 2021).

13. Kidney Research UK, *Ethnicity Adjustment for Kidney Function Testing Removed from NICE Chronic Kidney Disease Guidelines*, 25 August 2021.

14. Cartwright, *Report on the Diseases and Physical Peculiarities of the Negro Race*, p. 693.

15. Ibid., p. 707.

16. Ibid., p. 708.

17. Ibid., p. 710.

18. A. B. Evarts, 'Dementia Precox', *Psychoanalytic Review*, 1913, pp. 388, 394.

19. E. M. Green, 'Psychoses among Negroes – A comparative study', *Journal of Nervous and Mental Disease*, 41(2), 1914, pp. 697–708.

20. M. O'Malley, 'Psychoses in the colored race', *American Journal of Insanity*, 71(2), October 1914, p. 316.

21. Ibid., p. 311.

22. Ibid.

23. T. Rosenberg, 'Busting the myth that depression doesn't affect people in poor countries', *Guardian*, 30 April 2019.

24. Ibid.

25. Green, 'Psychoses among Negroes – A comparative study', p. 708.

26. T. Qassem, P. Bebbington, N. Spiers, S. McManus, R. Jenkins and S. Dein, 'Prevalence of psychosis in black ethnic minorities in Britain: analysis based on three national surveys', *Social Psychiatry and Psychiatric Epidemiology*, 50(7), 2015, pp. 1057–64.

27. American Psychiatric Association, fact sheet, *Mental Health Disparities: African Americans*, 2017.

28. GOV.UK, *Race Disparity Audit: Summary Findings from the Ethnicity Facts and Figures Website* (Cabinet Office, 2018).

29. Cartwright, *Report on the Diseases and Physical Peculiarities of the Negro Race*, p. 697.

30. B. Malzberg, 'Mental disease among native and foreign-born negroes in New York State', *The Journal of Negro Education* 25(2), 1956, pp. 175–81; Metzl, *The Protest Psychosis*, p. 108.

31. R. Abeles, 'Relative deprivation, rising expectation and Black militancy', *Journal of Social Issues* 32(2), 1976.

32. G. Kounani, *Living While Black: The Essential Guide to Overcoming Racial Trauma* (London: Penguin Books, 2021).

33. F. Fanon, *Black Skin, White Masks* (New York, NY: Grove Press, 1967), p. 113.
34. Ibid., p. 60.
35. Ibid., p. 100.
36. Kounani, *Living While Black*.
37. C. E. Matias and R. DiAngelo, 'Beyond the face of race: emo-cognitive exploration of white neurosis and racial cray-cray', *Educational Foundations*, 22 June 2013, p. 14.
38. R. Ellison, *Invisible Man* (London: Penguin Books, 2001), p. 7.
39. Quassem et al., 'Prevalence of psychosis in black ethnic minorities in Britain'.
40. *Psychosis and Me*, starring David Harewood, directed by E. Ottiewill, London: Films of Record, 2019.
41. D. Harewood, 'I feel no shame about my mental breakdown: it helped make me who I am', *Guardian*, 13 October 2017.
42. C. Rose interview with T. Morrison, PBS, 5 July 1993, available at https://charlierose.com/videos/18778, accessed 15 March 2023.
43. Fanon, *Black Skin, White Masks*, p. 60.
44. M. Vaughan, 'Colonial melancholia', *Raritan* 37(1), 2017, p. 118.
45. Metzl, *The Protest Psychosis*, p. 122.
46. K. Andrews, *The New Age of Empire: How Racism and Colonialism Still Rule the World* (London: Penguin Books, 2021).
47. C. Anderson, *White Rage: The Unspoken Truth of Our Racial Divide* (London: Bloomsbury Publishing, 2017), p. 40.
48. *Tulsa Race Riot: A Report by the Oklahoma Commission to Study the Tulsa Race Riot of 1921*, 28 February 2001, available at https://www.okhistory.org/research/forms/freport.pdf, accessed 27 February 2023.
49. Ibid., p. 43.
50. Anderson, *White Rage: The Unspoken Truth of Our Racial Divide*, p. 18.
51. Fanon, *Black Skin, White Masks*, p. 92.
52. C. Mills, *The Racial Contract* (Ithaca, NY: Cornell University Press, 1997), p. 97.
53. N. Ferguson, *Empire: How Britain Made the Modern World* (London: Penguin Books, 2017), p. 380.
54. Ibid., p. 298.
55. Andrews, *The New Age of Empire*.
56. Malcolm X, speech at the Ford Auditorium, 13 February 1965.
57. Ferguson, *Empire: How Britain Made the Modern World*, p. X.
58. L. Gordon, *Bad Faith and Antiblack Racism* (Atlantic Highlands, NJ: Humanities Press, 1995).

59. G. Beckles-Raymond, 'Implicit bias, (global) white ignorance, and bad faith: the problem of whiteness and anti-black racism', *Journal of Applied Philosophy* 37(2), 2020.

60. J. Lind, 'The color complex in the Negro', *Psychoanalytic Review* 1(4), 1913, pp. 404–14.

2: THE ANTI-RACISM INDUSTRIAL COMPLEX

1. UK Parliament, House of Commons, 'Black History Month', debated Tuesday 20 October 2020, vol. 682, Hansard historic record, https://hansard.parliament.uk/commons/2020-10-20/debates/5B0E393E-8778-4973-B318-C17797DFBB22/BlackHistoryMonth.

2. J. Diamond and J. Hoffman, 'Trump doubles down on divisive messaging on speech to honor Independence Day', CNN, 4 July 2020, available at https://edition.cnn.com/2020/07/04/politics/trump-july-fourth-remarks/index.html.

3. *Executive Order on Combating Race and Sex Stereotyping*, The White House, 22 September 2020, available at https://edition.cnn.com/2020/07/04/politics/trump-july-fourth-remarks/index.html.

4. D. S. Owen, 'Towards a critical theory of whiteness', *Philosophy & Social Criticism* 33(2), 2007, pp. 203–22, 203.

5. C. I. Harris, 'Whiteness as property', *Harvard Law Review* 106, 1993, pp. 1707–91.

6. S. Garner, *Whiteness: An Introduction* (London: Routledge, 2007); S. Gunew, 'Rethinking Whiteness', *Feminist Theory* 8, 2007, pp. 141–8; A. Moreton-Robinson, 'Towards a new research agenda? Foucault, Whiteness and indigenous sovereignty', *Journal of Sociology* 42, 2006, pp. 383–95.

7. K. Deliovsky and T. Kitossa, 'Beyond Black and White: when going beyond may take us out of bounds', *Journal of Black Studies* 44, 2013, pp. 158–81; M. Green, C. G. Sonn and J. Matsebula, 'Reviewing whiteness: theory, research and possibilities', *South African Journal of Psychology* 37(3), 2007, pp. 389–419; J. Warren and F. Twine, 'White Americans, the new minority? Non-Blacks and the ever-expanding boundaries of whiteness', *Journal of Black Studies*, 28(2), 1997, pp. 200–18.

8. R. L. Allen, 'The globalization of white supremacy: toward a critical discourse on the racialization of the world', *Educational Theory* 51, 25 January 2005, pp. 467–85.

9. K. P. Feldman, 'The globality of whiteness in post-racial visual culture', *Cultural Studies* 30(2), 2016, pp. 289–311.

10. Green, Sonn and Matsebula, 'Reviewing Whiteness', p. 390.

11. Owen, 'Towards a critical theory of whiteness', p. 213.

12. Z. Leonardo, 'The color of supremacy: beyond the discourse of "white privilege"', *Educational Philosophy and Theory* 36(4), 2002, pp. 137–52.

13. C. Mills, *The Racial Contract* (Ithaca, NY: Cornell University Press), p. 97.

14. For example, see N. Aveling, 'Critical whiteness studies and the challenges of learning to be a "white ally"', *Borderlands*, 3(2), 2004, pp. 1–43; D. Gillespie, L. Ashbaugh and J. Defiore, 'White women teaching white women about white privilege, race cognizance and social action: toward a pedagogical pragmatics', *Race, Ethnicity and Education*, 5(3), 2002, pp. 237–53; D. Nichols, 'Teaching critical whiteness theory: what college and university teachers need to know', *Understanding & Dismantling Privilege*, 1(1), 2010; S. Sharma, '*Crash* – towards a critical pedagogy of whiteness?', *Cultural Studies*, 24(4), 2010, pp. 533–52.

15. Mills, *The Racial Contract*, p. 132.

16. Leonardo, 'The color of supremacy: beyond the discourse of "white privilege"', p. 142.

17. D. Walker, *Walker's Appeal, in Four Articles; Together with a Preamble, to the Coloured Citizens of the World, but in Particular and Very Expressly, to Those of the United States of America* ([Boston, 1829] Chapel Hill, NC: University of North Carolina Press, 2011), p. 5.

18. A. Davis, *An Autobiography* (New York, NY: International Publishers, 2004), pp. 126–7.

19. Allen, 'The globalization of white supremacy', p. 482.

20. Gillespie, Ashbaugh and Defiore, 'White women teaching white women about white privilege, race cognizance and social action', p. 240.

21. C. Levine-Rasky, 'Framing Whiteness: working through the tensions in introducing whiteness to educators', *Race, Ethnicity and Education* 3(3), 2000, pp. 271–92, 277.

22. N. Ignatiev, *How the Irish Became White* (London: Routledge, 1995).

23. N. Ignatiev, *Treason to Whiteness Is Loyalty to Humanity* (London: Verso Books, 2022), p. 235.

24. Z. Leonardo, 'The souls of white folk: critical pedagogy, whiteness studies, and globalization discourse', *Race, Ethnicity and Education* 5(1), 2002, pp. 29–50, 37.

25. Ignatiev, *Treason to Whiteness*, p. 221.

26. S. Chan, 'Noel Ignatiev, scholar who called for abolishing whiteness, dies at 78', *Los Angeles Times*, 11 November 2019.

27. M. Kearney and B. Harris, 'Ten economic facts about crime and incarceration in the United States', The Brookings Institute, 2014.

28. Ignatiev, *Treason to Whiteness*, p. 235.

29. K. Andrews, *The New Age of Empire: How Racism and Colonialism Still Rule the World* (London: Penguin Books, 2021).

30. J. Ryde, *White Privilege: How to Be Part of the Solution* (London: Jessica Kingsley Publications, 2019), pp. 18, 123.

31. L. Saad, *Me and White Supermacy: How to Recognise Your Privilege, Combat Racism and Change the World* (Quercus Audio), 5:23:50.

32. R. DiAngelo, *White Fragility: Why It's So Hard for White People to Talk about Racism* (London: Penguin Books, 2019), pp. 2, 144 and 154.

33. R. DiAngelo, 'Accountability statement', 2002, at robindiangelo.com.

34. Trades Union Congress, *BME Women and Work: TUC Equality Briefing*, 26 October 2020.

35. W. Allen, R. Teranishi, G. Dinwiddie and G. Gonzalez, 'Knocking at freedom's door: race, equity, and affirmative action in US higher education', *Journal of Public Health Policy* 69(1/2), 2002, pp. 3–11.

36. Ryde, *White Privilege: How to Be Part of the Solution*, p. 18.

37. Saad, *Me and White Supremacy* (London: Quercus, 2019).

38. Malcolm X, 'The Black Man's History', speech at Muslim Mosque no. 7, New York, 12 December 1962.

39. A. Solomon and K. Rankin, *How We Fight White Supremacy: A Field Guide to Black Resistance* (New York, NY: Nation Books, 2019), p. 76.

40. I. Oluo, *Mediocre: The Dangerous Legacy of White Male Power* (New York, NY: Basic Books, 2020), p. 87.

41. I. Oluo, *So You Want to Talk About Race* (Blackstone Audio, 2018), 02:17:16

42. Ibid., 7:33:45.

43. Solomon and Rankin, *How We Fight White Supremacy*, p. 49.

44. I. Kendi, *How to Be an Anti-Racist* (New York, NY: One World, 2019), p. 32.

45. Ibid., p. 19.

46. Ibid., p. 7.

47. Ibid., p. 10.

48. D. Bell, *Faces at the Bottom of the Well: The Permanence of Racism* (New York, NY: Basic Books, 1992), p. 198.

49. C. M. Fleming, *How to Be Less Stupid About Race: On Racism, White Supremacy and the Racial Divide* (New York, NY: Beacon Press, 2018), p. X.

50. Solomon and Rankin, *How We Fight White Supremacy*, p. 97.

51. Ibid., p. 272.

52. Malcolm X, 'The ballot or the bullet', speech at Cory Methodist Church, Cleveland, Ohio, 3 April 1964.

53. Solomon and Rankin, *How We Fight White Supremacy*, p. 188.

54. A. M. Brown, *Pleasure Activism: The Politics of Feeling Good* (AK Press Audio), 00:28:40 and 00:26:09.

55. Solomon and Rankin, *How We Fight White Supremacy*, p. 68.

3: WEST INDIAN SLAVERY

1. J. Kincaid, *A Small Place* (London: Virago Books, 1988).

2. K. Andrews, *Back to Black: Retelling Black Radicalism for the Twenty-First Century* (London: Zed Books, 2020).

3. A. Pawlowski, 'Haiti cruise stops draw ire, support', CNN, 21 January 2010.

4. E. Duperil, 'What if I told you that tourism may be bad for Haiti?', *Haitian Times*, 14 August 2015.

5. Rose Hall's website, available at: https://rosehall.com/, accessed 28 February 2023.

6. O. Hosken, 'It was never OK to get married at a plantation. Here's why', *Town and Country*, 4 August 2020.

7. S. Grossbart, 'A look at Blake Lively and Ryan Reynolds' deeply controversial wedding', *E! Online News*, 9 September 2021.

8. V. Bevins, *The Jakarta Method: Washington's Anticommunist Crusade and the Mass Murder Program That Shaped Our World* (New York, NY: Public Affairs, 2020).

9. J. Eichstedt, and S. Small, *Representations of Slavery: Race and Ideology in Southern Plantation Museums* (Washington, DC: Smithsonian Institution Press, 2002).

10. A. Breed, 'Vacationers get cozy in slave cabins', Associated Press, 18 March 2002.

11. M. Yang, 'Airbnb apologizes for slave cabin for rent in Mississippi', *Guardian*, 3 August 2022.

12. S. Cashdan, *Abnormal Psychology* (Englewood Cliffs, NJ: Prentice Hall, 1972).

13. M. Apted (director), *Amazing Grace*, Fourboys Films, 2006.

14. A. Asante (director), *Belle*, Fox Searchlight, 2013.

15. O. Equiano, *The Interesting Narrative of the Life of Olaudah Equiano: or, Gustavus Vassa, the African* (London: [1789]).

16. S. Dadzie, *A Kick in the Belly: Women, Slavery and Resistance* (London: Verso Books, 2020).

17. D. Olusoga, *Black and British: A Forgotten History* (London: Macmillan, 2016).

18. D. Smith and S. H. Friedman, '"Let justice be done though the heavens may fall": the *Zong* in Amma Asante's *Belle*', *Journal of the American Academy of Psychiatry Law*, 42, 2014, pp. 530–32.

19. J. Krikler, 'The *Zong* and the Lord Chief Justice', *History Workshop Journal*, 64(1), 1 October 2007, pp. 29–47.

20. A. Rupprecht, 'A limited sort of property: history, memory and the slave ship *Zong*', *Slavery & Abolition*, 29(2), 2008, pp. 265–77.

21. A. Rupprecht, '"A very uncommon case": representations of the *Zong* and the British campaign to abolish the slave trade', *Journal of Legal History* 28(3), p. 330.

22. Krikler, 'The *Zong* and the Lord Chief Justice'.

23. Ibid., pp. 36 and 37.

24. P. Finkelman, '"Let justice be done, though the heavens may fall": the law and freedom', *Chicago-Kent Law Review* 70(2), 1994, p. 325.

25. L. Dearden, 'Scottish independence: full text of David Cameron's 'no going back' speech, *Independent*, 16 September 2014.

26. Rupprecht, 'A limited sort of property: history, memory and the slave ship *Zong*', p. 267.

27. J. Doward, 'British version of 12 Years a Slave to shed light on our role in Atlantic slave trade', *Observer*, 12 January 2014.

28. Finkelman, '"Let justice be done, though the heavens may fall": The law and freedom'.

29. G. Adams, 'Dido Elizabeth Belle, a Black girl at Kenwood: an account of a protegée of the 1st Lord Mansfield', *Camden History Review*, 12, 1984, pp. 10–14.

30. R. King, 'Belle, Dido Elizabeth (1761?–1804)', *Oxford Dictionary of National Biography* (Oxford: Oxford University Press, 2004).

4: SELF-SEGREGATION

1. E. Anderson, 'The iconic ghetto', *The ANNALS of the American Academy of Political and Social Science*, 642(1), 4 June 2012, p. 8.

2. S. Hall, C. Critcher, T. Jefferson, J. Clarke and B. Roberts, *Policing the Crisis: Mugging, the State and Law and Order* (London: Macmillan, 1978), p. 96.

3. D. P. Waddington, *Contemporary Issues in Public Disorder: A Comparative and Historical Approach* (London: Routledge, 1992).

4. GOV.UK, *The Lammy Review: Final Report. An Independent Review into the Treatment of, and Outcomes for Black, Asian and Minority Ethnic Individuals in the Criminal Justice System* (Home Office, 2017).

5. *Children in Custody 2017–18: An Analysis of 12–18-Year-Olds' Perceptions of Their Experiences in Secure Training Centres and Young Offender Institutions* (London: HM Inspectorate of Prisons, 2019).

6. S. Kumar, L. Sherman and H. Strang, 'Racial disparities in homicide victimisation rates: how to improve transparency by the Office of National Statistics in England and Wales', *Cambridge Journal of Evidence-Based Policing* 4: 2020, pp. 178–86.

7. C. Elton, 'How has Boston gotten away with being segregated for so long?', *Boston Magazine*, 12 August 2020.

8. A. Williams and A. Emamdjomeh, 'America is more diverse than ever – but still segregated', *Washington Post*, 10 May 2018.

9. G. Orfield, *Reviving the Goal of an Integrated Society: A 21st Century Challenge* (Los Angeles, CA: The Civil Rights Project/Proyecto Derechos Civiles, 2009).

10. Malcolm X, speech at the University of Columbia, 20 May 1963.

11. J. Givens, *Fugitive Pedagogy: Carter G. Woodson and the Art of Black Teaching* (Cambridge, MA: Harvard University Press, 2021).

12. C. Anderson, *White Rage: The Unspoken Truth of Our Racial Divide* (London: Bloomsbury Publishing, 2017).

13. K. Andrews, 'Minnijean Brown-Trickey: the teenager who needed an armed guard to go to school', *Guardian*, 26 November 2020.

14. M. Patillo, *Warriors Don't Cry: A Searing Memoir of the Battle to Integrate Little Rock's Central High* (New York, NY: Washington Square Press, 1994).

15. G. Panetta, 'Joe Biden worried in 1977 that certain de-segregation policies would cause his children to grow up "in a racial jungle"', *Business Insider*, 14 July 2019.

16. B. Gellerman, '"It was like a war zone": busing in Boston', *WBUR News*, 5 September 2014.
17. Ibid.
18. I. Wilkerson, *Caste: The Origins of Our Discontents* (London: Penguin Books, 2020).
19. Ibid., p. 119.
20. Anderson, *White Rage: The Unspoken Truth of Our Racial Divide*.
21. K. Yamatta-Taylor, *How Banks and the Real Estate Industry Undermined Black Homeownership* (Princeton, NJ: Princeton University Press, 2020).
22. M. Alexander, *The New Jim Crow: Mass Incarceration in the Age of Colorblindness* (New York, NY: The New Press, 2016).
23. K. Taylor, 'Why should we trust you? Clinton's big problem with young black Americans', *Guardian*, 21 October 2016.
24. The Ringer, J. R. Conn, 'What If? The Len Bias Story' (podcast), 2 June 2021.
25. Dead Prez, 'Sellin' d.o.p.e.', *Slam*, Soundtrack, 1998.
26. W. Grenade, *Grenada Revolution: Reflections and Lessons* (Jackson, MI: University Press of Mississippi, 2015).
27. Anderson, *White Rage: The Unspoken Truth of Our Racial Divide*, p. 128.
28. J. Rex and R. Moore, *Race, Community and Conflict: A Study of Sparkbrook* (Oxford: Oxford University Press, 1971).
29. Malcolm X, 'The ballot or the bullet', speech at King Solomon Baptist Church, Detroit, Michigan, 12 April 1964.
30. Office for National Statistics (2022) Ethnicity facts and figures: Regional ethnic diversity. Available at: https://www.ethnicity-facts-figures.service.gov.uk/uk-population-by-ethnicity/national-and-regional-populations/regional-ethnic-diversity/latest#:~:text=London%20(13.5%25)%20and%20the,1.6%25)%20had%20the%20lowest
31. M. Griffin, 'Where should I live in Birmingham? Find your part of town', *Guardian*, 9 September 2015.
32. M. Lawford, 'Britain's most liveable and affordable rural property hotspots', *Daily Telegraph*, 14 July 2021.
33. Birmingham City Council, *Big City Plan*, available at: https://www.birmingham.gov.uk/directory_record/264494/big_city_plan, accessed 23 February 2023.
34. The Canary, S. Purdy-Moore, 'London's luxurious "Sky Pool" is peak gentrification', 4 June 2021.

35. L. Casey, *The Casey Review: A Review into Opportunity and Integration* (London: Department for Communities and Local Government, 2016).

36. T. Dunn, 'GHETTO BLASTER: mass immigration to Britain has changed it beyond recognition and turned communities into ghettos, reveals damning report', *Sun*, 5 December 2016.

37. Geni, *100 Greatest Britons* (BBC Poll, 2002), available at: https://www.geni.com/projects/100-Greatest-Britons-BBC-Poll-2002/15375, accessed 23 February 2023.

38. A. Richards, 'Enoch Powell: what was the "Rivers of Blood" speech? Full text here', *Birmingham Mail*, 30 March 2015.

39. Interview with Margaret Thatcher, *World in Action*, Granada, 27 January 1978.

40. The Runnymede Trust, Commission on the Future of Multi-Ethnic Britain (chair: B. Parekh), *The Future of Multi-Ethnic Britain* (London: Profile Books, 2000).

41. *Community Cohesion: Report of the Independent Review Team* (chair: T. Cantle), Home Office, 2001.

42. Ibid., p. 20.

43. R. Norton-Taylor, 'Iraq war "motivated London bombers"', *Guardian*, 3 April 2006.

44. T. Blair, 'A battle for global values', *Foreign Affairs*, 1 January 2007.

45. BBC News, 'Conform to our society, says PM', 8 December 2006.

46. N. Ferguson, *Empire: How Britain Made the Modern World* (London: Penguin Books, 2004).

47. T. Blair, 'Tony Blair's Britain speech', *Guardian*, 28 March 2000.

48. Blair, 'A battle for global values'.

49. P. Thomas, 'Prevent and community cohesion in Britain – the worst of all possible worlds?', in C. Baker-Beall, C. Heath-Kelly and L. Jarvis (eds) *Counter Radicalization – Critical Perspectives* (London: Routledge, 2014).

50. P. Lewis, 'Surveillance cameras in Birmingham track Muslims' every move', *Guardian*, 4 June 2010.

51. GOV.UK, *Promoting Fundamental British Values as Part of SMSC in Schools: Departmental Advice for Maintained Schools* (Department for Education, 2014), p. 3.

52. BBC News, S. Kotecha, 'More than 400 children under 10 referred for "deradicalisation"', 21 January 2016.

53. D. Lundie, 'Building a terrorist house on sand: a critical incident analysis of interprofessionality and the Prevent programme', *Journal of Beliefs and Values* 40(3), 2019, pp. 321–33.

5: WE'RE LOSING THE COUNTRY

1. J. Stolworthy, 'Jamiroquai star Jay Kay addresses comparisons to Capitol rioters: "I wasn't with all those freaks"', *Independent*, 7 January 2021.
2. A. Serwer, 'Bitherism of a nation', *Atlantic Magazine*, 14 May 2020.
3. A. Barr, '51% of GOP voters: Obama foreign', *Politico*, February 2011.
4. D. Trump, 'Address to the Republican National Conference', 21 July 2016.
5. K. Rogers, 'Protesters dispersed with tear gas so Trump could pose at church', *The New York Times*, 1 June 2020.
6. D. Trump, 'Salute to America', The White House, 4 July 2020.
7. NPR, D. Gonyea, 'Majority of white Americans say they believe whites face discrimination', 24 October 2017.
8. D. Massey, 'White women benefit most from affirmative action – and are among its fiercest opponents', *Vox*, 23 June 2016.
9. Pew Research Center, J. Horowitz, A. Brown and K. Cox, *Race in America 2019*, 9 April 2019.
10. Politifact, K. Sanders, 'NBA legend Abdul-Jabbar: "More whites believe in ghosts than believe in racism"', 4 May 2014.
11. A. Saini, *Superior: The Return of Race Science* (Boston, MA: Beacon Press, 2019), p. 47.
12. J. Gabbatiss, 'James Watson: The most controversial statements made by the father of DNA', *Independent*, 13 January 2019.
13. R. Dennis, 'Social Darwinism, scientific racism, and the metaphysics of race', *The Journal of Negro Education* 64(3), 1995, pp. 243–52.
14. [to come]
15. T. Sewell, 'Black boys are too feminized', *Guardian*, 15 March 2010.
16. GOV.UK, *The Forgotten: How White Working-Class Pupils Have Been Let Down, and How to Change It* (London: Department of Education, 2021).
17. J. Oldham, 'Trojan Horse Jihadist plot to take over Birmingham schools', *Birmingham Mail*, 7 March 2014.

18. J. Haynes and R. Stoere, 'Michael Gove on Trojan Horse: "A sustained effort to change character of Birmingham schools"', *Birmingham Mail*, 1 March 2022.
19. Ofsted, Nansen Primary School – A Park View Academy, full inspection, 9 June 2014.
20. L. Tikly, A. Osler and J. Hill, 'The ethnic minority achievement grant: a critical analysis', *Journal of Education Policy* 20(3), 2005, pp. 283–312.
21. K. Andrews, *Resisting Racism: Race, Inequality and the Black Supplementary School Movement* (London: Institute of Education Press, 2013).
22. GOV.UK, *Aiming High: Supporting Effective Use of EMAG* (Department for Education and Skills, 2004).
23. Andrews, *Resisting Racism: Race, Inequality and the Black Supplementary School Movement*.
24. GOV.UK, *Ethnicity Facts and Figures: Permanent Exclusions* (Department of Education, 7 February 2023).
25. J. Boakye, *I Heard What You Said* (London: Picador, 2022).
26. National Education Opportunities Network (NEON), G. Atherton and T. Mazhari, *Working Class Heroes – Understanding Access to Higher Education for White Students from Lower Socio-economic Backgrounds* (London: National Education Opportunities Network, 2019).
27. Ibid., p. 11.
28. P. Curtis, 'Black students failing to get into top universities', *Guardian*, 3 January 2006.
29. Higher Education Statistics Authority, *Higher Education Graduate Outcomes Statistics: UK, 2017/18 – Graduate Activities and Characteristics*, available at https://www.hesa.ac.uk/news/18-06-2020/sb257-higher-education-graduate-outcomes-statistics/activities, accessed 23 February 2023.
30. V. Amos and A. Doku, *Black, Asian and Minority Ethnic Student Attainment at UK Universities* (London: Universities UK, 2019).
31. Advance HE, 'Advance HE launches *Ethnicity Awarding Gaps in UK Higher Education in 2019/20* report', 13 October 2021.
32. C. Rock, *Bring the Pain*, HBO TV special, 1996.
33. L. Thomas, 'Do pre-entry interventions such as "Aimhigher" impact on student retention and success? A review of the literature', *Higher Education Quarterly* 65(3), 1 July 2011, pp. 230–50.
34. A. Coulter, 'Bush's America: Roach Motel', Universal Press Syndicate, 6 June 2007.

35. C. Anderson, *One Person, No Vote* (London: Bloomsbury Publishing, 2018).

36. A. Dulitzsky, 'A region in denial: racial discrimination and racism in Latin America', in A. Dzidzienyo and S. Oboler (eds), *Neither Enemies Nor Friends: Latinos, Blacks, Afro- Latinos* (Basingstoke: Palgrave Macmillan, 2005), pp. 39–59.

37. Pew Research Center, D. Cohn, A. Brown and H. Lopez, Chapter 3: 'Hispanic Identity and Immigrant Generations', in *Black and Hispanic Americans See Their Origins as Central to Who They Are*, 14 May 2021. Available at: https://www.pewresearch.org/social-trends/2021/05/14/hispanic-identity-and-immigrant-generations/, accessed 27 February 2023.

38. G. Coronado, '"The police come here to hunt": Brazilian cops kill at 9 times the rate of U.S. law enforcement', *Los Angeles Times*, 1 October 2022.

39. J. W. Warren and F. W. Twine, 'White Americans, the new minority? Non-Blacks and the ever-expanding boundaries of Whiteness', *Journal of Black Studies* 28(2), 18 November 1997, pp. 200–18, 201.

40. N. Ignatiev, *How the Irish Became White* (New York, NY: Routledge, 1995).

41. S. Hitlin, J. S. Brown, G. H. Elder, 'Measuring Latinos: racial vs. ethnic classifications and self-understandings', *Social Forces* 86(2), 2007, pp. 587–611, 603.

42. F. A. Rosales, *Chicano! The History of the Mexican American Civil Rights Movement* (Houston, TX: Arte Público, 1997).

43. F. F. Montalvo, 'Skin color and Latinos in the United States', *Ethnicities* 1(3), 2001, pp. 321–41.

44. G. A. Martinez, 'African-Americans, Latinos, and the construction of race: toward an epistemic coalition', *Chicano-Latino Law Review* 19, 1998, pp. 213–22.

45. I. H. Lopez, 'White Latinos', *Harvard Latino Law Review* 6(1), 2003, pp. 1–7, 3.

46. A. Waterson, 'Are Latinos becoming "white" folk? And what that still says about race in America', *Transforming Anthropology* 14(2), 2006, pp. 133–50.

47. K. Deliovsky and T. Kitossa, 'Beyond Black and White: when going beyond may take us out of bounds', *Journal of Black Studies* 44 (2), March 2013, pp. 158–81.

48. Montalvo, 'Skin color and Latinos in the United States', p. 324.

49. BBC News, A. Gregorious, 'The black people "erased from history"', 10 April 2016.

50. H. Llorens, *Imaging the Great Puerto Rican Family: Framing Nation, Race, and Gender during the American Century* (Washington, DC: Rowman & Littlefield, 2014).

51. *Closer* staff, 'Martin Sheen reveals changing his name from Ramon Estevez for Hollywood is "one of my regrets"', *Closer Weekly*, 18 June 2022.

52. A. Randolph, 'Race as a resource? School composition and teachers' disparate discourse on school quality'. Paper presented at the First Forum of Sociology of the International Sociological Association, 5–8 September 2008, Barcelona, Spain.

53. Pew Hispanic Center, *Shades of Belonging*, 6 December 2004.

54. M. L. Clemons, C. E. Jones, 'Global solidarity: the Black Panther Party in the international arena', *New Political Science* 22(2), 1999, pp. 177–203.

55. S. Vidal-Ortiz, 'On being a white person of colour: using autoethnography to understand Puerto Ricans' racialization', *Qualitative Sociology* 27(2), 2004, pp. 179–203, 196.

56. Martinez, 'African-Americans, Latinos, and the construction of race', p. 222.

57. L. Shriver, 'Would you want London to be overrun by Americans like me?', *Spectator*, 26 August 2021.

58. The Migration Observatory, C. Vargas-Silva and P. Walsh, *EU Migration to and from the UK*, 15 February 2020, available at https://migrationobservatory.ox.ac.uk/resources/briefings/eu-migration-to-and-from-the-uk/, accessed 27 February 2023.

59. G. Jones, T. Helms and G. Wilson, '"British workers for British jobs," says Brown', *Daily Telegraph*, 6 June 2007.

60. R. Taylor, 'Cameron refuses to apologise to Ukip', *Guardian*, 4 April 2006.

61. Office for National Statistics, *International Migration, England and Wales: Census 2021*, available at https://www.ons.gov.uk/peoplepopulationandcommunity/populationandmigration/internationalmigration/bulletins/internationalmigrationenglandandwales/census2021#country-of-birth, accessed 13 March 2023.

62. W. E. B. DuBois, *Black Reconstruction in America 1860–1880* (New York, NY: The Free Press, 1998).

63. K. Andrews, *The New Age of Empire: How Racism and Colonialism Still Rule the World* (London: Penguin Books, 2021).

64. The Conversation, C. Lawton and R. Ackrill, 'Hard evidence: how areas with low immigration voted mainly for Brexit', 8 July 2016.
65. Bulletin of the Atomic Scientists, M. Riordan, 'The human cost of the Trump pandemic response? More than 100,000 unnecessary deaths', 30 September 2020.
66. A. Sullivan, 'Explainer: More guns than people: why tighter U.S. firearms laws are unlikely', Reuters, 14 April 2021.
67. J. Metzl, *Dying of Whiteness: How the Politics of Racial Resentment Is Killing America*. (New York, NY: Basic Books, 2019).
68. Ibid.
69. S. Woolhandler et al., *Public Policy and Health in the Trump Era*, The *Lancet Commission* 297(10275), 20 February 2021, pp. 705–53.
70. E. Eze, 'The color of reason: The idea of "race" in Kant's *Anthropology*', in E. Eze (ed.), *Postcolonial African Philosophy: A Critical Reader* (Oxford: Blackwell Publishers, 1997), p. 117.
71. A. E. Miller and L. Josephs, 'Whiteness as pathological narcissism', *Contemporary Psychoanalysis* 45(1), 2009, pp. 93–119.

6: CULTURAL MISAPPROPRIATION

1. B. Phillips, *Loot: Britain and the Benin Bronzes* (London: Oneworld, 2021)
2. M. Brown, 'New museum in Nigeria raises hopes of resolution to Benin bronzes dispute', *Guardian*, 14 November 2020.
3. Ibid.
4. V. Ehikhamenor, 'Give us back what our ancestors made', *The New York Times*, 28 January 2020.
5. D. Hicks, *The Brutish Museums: The Benin Bronzes, Colonial Violence and Cultural Restitution* (London: Pluto Press, 2020), p. 4.
6. K. Nzerem, 'Benin Bronzes "properly reside" in British Museum, says Culture Secretary', *Channel 4 News*, 10 September 2021.
7. D. Faloyin, *Africa Is Not a Country: Breaking Stereotypes of Modern Africa* (London: Penguin Books, 2020).
8. M. Gladwell, 'Dragon Psychology 101: Revisionist History' (Pushkin podcast), 20 June 2020.
9. A. Procter, *The Whole Picture: The Colonial Story of the Art in Our Museums and Why We Need to Talk about It* (Sydney: Hachette Australia, 2020).
10. Ibid.

11. Ibid., p. 132.

12. R. Maclean, 'Bronzes to Benin, gold to Ghana . . . museums under fire on looted art', *Guardian*, 2 December 2018.

13. M. Kram, 'Long overdue statue of Joe Frazier a sign of love from Philadelphia', *Sports Illustrated*, 11 September 2015.

14. See www.humanzoos.net.

15. A. Jama, 'Black people on display: the forgotten history of human zoos', *Rife Magazine,* 30 April 2019.

16. D. Olusoga, *Black and British: A Forgotten History* (London: Macmillan, 2016).

17. I. Kendi, *Stamped from the Beginning: The Definitive History of Racist Ideas in America* (London: Bodley Head, 2017), p. 139.

18. K. Andrews, 'Exhibit B, the human zoo, is a grotesque parody – boycott it', *Guardian*, 12 September 2014.

19. J. O'Mahony, 'Edinburgh's most controversial show: Exhibit B, a human zoo', *Guardian*, 11 August 2014.

20. S. Odunlami and K. Andrews, 'Is art installation Exhibit B racist?', *The Observer*, 27 September 2014.

21. Akala, 'The human zoo and the masturbation of white guilt', *HuffPost*, 13 September 2014.

22. For instance: C. Bennett, 'What price artistic freedom when the bullies turn up?', *Guardian*, 28 September 2014; K. Malik, Pandaemonium, 'Exhibit B and thinking for oneself', 2014.

23. H. Muir, 'The Exhibit B slavery show has value – but who was it aimed at?', *Guardian*, 26 September 2014.

24. 'Exhibit B performer Stella Odunlami: "We were terrified"', BBC News, 24 September 2014.

25. A. Abbott, 'Traces of paint confirmed on Parthenon sculptures', *Nature*, 15 June 2009.

7: THE POST-RACIAL PRINCESS

1. Linton Kwesi Johnson, *Inglan Is a Bitch* (London: Penguin Books, 1980).

2. Statement by His Royal Highness Prince Harry, Duke of Sussex, 1 October 2019, available at https://sussexofficial.uk/, accessed 27 February 2023.

3. A. Bland, 'Society of Editors in turmoil over its statement on Meghan', *Guardian*, 9 March 2021.

4. R. Styles and S. Bathia, 'Harry's girl is (almost) straight outta Compton: gang-scarred home of her mother revealed – so will he be dropping by for tea?', *Daily Mail*, 2 November 2016.

5. R. Booth and L. O'Carroll, 'Prince Harry attacks press over "wave of abuse" of girlfriend Meghan Markle', *Guardian*, 8 November 2016.

6. L. Clancy and H. Yelin, 'Monarchy is a feminist issue: Andrew, Meghan and #MeToo era monarchy', *Women's Studies International Forum*, 84, January–February 2021.

7. T. Sykes, 'Prince Harry and Meghan Markle might spark a royal cultural revolution', *Daily Beast*, 5 November 2016.

8. K. Andrews, 'Fear of a Black princess: Britain's royal racial problem', *Ebony Magazine*, 10 November 2016.

9. E. Bonilla-Silva, *Racism without Racists: Color-Blind Racism and the Persistence of Racial Inequality in America* (Lanham, MD: Rowman & Littlefield, 2017).

10. K. Taylor, *From #Blacklivesmatter to Black Liberation* (Chicago, IL: Haymarket Books, 2016).

11. C. West (ed.), *The Radical King* (Boston, MA: New Beacon Press, 2015), p. 332.

12. D. Bell, *Faces at the Bottom of the Well: The Permanence of Racism* (New York, NY: Basic Books, 1992), p. 3.

13. J. Sumption, 'Brexit and the British constitution: reflections on the last three years and the next fifty', *Political Quarterly* 91(1), 2020, pp. 107–15.

14. R. Tingle and T. Pyman, 'Education Secretary slams "absurd" cancelling of the Queen as students at Oxford's Magdalen College vote to take down "unwelcoming" portrait of the monarch from graduates' common room because she "represents recent colonial history"', *Daily Mail*, 8 June 2021.

15. 'Good Morning Britain's removal of portrait of the Queen at Oxford University sparks heated debate', 9 June 2021, available at Removal of Portrait of The Queen at Oxford University Sparks Heated Debate | Good Morning Britain - YouTube.

16. GOV.UK, *Race Disparity Audit: Summary Findings from the Ethnicity Facts and Figures* (Cabinet Office, 2017).

17. N. Iqbal, 'Has Meghan Markle changed Britain's attitude to race and royalty?', *Guardian*, 13 May 2018.

18. J. Burnett, 'Racial violence and the Brexit state', *Race & Class* 58(4), 2017, pp. 85–97.

19. M. Goodfellow, *Hostile Environment: How Immigrants Became Scapegoats* (London: Verso Books, 2019).

20. L. Staples, 'A really, really long list of awful things Boris Johnson has said about women, LGBT+ people and people of colour', *Indy 100*, 24 November 2019.

21. D. Carbado and K. Crenshaw, 'An intersectional critique of tiers of scrutiny: beyond "either/or" approaches to equal protection', *Yale Law Journal Forum* 108, 6 November 2019, pp. 19–44.

22. M. Jacobs, 'The violent state: Black women's invisible struggle against police violence', *William & Mary Journal of Race Gender and Social Justice*, 24(1), 2017.

23. K. Crenshaw, K. Andrews and A. Wilson, *Blackness at the Intersection* (London: Bloomsbury Publishing, 2021).

24. M. Hunter, 'The persistent problem of colorism: skin tone, status, and inequality', *Sociology Compass* 1(1), 2007, pp. 237–54.

25. I. Law and S. A. Tate, *Caribbean Racisms: Connections and Complexities in the Racialization of the Caribbean Region* (London: Routledge, 2015).

26. A. Phoenix, 'Colourism and the politics of beauty', *Feminist Review*, 108(1), 2014, pp. 97–105.

27. K. Andrews, *The New Age of Empire: How Racism and Colonialism Still Rule the World* (London: Penguin Books, 2021).

28. B. Higman, *Slave Population and Economy in Jamaica, 1807–1834* (Kingston: Press of the University of the West Indies, 1976).

29. K. Walsh, 'Meghan Markle says she was treated "like a black woman" for the first time when dating Prince Harry', *Vogue*, 31 August 2022.

30. P. Fryer, *Staying Power: The History of Black People in Britain* (London: Pluto Press, 1984).

31. E. Nascimento, *The Sorcery of Color: Identity, Race, and Gender in Brazil* (Philadelphia, PA: Temple University Press, 2007).

32. The Commonwealth, Our History. Available at https://thecommonwealth.org/about-us/history, accessed 28 February 2023.

33. The Conversation, P. Murphy, 'The Commonwealth: rediscovering its radical voice could make it relevant again', 7 March 2021.

34. Commonwealth Games Federation, About Us, Who We Are. Available at https://thecgf.com/about, accessed 28 February 2023.

35. Constitutional Documents of the Commonwealth Games Federation, Company No: 10449637, p. 33, available at get_file.cgi (mygameday.app), accessed 28 February 2023.

NOTES

36. J. Hayes, 'Birmingham Commonwealth Games 2022 diversity row – with 19 of 20 leaders white', *Birmingham Mail*, 5 July 2020.

37. D. Woode, 'Meghan Markle's tell-all Oprah interview prompts questions over the future of the Commonwealth', *iNews*, 8 March 2021.

38. K. Andrews, 'Harry and Meghan, Africa doesn't want you', CNN, 24 April 2019.

39. R. Hall and A. Gentleman, '"Perfect storm": royals misjudged Caribbean tour, say critics', *Guardian*, 25 March 2022.

40. M. Bryant, 'Caribbean: William suggests monarchy will respect any decision to become republic', *Guardian*, 22 March 2022.

41. T. Mundle, 'Queen's death end of an era', *Jamaica Gleanor*, 9 September 2022.

42. A. Mersie and C. Uwiringiyimana, 'Commonwealth's royal succession stirs unease among Caribbean members. Reuters, 24 June 2022.

43. BBC News, 'Queen's lying-in-state: how long was the queue?', 19 September 2022.

8: BLACK SKIN, WHITE PSYCHOSIS

1. GOV.UK, The Right Hon. Boris Johnson MP, *Prime Minister Message on Black Lives Matter*, transcript of the speech exactly as it was delivered (Prime Minister's Office, 8 June 2020).

2. N. Parveen, 'Priti Patel describes Black Lives Matter protests as "dreadful"', *Guardian*, 12 February 2021.

3. J. Stone, 'Priti Patel says fans have right to boo England team for "gesture politics" of taking the knee', *Independent*, 14 June 2021.

4. N. Thomas-Symonds, 'Putting statues before women, the Tories could end up on the wrong side of history', *Guardian*, 15 March 2021.

5. R. Merrick, 'Migrants at risk of drowning if Priti Patel sends Navy warships to Channel, warns ex-home secretary', *Independent*, 8 August 2020.

6. A. Saini, *Superior: The Return of Race Science* (London: HarperCollins, 2019).

7. A. Woodcock, 'Home secretary Priti Patel admits own parents might not have been allowed into UK under her new immigration laws', *Independent*, 19 February 2020.

8. R. Sayal, '"Invasion" of the UK? Experts dubious of Suella Braverman's claim', *Guardian*, 1 November 2022.

227

9. R. Merrick, 'Priti Patel blames Suella Braverman for failure to prevent Kent asylum centre crisis', *Independent*, 31 October 2022.

10. Commission on Race and Ethnic Disparities (chair: T. Sewell), *Commission on Race and Ethnic Disparities: The Report* (2021), p. 8, available at Commission on Race and Ethnic Disparities – Commission on Race and Ethnic Disparities: The Report – March 2021 (publishing.service. gov.uk), accessed on 28 February 2023.

11. N. White, 'Author of controversial race report invokes Bob Marley's anti-oppression lyrics to defend slavery remarks', *Independent*, 29 April 2021.

12. T. Sewell, 'British education does NOT perpetuate racism', Debate, Oxford Union, 19 April 2017, available at British Education Does NOT Perpetuate Racism | Dr Tony Sewell CBE | Part 4 of 6 - YouTube, accessed 28 February 2023.

13. B. Marley, 'Babylon System', *Survival*, 1979.

14. S. Sanghera, *Empireland: How Imperialism Has Shaped Modern Britain* (London: Penguin Books, 2021).

15. F. Fanon, *Black Skin, White Masks* (New York, NY: Grove Press, 1967), p. 148.

16. Malcolm X, Excerpt of speech 'Who taught you to hate yourself?', 5 May 1962.

17. K. Andrews, 'From the "Bad Nigger" to the "Good Nigga": an unintended legacy of the Black Power movement', *Race & Class*, 55(3), 2014, pp. 22–37.

18. A. Wilson, *Black on Black Violence: The Psychodynamics of Black Self-Annihilation in the Service of White Domination* (New York, NY: Afrikan World Infosystems, 1994).

19. Fanon, *Black Skin, White Masks*, p. 192.

20. F. Fanon, *Towards the African Revolution* (New York, NY: Grove Press, 1967), p. 26.

21. Malcolm X, 'Message to the grassroots', Negro Grass Roots Leadership Conference, Michigan, 10 November 1963.

22. Ibid.

23. T. Thomas, 'Black youth unemployment rate of 40% similar to time of Brixton riots, data shows', *Guardian*, 11 April 2021.

24. World Bank Blogs, D. Wadhwa, 'The number of extremely poor people continues to rise in sub-Saharan Africa', 19 September 2018.

25. W. E. B. DuBois, *The Souls of Black Folk* (Mineola, NY: Dover Publications, 1994), p. 225.

26. C. Rock, *Bring the Pain*, HBO TV special, 1996.

27. T. Shakur, 'I Wonder if Heaven Got a Ghetto', *RU Still Down*, Amaru Records, 1997.

28. Taylor, *From #Blacklivesmatter to Black Liberation*, p. 140.

29. B. Obama, 'Remarks to the Democratic National Convention', *The New York Times*, 27 July 2004.

30. E. Pilkington, 'The Black Panthers still in prison. After 46 years, will they ever be set free?', *Guardian*, 30 July 2018.

31. K. Crenshaw, 'The girls Obama forgot', *The New York Times*, 29 July 2014.

32. K. Crenshaw, 'Demarginalizing the intersection of race and sex: a Black feminist critique of antidiscrimination doctrine, feminist theory and antiracist politics', *University of Chicago Legal Forum* 1(8), 1989, pp. 139–67.

33. Taylor, *From #Blacklivesmatter to Black Liberation*.

34. K. Evelyn, 'Barack Obama criticizes "Defund the Police" slogan but faces backlash', *Guardian*, 2 December 2020.

35. Malcolm X, 'Message to the grassroots'.

36. Malcolm X, Excerpt from interview with Louis Lomax (Greenwood, IN: Educational Video Group, 1963).

37. K. Andrews, *Back to Black: Retelling Black Radicalism for the 21st Century* (London: Zed Books, 2018).

38. N. Mandela, *Long Walk to Freedom* (New York, NY: Hachette Book Group, 1994).

39. Quartz, L. Chutel, 'Post-apartheid South Africa is failing the very people it liberated', 25 August 2017.

40. Human Rights Watch, 'They have robbed me of my life: xenophobic violence against non-nationals in South Africa', 17 September 2020.

41. K. Andrews, *The New Age of Empire: How Racism and Colonialism Still Rule the World* (London: Penguin Books, 2021).

42. Reuters staff, 'Mandela visits Apartheid die-hards', *The New York Times*, 16 August 1995.

EPILOGUE: BEYOND THE RABBIT HOLE

1. S. Poole, 'Jean Baudrillard: obituary', *Guardian*, 7 March 2007.

2. K. Andrews, *The New Age of Empire: How Racism and Colonialism Still Rule the World* (London: Penguin Books, 2021).

3. H. Shroff, P. Diedrichs and N. Craddock, 'Skin color, cultural capital, and beauty products: an investigation of the use of skin fairness

products in Mumbai, India', *Frontiers in Public Health*, 23 January 2018, available at https://doi.org/10.3389/fpubh.2017.00365 , accessed 28 February 2023.

4. F. Lawrence, 'Can the world quench China's bottomless thirst for milk?', *Guardian*, 29 March 2019.

5. Ibid.

6. Statista, A. Blazyte, 'Number of Starbucks stores in China from fiscal year 2005 to 2020', 23 November 2022, available at: https://www.statista.com/statistics/277795/number-of-starbucks-stores-in-china/, accessed 28 February 2023.

7. D. Bell, 'Brown vs Board of Education and the interest-convergence dilemma', *Harvard Law Review* 93(3), 11 January 1980, pp. 513–18.

8. A. Shakur, *Assata: An Autobiography* (London: Zed Books, 2014).

9. C. Anderson, *Eyes Off the Prize: The United Nations and the African American Struggle for Human Rights, 1944–1955* (New York, NY, and Cambridge: Cambridge University Press, 2003).

Index

Abolition of the Slave Trade Act (1807) 61
Abraham Lincoln: Vampire Hunter (film) 58–9
affirmative action 41–2, 103–4, 124, 158
African Americans 3, 13, 18, 34, 43, 44, 62; affirmative action and 41–2, 103–4, 124, 158; civil rights movement and *see* civil rights movement; ghettoization and 85–6; kidney function of 5; Latinx communities and 121, 123; lynching of xi, 19–20, 26, 79; mass incarceration of 37, 45, 85–6, 98–9, 104, 158; mental health of 10; Obama and 188–90; Philadelphia and 140–2; segregation in cities and 78–85; university enrolment of 41
Africa at the Palace 143
African National Congress (ANC) 193, 194, 196
Afrikaners 195, 196, 197
Aim Higher 116–17
Airbnb 57
Akala 146–7
Alexandra Stadium, Perry Barr 170

A Levels 108
allies, White anti-racist 33, 35, 43, 44, 83, 146, 201–3
Amazing Grace (film) 59–72
Amazon (online retailer) xiii, xiv
American Dream 185
Amistad (film) 58, 59
Amritsar Massacre, India (1919) 178
Anderson, Carol: *White Rage* 19, 79, 87
Anderson, Elijah 74, 77; *Code of the Street* 140
Antigua x, 54
anti-racism 24, 29, 121, 124, 144–5, 146, 148, 155, 172, 174, 198, 200, 203, 204; anti-racist industrial complex 31–51, 199; critical pedagogy and 34–8; critical Whiteness studies, backlash against 31–3; self-help books and 39–51
apartheid, South Africa 85, 120, 158, 193, 194, 195, 197, 198
Asante, Amma 60, 67
asylum seekers 176
austerity policies 41, 111, 117, 127
Azania (South Africa) 194

Baartman, Saartjie 143–4
Babylon System 178
Badenoch, Kemi 31–2, 33, 46, 50
bad nigger 22, 179
Bailey, Brett 144, 145, 146, 148
Bali 56
Barbican 147, 148, 149
Baudrillard, Jean 199, 204–5
BBC viii–ix, x, xi, 40–1, 125
BBC Breakfast xi
Bell, Derrick 46–7, 158, 162
Belle (film) 59–72
Benin Bronzes 133–7, 141–2,
    150, 151
Benin City, Nigeria 133–7, 141–2,
    150, 151
Benin Dialogue Group 133–4
Beresford, Alex 154
Bezos, Jeff xiii
Bias, Len 85, 86
Biden, Joe 82
Birmingham 75, 87, 88, 89, 91–3,
    96, 109, 124, 127, 139–40, 156,
    170–1
Birmingham City Council 91, 109
Birmingham City University 91,
    156, 170–1
Birmingham Museum 139–40
'birther' movement 102
Birth of A Nation (film) 58
Bishop, Maurice 87
Black and White Minstrel Show
    vii, viii
Black Entertainment Television
    (BET) 157
blackface viii, ix, 186
Black History Month 31–2,
    111–12, 165
black inferiority 46

Black Lives Matter xi, 5, 31, 102,
    103, 106, 153, 175–7, 189, 194
Black Power movement 3, 11, 50,
    112, 121, 181, 188
Black Studies 112, 115, 156, 203
Black Panthers 48–9, 123
Blair, Tony 93, 95, 96
Blue Origins xiii
Bolsonaro, Jair xiv, xv, 119,
    120, 129
Boone Hall Plantation, South
    Carolina, US 56
Boshoff, Carel 195
Boshoff, Wynand 195, 196
Boston, US 78, 82–5, 89
Boyd, Rekia 163
Bradford riots (2001) 93–4
Bradford World Fair (1804) 143
Branson, Richard 191
Braverman, Suella 176
Brazil xiv, 21, 119–20, 156, 167–8
Brexit xv, 126, 127–8, 159,
    162, 169
Bristol 167, 202
British empire: apologists for 23–5;
    British monarchy and 21–2,
    160–1, 169–74; Churchill and x;
    diversity used in service of 178;
    education and 22–5; Jamaica and
    57; museum/heritage sector and
    see museum/heritage sector;
    slavery and *see* slavery
British Empire Games 170
British Museum 133–9, 150, 151
British Museums Act (1963) 137
Bromberg, Walter 3–4
Brown, Adrienne Marie 48;
    Pleasure Activism 48
Brown Berets 123

Brown, Elaine 48–9
Brown, Gordon 125
Brown, Henry 'Box' 62
Brown, Mike 163
Brown-Trickey, Minnijean 80–1
Brown vs the Board of Education
    ruling, US (1955) 79–80
Burke, Aggrey 2
Burke, Vanley 139
Bush, George W. xiv, 95, 117, 181

Caledonia Farm, Virginia, US 56
Cambridge University 114
Cameron, David 66, 97, 127
Campbell, Lady Colin 157
cancel culture viii
Cantle Report (2001) 93–5
capitalism 37–8, 107
Capitol riot, US (6 January 2021)
    101
Caribbean 54, 55, 68, 87, 88,
    107–8, 111, 112–13, 149, 165,
    167, 172, 176, 177, 179, 191,
    192. See also individual nation
    name
Carlson, Tucker 118
Carothers, J. C. 9
Cartwright, Samuel 4–8, 10, 11,
    104–5
Casey, Dame Louise 92, 96
Catherine, Princess of Wales 172
Central High School, Little Rock,
    Arkansas 80–1
Centre for Contemporary Cultural
    Studies, Birmingham 75
Channel 4 viii, 156
Charles III, King 169, 172
Charlottesville Unite the Right rally
    (2017) 118

Chauvin, Derek xi
Chicago, US 78–9, 83, 102
Chicano Movement 121
China 200–1
Churchill, Winston x–xi
CIA 87
civil rights movements, US:
    affirmative action and 41, 158;
    Black History Month and 165;
    ghettoization and 85; Great
    Migration and 11; mental health
    and 3, 18; minimizing importance
    of racism and 69; Montgomery
    Bus Boycott and 202; Obama and
    189; origins 50; Republicans and
    104; success of 157–8
class: African Americans and 188–9;
    house negro 184, 186; housing
    segregation and 88, 89, 92, 94;
    mental health and 3, 9; racism
    and 84; Thatcher and xiv; US
    Civil war and 4–5; white
    working-class and
    delegitimization of racism
    complaints 69–71, 105–17,
    125, 127
cleaning jobs ix, 41, 92
Clinton, Hilary 85
Coates, Ta-Nahesi: We Were Eight
    Years in Power 190
cocaine 85–7
'Coconut' 180, 187, 193
Cold Spring Harbor Laboratory,
    New York, US 105
colonialism: 'benevolent' 25;
    capitalism and 37–8; end of 202;
    immigration and 88; Industrial
    Revolution and 22–3; Israel and
    120; Latin America and 119;

monarchy and 21–2, 161, 169–73; museum/heritage sector and 133–51; nostalgia for 57; Second World War and x, 24; violence of 17, 18–19, 21–5, 27, 96

colourism 165–7

Columbus, Christopher 20, 103

Common: *Like Water for Chocolate* 181

Commonwealth 22, 160, 168–74

Commonwealth Games 170–1

Commission on Race and Ethnic Disparities report (2021). *See* Sewell Report

'communities of communities' 93

'community cohesion' 94

Compton, L.A., US 156, 187

Congo Free State 20

Conservative Party xv, 41, 88, 93, 97, 128

consumer city 90

Contras 86–7

Coulter, Ann 117–18

counter-terrorism 96

Covid-19 pandemic xiv–xv, 74, 103, 107, 129, 171, 184

crack cocaine 85–6

Crenshaw, Kimberlé 163–4

critical pedagogy 34–8, 43

Critical Race Theory (CRT) 28, 32, 46–7, 50, 103, 104, 158, 164, 202

Crystal Palace 142–3

Cugoano, Ottabah 62

cultural appropriation 42

cultural imperialism 135–6

culture war ix, xi, xii, 185–6, 192

Curvier, George 143

Daily Mail 156, 160, 164, 178

Daily Telegraph 90

Danczuk, Simon 126

dark hordes 98, 131

Davinier, John 63, 70

Davis, Angela 34–5

Davis, Shantel 163

Dead Prez 86

delusions of grandeur xii, xiv, xv, 28, 131

Department for Education 109

depression viii, 9, 14

Desmond's (TV show) viii, 18

Detroit, US 84

Diana, Princess of Wales 164

DiAngelo, Robin: *White Fragility* 13, 39–40, 44

Dido, Belle Elizabeth 62

digital hallucinations 58–60, 71–2

Dillon, C. Douglas 137

diversity training 40

DNA 42, 105

Dominions 168

double consciousness 185

Douglas, Frederick 62

Dowden, Oliver 135–6

Drapetomania 6

drill music 179

DuBois, W. E. B. 34, 127, 185; *The Philadelphia Negro* 140

Dunbar, Alexander 84

dysesthesia Aethiopis 6

Ebony 155–6

Edinburgh Festival 144, 145, 149

Edo Museum of West African Art, Benin City, Nigeria 133–4, 151

Education Funding Agency 110

Education Select Committee: 'The Forgotten' report 107, 112
Egypt 150
Ehikhamenor, Victor 134
Eisenhower, Dwight D. 81
Elgin, Lord 150
Elizabeth II, Queen 22, 54, 154, 159, 160–1, 169, 172–3, 186
Ellison, Ralph: *Invisible Man* 14
Enlightenment 66, 131
'epistemology of ignorance' 22, 34, 203
Equiano, Olaudah 60, 62, 139
Estevez, Emilio 122
Ethnic Minority Achievement Grant (EMAG) 110–11
eugenics movement x, 5, 104–5
Euro 2020 175
European Union (EU) 125–8, 159, 162, 169
Evarts, A. B. 7
Exhibit B 144–50

Fair Sentencing Act (2010) 86
Fanon, Franz: *Black Skin, White Masks* 12–13, 16–17, 22, 178–81
Farage, Nigel 125–6, 127
Ferguson, Niall: *Empire: How Britain Shaped the Modern World* 23–5
field negro 182–4
Financial Accounting Standards Board 136
financial crisis (2008) 127
First World War (1914–18) 83, 129, 167
Fisher, Abigail 103–4
Fisher, Hartwig 133
Fleming, Crystal 47

Flint Michigan water crisis 190–1
Flitch Green, Essex 90
Floyd, George ix, xi, 31, 43, 56, 103, 134, 165, 175, 199
Foreign Affairs 96
Foreman, Stanley 82
Fox News 118, 124
Frazier, Joe 141
Free at Last: The Spirit of Wilberforce 66–7
Freedom Front Plus 195
free school meals 105–8, 112–13, 117
free trade 23–5
Fresh Prince of Bel-Air (TV show) 18, 140
Frey, Shelley 163

Garner, Eric 163
Garvey, Marcus 177
GCSE 107, 108–9, 110, 112–13
general elections, UK: (1945) x; (1997) 93; (2017) 159; (2019) 128, 162
gentrification 90, 91
George VI, King 169
ghetto 27–8, 83, 92, 98, 123, 183; ghettoization 85–7; 'iconic ghetto' 74–6, 77–8, 79, 82, 84, 85–6, 130, 179, 181
Gladwell, Malcolm 136, 137
golliwog toys 11
Gone With the Wind (film) 59
Gonsalves, Camillo Michael 173
Good Morning Britain (TV show) viii, ix, 154, 156, 160
'good Negro' 11, 190
Gordon, Lewis 25
Gould, Benjamin 4–5

Gove, Michael xv, 109
Great Exhibition (1851) 142–3
Great Migration (1910–70) 11, 83
Greece, ancient 150–1
Green, E. M. 10
Grenada 87
Griffiths, Peter 88
grime music 73–4, 179
Groenewald, Pieter 197
Guardian, The 80, 89, 106, 156
guns, US ownership of 129–30

Haiti 54
Hall, Professor Stuart 75
Handsworth 75–6, 88
Harwood, Tom ix, xiii
Harewood, David 15–16
Harriet (film) 58
Harvard University 41
Hemmings, Sally 48
Henry, Sir Lenny vii–viii, 186
Hicks, Dan 135
high culture 142
higher education: affirmative action
    and 41–2, 104; Black Studies
    Degree in 203; Black student
    representation in 79, 106,
    113–17; Babylon System and 178;
    gentrification and 91, 170–1;
    study of Whiteness in 50; White
    women representation in 41–2;
    White working-class boys and
    105–6, 108, 113–17; working in
    13–14, 25
High Speed 2 (HS2) 91
Hirsch, Afua 156
Hitler, Adolf x, 24, 182; Mein
    Kampf 176
Holocaust x, 105

Hopkins, Bernard 141
Hopkins, Katie xv, 124
'Hottentot Venus' 143–4
house negro 182–91, 192, 193
House of Lords 92
Houses of Parliament 31; Black
    History Month debate 31;
    prorogued 159
housing 77–92, 94, 113, 127, 171
human zoos 142–50
humanitarian imperialisms 147

iconic ghetto 74–6, 77–8, 79, 82,
    84, 85–6, 130, 179, 181
Ignatiev, Noel 35–8; How the Irish
    Became White 35
immigration 3, 11, 32, 41, 75, 83,
    88, 92, 93, 99, 116, 117–18, 120,
    123–8, 155, 162, 167, 176
Imperial Conference (1926) 168
India x, 92, 126, 143, 168–9, 175,
    176, 178, 200
individualism 48, 49
Industrial Revolution 22, 51, 66
institutional racism 3, 38, 41, 45,
    76, 119, 177, 178
interest convergence 202, 203
internalized racism 12–16
interracial love 48
intersectionality 53, 70, 163–8;
    intersectional failure 163–8
IQ 104, 105
Iraq War (2003-11) 95
Ireland 35, 88, 120, 122, 168

Jabbar, Kareem Abdul 104
Jamaica vii, x, 48, 53–8, 61, 65, 76,
    172, 177, 179–80
Jay Kay 101

Jefferson, Thomas 4, 48
Jews x, 105, 120, 146
Jian Yi 201
Jim Crow laws 38, 79, 83, 88
'Jimmy Savile defence' 136
Johnson, Andrew 21
Johnson, Boris xiv, xv, 128, 129,
    159, 162, 175, 176
Johnson, Linton Kwesi 153
Johnson, Sidney 19
Jonathan, Goodluck 194
Jones, Nikki: *Between Good and
    Ghetto* 140

Kant, Immanuel 131
Kendi, Ibram X.: *How to Be An
    Anti-Racist* 45–6
Khanom, Aysha 183
kidney function 5
Kimberley, South Africa 195
King, Gayle 154
King, Martin Luther 15–16, 156,
    165, 189, 192; 'I Have a Dream'
    speech 158
Kings Heath 89
KKK xi, 43, 118
knife crime 73–4, 77, 96; #knifefree
    campaign 73–4, 77, 96
Koh-i-Noor diamond 143
Krikler, Jeremy 64

Labour Party x, 4, 88, 93, 110,
    126, 128
lactose intolerance 200–1
Ladywood 91
Last Poets: The White Man's Got a
    God Complex' xiii
Latinx population 119–24, 129
Lawrence, Jacob 140, 141

Leeds Beckett University Centre for
    Race, Education and Decoloniality
    183
Leonardo, Zeus 34, 36
Leopold II, King 20
Lil Wayne 187
Lincoln, Abraham 202
Lincoln (film) 58
Lind, John 26
Little Britain viii, ix
Little Italy, New York 122
Little Rock Nine 80–1
Lively, Blake 56
Liverpool 167
Livingstone, David 23–4
Lodge, Reni Eddo: *Why I Am No
    Longer Talking to White People
    About Race* 204–5
London Metropolitan University 114
lynching xi, 19–20, 26, 79

MacDonald, Sir Trevor viii
Madeley, Richard 160
Magnolia Hill Plantation Hotel,
    Natchez, Mississippi 56
majority-minority 118, 124, 127
'Make America White Again' 103
Malcolm X xiii, 25, 34–5, 43–4, 47,
    48, 79, 88, 112, 156, 179, 182,
    184, 185, 192–3, 197
Malthouse, Kit 73
mandatory minimum sentences
    85–6
Mandela, Nelson 193–6
Mandigo (film) 58
Mansfield Estate 69, 70
Mansfield, Lord 62–5, 68, 69–70,
    71
Maoris 138

March on Washington (1963) 158
Marley, Bob: 'Redemption Song'
    177–8
Marshall, Thurgood 182
Martin, Trayvon 18, 189–90
Marvel 49
Marx, Karl/Marxism 37, 86–7, 107
Matias, Cheryl E. 13
Matrix, The 199
May, Theresa 159
mediocre White man xii–xvi, 23, 160
mestizo 167
Metropolitan Museum of Art, New
    York, US 136–7
Metzl, Jonathan: *Dying of
    Whiteness* 130; *The Protest
    Psychosis* 3
Mexican Americans 121–2
Mexican War of Independence
    (1810–21) 121
microaggresions 13, 18
Mills, Charles 22, 34
minstrel shows vii–viii, 186
mixed-race 162, 166, 171
Mobutu 194
Mokae, Dr Sabatampho 195
Mokomokai 138
monarchy 21, 22, 151, 153–68,
    171–2, 174
Montgomery Bus Boycott, US
    (1955–6) 202
Morgan, Piers x, xii, 154, 157,
    160, 193
Morrison, Toni 16
Moseley 89
Mozambique 169
mugging 75, 76, 88
Muir, Hugh 149
mulatto 166

Mullis, Brian 54
multiculturalism 45, 77, 88–9, 91,
    93–4, 97, 125
murder 51, 55–6, 63, 64–5, 76–7,
    86, 103, 120, 165, 178, 179,
    193, 194
Murdoch, Rupert 75
Murray, Elizabeth 69, 70
museum/heritage sector 28, 133–51
Muslims 92–8, 109, 110, 162
My Brother's Keeper (MBK) 189
Myers, Sara 147

Nanny of the Maroons 48
narcissism 28, 131
NASA xiii
National Education Opportunities
    Network 114
National Institute for Health and
    Care Excellence (NICE) 5
NBA 85, 104
Neeson, Liam xi
Negritude movement 180
'Negro villages' 143–4
neo-liberalism 127–8
neo-Nazis 118
new abolitionists 35, 38
New Labour 93, 110
Newsnight (TV show) 147, 156
New Zealand 138, 168
Nicaragua 86–7
Niggaz Wit Attitudes (N.W.A.) 187
'nigger moment' 77
9/11 95
Nixon, Richard 86
Njole, Berthe 145
Northern Fox 79, 83
Nottingham Council 93
Nulman, Dr Eugene 59

Oba (King) of Benin 135
Obama, Barack 86, 101–2, 130, 157, 158–9, 161, 187, 188–91
Obamacare 130
objectification 145
Odunlami, Stella 146
Oldham riots (2001) 93–4
Oluo, Ijeoma 44; *So You Want to Talk About Race* 44–5
Olympic Games (1984) 201
O'Malley, Mary 8
'one drop rule' 42, 167
On Stage with the George Mitchell Minstrels vii
Oprah Show 153, 154–5, 168, 171
Orania, South Africa 195–8
'Other' 27–8, 98, 126
Owens, Candace 192
Oxford University 97, 114, 117, 160

Palmer, Annie 55
Pan African Congress 194, 195
paranoia xv, 6, 28, 124, 130–1
Parekh, Lord Bhiku 93
Paris World Fair: (1878) 143; (1889) 143
Parthenon Marbles 150
Patel, Priti 175–6
Patel, Vickram 9
Peasemore, West Berkshire 97
'people of colour' 119–21, 124
Peterson, Marlon 45
Philadelphia 78, 140–2
Philadelphia Museum of Art 140, 141
Phillips, Vice-Consul General James Robert 135
Phillips, Trevor 147

'Pimp' 179
plantation weddings 56–7
pleasure activism 48–9
Poland 126, 145
police: defunding xi, 191; harassment/brutality 11, 14–16, 18, 36–7, 45, 73–6, 83, 84, 92, 96–8, 120, 162, 163, 165, 175, 184, 202; stop and search 73, 76
Policing the Crisis 75
populism xiv, xv, 119, 126, 128
positive law 65
Post-92 institutions 114, 117
post-race/post-racial society 28, 68–9, 85, 104, 105, 147, 151, 157, 161, 163, 164, 173–4, 189, 198
poverty xiii, 9, 53, 71, 91, 104, 105, 106, 156, 158, 170, 184, 193
Powell, Colin 188
Powell, Enoch: 'Rivers of Blood' speech 92–3, 125, 126
Powell, Ted 162
presidential elections, US: (1996) 188; (2008) 101–2, 158, 188–9; (2016) xv, 128, 230; (2020) 82, 102, 103, 128, 129
Preventing Violent Extremism and Terrorism ('Prevent') strategy 96–7
Prince, Mary 62
prison 2, 22, 36, 73, 76, 177, 189; mass incarnation 37, 45, 85–6, 98–9, 104, 158; prison industrial complex 85–6
Procter, Alice 138
psychiatry 2, 3–12, 16, 26, 130
'psychological wage' of Whiteness 34, 127, 128

psychosis: delusions of grandeur
and xii, xiv, xv, 28, 131;
internalized racism and 12–16;
psychiatry, racist 2, 3–12, 16, 26,
130; 'psychosis of Whiteness'
term xii, xv–xvi, 1–29;
schizophrenia and 1–2, 3, 10, 11
Psychosis and Me (documentary)
15–16
Puerto Rico 122

quadroons 167

race riots 83, 120, 167
'racial cray-cray' 13
racial science 104–17
racial segregation 3, 77–80, 81,
82, 83, 84, 85, 89, 90, 96–7,
109–10, 194
racism: anti-racism 24, 29, 31–51,
121, 124, 144–5, 146, 148, 155,
172, 174, 198, 199, 200, 203,
204; anti-racist industrial complex
31–51, 199; black people, racist
46; institutional 3, 38, 41, 45, 76,
119, 177, 178; internalized 12–16;
psychiatry and 3–12; psychosis of
Whiteness minimizes importance
of 68–72; structural xi, 45, 110,
162, 168, 173
radicalization 96, 97–8
Rankin, Kenrya 44, 47
'rascality' 7, 10
Rashford, Marcus 112
Rastafarians 2, 178
Reagan, Ronald 87, 127
Real McCoy, The (TV show) viii
Republican Party 102, 104, 118,
130, 188

Revisionist History (podcast) 136
Reynolds, Ryan 56
Rice, Tamir 163
RightMove 90
Robben Island, South Africa 193
Robinson, Calvin 183, 185–6
Rock, Chris xiv, 116, 188
Rocky (film) 141
Romania 126
Royal African Company 66
Royal Caribbean 54
royal family, UK. *See* monarchy
Rule Britannia (song) xi
Rupprecht, Anita 66–7
Rushdie, Salman: *The Satanic
Verses* 148
Russell Group 114, 115
Rwanda 169, 178, 198
Ryan, Jan 146

Saad, Layla F.: *Me and White
Supremacy* 42
sambos 166
Samuels, Dominque ix
savages 6, 17, 18, 19, 20, 25, 75, 78,
79, 98, 131, 135, 142, 143, 163
#SayHerName campaign 163
schizophrenia 1–2, 3, 10, 11
schools 17, 28, 31, 32, 33, 37, 40,
41, 46, 88, 90, 127, 129–30, 165,
181, 193, 198, 203; class and
105–17; de-radicalization in
97–8; faith schools 109, 110; free
school meals 105–8, 112–13, 117;
school bussing 17, 82; segregation
in US 79–83; Trojan Horse
Jihadist plot to take over
Birmingham schools 109
Schwegler, Amanda 56–7

Second World War (1939–45) x, 24, 87–8, 124
security jobs ix, 13, 41, 92
self-help, Whiteness 39–51, 205
'sell-out' 181–2, 193, 194–5, 196 7/7 95, 96
Sewell Report (Commission on Race and Ethnic Disparities report) (2021) 106, 108, 113, 177–8, 186
Sheen, Martin 122–3
Shriver, Lionel 124–5
Simon, Franck 3, 4
skin tone 165–6
Sky News viii, ix, 139, 156
slavery: abolition of 7, 21, 34, 35, 36, 38, 57, 60–8, 119–20, 139, 202; abolitionists 34, 35, 36, 38, 61, 62, 63–5, 67, 69, 70; Atlantic system 27; Brazil and 119–20; British empire and 22–3; education and 31–2, 165; field negro and 182–3; film and 58–72; Industrial Revolution and 22, 51; Jamaica and 48, 53–72; Lincoln and 202; mental health and 4–12; Mexico and 121; mixed-race and 166–7; racial science and 104–5; sexual violence and 20; 13th Amendment outlaws 21; tourism and 56–8; US Civil war and 4–5, 202; West Indian 53–72; Wilberforce and 60–2, 66, 67–8
Smethwick by-election (1964) 88
Smethwick Council 88
Smith, Rickell Howard 47
Smits, Jimmy 122
Sobekwe, Robert 195
social democracy 127
social housing 88, 127

Society of Editors 155
Somerset, James 65
South Africa 76, 85, 120, 143, 144, 146, 158, 168, 169, 193–8
South Boston Public High School 82
Southern Wolf 79, 81, 82, 85
Sparkbrook 96–7
Spectator 124–5
spirometers 5
Spoiling Old Glory (photograph) 82
Spring, Chris 138
Stannus, Dr Hugh 17
Starbucks 201
statement of allegiance 94–5
state multiculturalism 97
Stephen, James 61
stop and search 73, 76
Stormzy 74, 117
suicide 36, 95, 129
Sun, The 75, 92
'super-predators' 85
Supreme Court, UK 159
Supreme Court, US 182, 198
sus laws 75–6
Sussex, Prince Harry, Duke of 151, 153–7, 161, 163, 164, 167, 171, 172
Sussex, Meghan Markle, Duchess of 151, 153–68, 171–2, 174
Sustainable Travel International 54
Sutton Coldfield 89, 90

TalkRadio xi, xii
Tatum, Professor Beverly Daniel: Why Are All the Black Kids Sitting Together in the Cafeteria? 17
terrorism 50, 95–8, 102, 103, 125
Tezcuco Plantation, Louisiana 56

Thatcher, Margaret xiv, 93, 127–8
Thomas, Clarence 182
Thompson, Steven 2
threat, black 11, 14, 79, 95
token Black 77
token integration 184, 192–3
tourism 53, 54–5, 56, 140–1, 193
tropical neurasthenia 17, 18, 24,
  98, 150
Trump, Donald xiv, xv, 28–9, 32,
  33, 41, 46, 50, 101–2, 103, 118,
  119, 123, 128–9, 130, 131, 182,
  187, 189, 194
Tubman, Harriet 48
Turner, Mary 19
Twelve Years a Slave (film) 58, 67
Twitter 124, 125, 183

UK Arts International 146
Uncle Tom 191, 192–8
unconscious bias 40, 41, 203
Union Army 202
United Kingdom Independence
  Party (UKIP) 125–6
universities. *See* higher education
University of Chicago 79
University of Texas 104
US Civil War (1861–5) 4–5, 7,
  19, 202

Verwoerd, Betsie 196
Verwoerd, Hendrik 195, 196
Voltaire 166

Walker, David: *Appeal* 34
'war on drugs' 85, 87
Warren, Elizabeth 41–2
Washwood Heath 96–7
Watson, James 105

We Are Black and British (TV
  show) ix, 40–1
West, Kanye 181, 182
West Wing, The (TV show)
  122–3, 124
White (documentary series) 125
white flight 79, 82–3, 88–90,
  109–10
white fragility 13, 32, 39, 40, 154
white genocide 117–24, 131
White House negro 188–91
White, Jean 82
white nationalism 32
whiteness studies 32–3, 34, 35, 38,
  39, 43, 46–7, 49, 50, 145–6
white privilege 32, 34, 39, 101, 103,
  104, 107, 148, 200
white supremacy: Atlantic system
  and 27; Caribbean and 55;
  Churchill and x; civil rights and
  11; Columbus and 20; damage to
  psyche of 12, 13, 15; diversity
  used in service of 178; economic
  system and 16; epistemology of
  ignorance and 34; film production
  and 58; guns and 129; Latinx
  communities and 123; museum/
  heritage sector and *see* museum/
  heritage sector; police and 18–19;
  racial science and 104–5;
  segregation and 98; society based
  on 25–6; strongmen leaders and
  xv, 129, 182; university league
  tables and 114; violence and 21;
  world defined by 24
white working-class 105–8, 112,
  114–17
Wilberforce, William 60–2, 66, 67–8
William, Prince of Wales 172

Williams, Eugene 83–4
Williams, Robert 18
Windrush scandal 31, 162
women: affirmative action and
    41–2, 103–4; austerity policies
    and 41; childbirth fatalities 76;
    intersectionality and 163; Markle
    and marginalization of Black
    153–74; presidential election
    voting and xiv, 102; slavery and
    20; suicide and 129; violence
    against Black 163–4; WWII and x
Women of the World Festival 163
Wright, Jeremiah 190

Xhosian people 143–4
Xi Jinping 201

Yahmatta-Taylor, Keeanga: *Race for
    Profit* 85
Young Guns (film) 122

Zimbabwe 169, 194
Zimmerman, George 18
Zong (slave ship) 62–8, 71